305

Pte de la Roch
le Petit Trou
Pointe de la Petite Saline
La Grange
Port de Paix
Petit S.t Louis
Camp de Louise
Cap Haïtien
les 7 Freres
Bay.
Isabelique
ne de
Rabel
polis
Petit Paradis
Petit le Gros Morne
le Borgne
Lumbé
Morne
Plaine du Nord
Acul P. Ance
Plaisance
Limonade
Dondon
Trou
Q. du Trou
Mont Christ
le Terre neuve
Fort
Dauphin
Ouanaminthe
R. de Monte Christ ou des
Isabelique
la Gonaives
Palas
PARTIE
Plaine de l'Artibonite
le Petit Fond
Atalaye
Plaine et
Savannes
Hincha ou S.t
Jean de Goava
M. de
Ciboa
aibonit
le Tapion
M. du Mardi gras
les Montes de
Montrouy
Arahuy
le Mirebalais
l'Artibonite
Banixa
des
G. Savannes
S.t Thomé
ou
Prairies naturelles
de la Gonave
R. du Fer a Cheval
Passage Bien
Rio du Fossé
Île Cul de Sac
Etang du
Cul de Sac
S.t Juan de
Maguano
R. de Neybe
Gonave
Rochelois
G.e Gouve
P. Percé
Etang de Roquille
Port au Prince
Laxame
Lamentin
M.
Noire
COISE
le Eton
P. Suve
Michel
Benes
Jacmel
Cayes
Festro
Sale Trou
Petit Trou
Ance
a l'Etre
Cul Brmet
C. Jacmet
C. Marrchauce
Montagne
de
Baharuco
B. d'Oca
du N
ache
B. Nayanco
C. de la Beate
I. de la Beate

75

Wenda Parkinson was born in Kent, England, in 1923. From the
age of nine she trained for the theatre and at fifteen
she was offered a job in a repertory company. A year later she won
the Leverhulme Scholarship to the Royal Academy of Dramatic
Art. She gave up her acting career on her marriage to
photographer Norman Parkinson.

Since 1963 Wenda Parkinson's home has been Tobago, West Indies.
She has explored every island in the Caribbean and
her travel articles have been widely published in many magazines.
This is her first book.

Toussaint L'Ouverture
COURTESY OF THE BRITISH LIBRARY

'THIS GILDED AFRICAN'
Toussaint L'Ouverture

Wenda Parkinson

QUARTET BOOKS

LONDON · MELBOURNE · NEW YORK

First published by Quartet Books Limited 1978
A member of the Namara Group
27 Goodge Street, London W1P 1FD

Copyright © 1978 by Wenda Parkinson
ISBN 0 7043 2187 4

Distribution in the USA by
Horizon Press, 156 Fifth Avenue
New York, NY 10010

Typeset by Clerkenwell Graphics
Printed by
Newgate Press Limited,
London EC1, England

I dedicate this book
to the Citizens of
the Republic of Trinidad and Tobago,
who, I believe, are proving
that the dream of
Toussaint L'Ouverture
is indeed possible.

Contents

Illustrations

Acknowledgements

Many people have been generous enough to help me with this book and I would like to thank them. Particularly the Father in charge of the Bibliothèque des Frères d'Instruction Chrétienne in Port au Prince, Haiti; this Library contains a collection of books on this subject which are hard to find elsewhere. I would also like to thank the family of the late General Nemours of Haiti (an acknowledged authority), who suggested sources of information which would otherwise have been unavailable to me. In fact I would like to thank all those whom I met on my many visits to Haiti, who helped to make the island and its people come alive for me.

Monsieur de Marche of the Bibliothèque de L'Armée at Les Invalides in Paris was of great assistance and his cheerful presence made research a pleasure.

Monsieur Michel Villemont, also of Paris, kindly took days searching for particular books that I needed, withstanding unsympathetic rebuffs from men of letters who wished to know why anyone was interested in a man who caused so much trouble to Napoleon.

To all those dedicated librarians in the Official Publications section of the British Library, I would also like to say, thank you.

The Right Honourable Dr Eric Williams, P.C., the Prime Minister of the Republic of Trinidad and Tobago, was kind enough to spare me some of his valuable time and his experience as an historian in guiding me upon the bibliography.

Mr Aarons of the Jamaica Institute in Kingston for his kind assistance, many thanks.

I would also like to thank those who have assisted me with the translation of difficult, Creole and archaic French. Mrs Pamela Rathbone above all, who not only helped with this but battled with my impossible handwriting while typing the manuscript. Mrs Marion Mackenzie-Johnstone and my daughter-in-law Kathryn Parkinson also translated for me and I would like to thank them.

My friend Olga Mavrogordato of Port of Spain, Trinidad, kindly allowed me to make use of her beautiful house and her extensive library. And, of course, I would like to thank my husband for his patience and encouragement.

Introduction

On the sixteenth day of December in the year 1492 Christopher Columbus, triumphant from his first landing in the New World on the island of San Salvador, sighted from the deck of his flagship, the *Santa Maria*, a small island to the south, behind which there loomed a large land mass, its mountains dark green against the sky. Columbus threaded his little fleet through the coral reefs, landed briefly on the smaller island, which he named Tortuga, and then sailed towards the land he was later to christen Hispaniola.

He had discovered an island of magnificent grandeur, one of the most beautiful tropical islands in the world: of high, crumpled mountains, creased like linen that has been crushed by a giant hand; of gorges so deep that the forests of crowded trees appear from above to be only moss. The mountain tops conceal a secret world of lush valleys and slate-black lakes. Waterfalls spill down steep slopes into boulder-strewn rivers which flow through plains bleached colourless by the sun, and where the air shimmers in glassy mirages that dance in the stifling heat. Lagoons of mutton-fat water edge a sea so clear that the white sand glitters full fathom five below.

This is the island of Hispaniola, divided into the Dominican Republic in the east and Haiti in the west. Its length is 400 miles, its breadth 150, about the same size as Ireland.

As Christopher Columbus approached the northern coast of Hispaniola and his men rowed him through the pale, clear water there came to meet him dug-out canoes, filled with brown, naked men, their bodies and faces painted in swirling patterns. When he landed he was led towards a chieftain, a Cacique, who stood waiting to receive him surrounded by a timid, wondering crowd of men and women. The Cacique welcomed Columbus and his men with grace, offering them gifts of fruit, vegetables, fish, parrots and the bright feathers of unknown birds. He also gave them arm-bands and anklets of gold.

So the people of the New World welcomed with guileless warmth these strange, pale men who had come out of the ocean. The Indians chattered and laughed with embarrassed excitement as they gazed with curious eyes into the white faces, some of which were the colour of the sea itself. They could not know that they were confronting the first of those who were to bring about the destruction of their race, and obliterate for ever the tranquil world in which they lived.

That night, in perfect weather, whilst the crew was asleep the *Santa Maria* drifted and foundered on the rocks of the reef. From its salvaged timbers Columbus and his men constructed a small fort; the first known European structure to be built in the New World.

Columbus sailed back to Spain in his second ship, the *Tinto*, to bring the news of his discovery and to seek more men, ships and provisions. He left behind him in the little fort forty men. He cautioned them as he left to stay close to the fort, and to behave with discretion towards the native women. But the Spaniards had seen gold in the Cacique's long house, they saw gold on the bodies of those who brought them food and they saw the beauty of the women, with their long black hair, soft rounded bodies and red-gold skin of an amazing silky smoothness. They attempted to seize both the gold and the women. When Columbus returned he found the fort had been burned and of the men there was no trace.

Gold and money meant nothing to the Indians, for they had never known poverty. But it meant a great deal to Columbus. His reputation, the justification for his voyage depended upon the discovery of gold. It was essential for him to be the means by which the coffers of Spain would be filled, essential that these islands should provide the key which would open the door to El Dorado, the legendary city of gold. Then he would be vindicated, then and only then would he receive from a duly grateful Spain the honours, respect and financial reward that his discovery merited.

Initially he was fortunate for there was gold on Hispaniola. Columbus realized that to work the gold-mines labour would be needed, and it was available. To him it seemed fortuitous that the island was inhabited by pagans who could be used as a slave work force, and incidentally at the same time be brought to the true faith, their souls saved for the greater glory of God and of Spain. Although Queen Isabella's conscience had misgivings at enslaving her new subjects Columbus's arguments were persuasive and there were certainly no doubts in the minds of the merchant adventurers who were to follow him to the New World.

In 1492 the peace-loving population of the Indians of Hispaniola numbered perhaps over a million. Twenty-five years later there were less than 60,000 and forty years later no more than 200. The discovery of the island began the genocide of its people.

Unused to labour, indolent, pleasure-loving, the people were driven through force and fear to work as slaves in the mines and on the land by their new masters. Their heritage was seized, their women raped or at best taken as concubines. The very gentleness and recessiveness of the Indians' nature produced a reaction in the Spaniards of sadistic savagery, made more appalling by the fact that it was so senseless. They destroyed the very work force they needed.

To escape from the whip, the flames, the wheel, the dogs that tore them to pieces, and from near starvation, the Indians committed mass suicide, clubbing their own children to death as they were born. The priests who held the cross on high called upon them to save their souls as the faggots were lighted, but they remembered that their own gods had been kinder. As they died in their hundreds they turned their faces away from this new religion which allowed man to behave to man in such a way: 'The gods they worshipped were as simple and gentle as they were themselves. Both gods and people formed in common childishness.' (Métral)

When help came it was already too late. Las Casas, a Dominican priest, pleaded the Indians' cause in Spain, against 'cruelties more atrocious than any recorded by savage barbarians'. To preserve the prosperity of the colony he suggested as a solution that the 'labour force of the Negro is more valuable than your Indians'. In 1577 it was decreed that 15,000 Negro slaves should be shipped from Africa to Hispaniola. Las Casas fought for the liberty of the Indian, but thereby promoted the slavery of the African in the Spanish West Indies.

The Africans who were forced to cross the sea to slavery in Hispaniola were not gentle complaisant Indians, they were warriors who fought for their freedom. In the first year 7000 escaped into the fastnesses of the mountains and there returned to the life they had lived in their distant homeland.

The Spaniards, finding their gold mines – never of great importance – were becoming exhausted, the Indian labour worn out by hardship and sickness and the new African slaves intractable, looked now towards South America to Peru and Mexico, and gradually abandoned large tracts of the island which soon became a natural game park of once domesticated animals. The only city remaining was San Domingo whose neglected ruins served merely as a shelter for herdsmen.

The remaining Spaniards were further troubled by marauding bands who settled on the island of Tortuga, men of mixed nationalities who were escaping from justice, from indentured labour, from religious persecution, desperate men seeking a rough sanctuary, who were prepared to stay alive by any means. These 'boucaniers' or buccaneers were originally hunters of the wild oxen and barbecued their meat – their only food – on gridirons or 'boucans', but they soon took to more lucrative game: they raided the remaining Spanish settlements and turned pirate, seizing the trading ships that were the Spaniards' life-line. Gradually they penetrated deeper and deeper into the mainland, settling and cultivating crops of indigo, cotton and sugar. The Spaniards attempted to drive them off, but their hold was firm.

All that the buccaneers now lacked was women. As most of them were French in origin a delegation of them travelled to France where in the ports they rounded up numbers of prostitutes whom they brought back to Hispaniola and sold them in the market to eager bidders. 'They received with joy prostitutes as wives, so revenging the former injury.' (Métral) These well-matched couples and their subsequent families prospered and formed small settlements throughout the island.

In 1640 Levasseur was sent from France as Governor to this lightly acquired colony.

In 1695 by the Treaty of Ryswick the western half of the island of Hispaniola was officially ceded to France by Spain. And the greatest colony of France, her richest colony in the world, St Dominigue, was born.

I St Dominigue: The Background

In its earliest years St Dominigue was a simple rural community. The farmers worked the land themselves together with their families and perhaps one to two slaves or hired white labourers. To the slaves they were paternal rather than oppressive. If you work in a field side by side with a man it is hard to wield a whip over him. They grew cocoa, indigo and tobacco, and the land was fertile so they prospered. But as they cleared more land they needed more labour; so the Compagnie de St Louis was approached and a consignment of 1500 white indentured labourers and 3000 slaves was brought to the island.

The whites worked for a period of five years bonded to their master, then they gained their freedom. For the slaves manumission was sometimes, but seldom, given. Among both whites and blacks there was a percentage of women.

When he was freed from bond the white labourer – if he survived (the death rate was particularly high among whites owing to the climate and disease) – would often buy a black woman to be his housekeeper, companion and mistress rather than a freed white servant, who would be worn out by a former life of prostitution and poverty in France, followed by five years of working under a tropical sun. In this way there came into being three classes, the white, the mulatto and the black, which in those days implied no particular evil, except the basic one of slavery which was generally accepted.

Unlike the other Caribbean islands St Dominigue had begun as a poor man's land. It was not settled by men of noble birth or wealth. Here there was no rich man sitting up in the great house. Here the slave was a valuable commodity, an expensive item in a poor man's budget, and only the rich could afford to make them expendable. Here all were humble; the child of prostitute and buccaneer, of labourer and slave, of slave and slave. This state of affairs was to change.

In 1644 Benjamin da Costa had brought the sugar-cane plant from Java to Brazil; from there it was brought to the Antilles, and with the increasing demand for sugar in Europe a social and economic revolution came to St Dominigue. The small 'gardens' were swallowed up in vast sugar plantations with their own boiler houses and factories, farms, stables and warehouses, each plantation a world on its own. Men of substance from the 'metropole' saw a new opportunity for investment, 'cadets de familles' saw the chance of making a fortune on their own account; soon the estates began to bear the great names of France, de Gramont, Noailles, Fronsac, and the slave traders moved in, ready to flood this profitable new market with human merchandise.

In the African colonies of Guinea, Senegal, the Congo and Dahomey men and women were hunted down and seized to provide for the new-found prosperity of St Dominigue. Sugar needed men, without men there could be no sugar and no profits, so what man was doing to man in order to gain those profits concerned no one. 'They had lived in an honourable frugality; but as soon as they had acquired great riches and saw themselves surrounded by numbers of slaves prosperity corrupted them; they abandoned themselves to the most shameful vices, they lived in idleness, luxury and indolence, they passed their time at table, in the bath and lying in the shade of their groves. In place of wooden houses they built magnificent residences where like absolute princes they reigned over thousands of slaves.' (Métral)

That the treatment of slaves while these riches were being acquired, and after, was worse in the French colonies than in the Spanish, British or Dutch is a recorded fact; perhaps this was due to a dedicated acquisitiveness that is a part of the French character, but in this case it was turned, in the fierce struggle for wealth, to terrorization of those who were the means of making it.

The Africans themselves did not hesitate to take part in the general scramble for gain. They sold their prisoners taken in skirmishes, sold them to the white traders, even men of their own tribes, even families betrayed their own brothers.

Black may have traded black, but the ultimate winner was always the white man; he bought cheap and sold dear.

Thousands upon thousands of men and women were whipped and prodded across the trails of West Africa, roped together, weighted with stones to prevent their escape they stumbled towards the coastal ports and the sea. In the slave-trading centres, Benin and Wydah, they were herded into warehouses. Their strength, their health, their worth were all assessed; their muscles were prodded and their teeth inspected like horses at a fair. Women, even young girls were examined for pregnancy and the intimate parts of their bodies handled by the prying hands of brutal, prurient men. They had no redress. All were helpless.

Three hundred ships a year sailed to St Dominigue with their human cargo of misery and despair. They lay strapped down in the holds side by side, head to toe. The ships' designers had shown ingenuity in working out specifications to fit in as much cargo as possible. The slaves had no freedom even to turn their bodies; they lay trapped in the stifling, stinking dark, helpless in their own excrement and vomit.

When the sailors sluiced down the holds with sea water and com-plained of the stench, they gave no thought to those who endured this day after day, who lay there degraded and afraid, sweating not only with the heat but with fear. The human cargo in the hold did not know what lay beyond the measureless heaving sea, no one had ever returned to tell them. They knew only their village, the water hole, the distant blue hills and the long stretch of plain where the animals ran free. They lay in the dark, suffocated by the terror of the unknown.

Now and then they were brought up on deck, staggering and blinking in the sudden glare of the sun, weak with both sea sickness and lack of food and water. Still in their chains 'they were forced to dance to calm their distress, the music an added insult to them . . . the innocence and the chastity of their women was outraged by gross vices. When they were found to be too ill to cure they were thrown alive into the sea like so much spoiled merchandise. Fifteen thousand corpses were strewn over the ocean, and floating there between the shores of two worlds marked the funeral route of the slave trade.' (Métral)

Twenty thousand slaves a year reached St Dominigue alive; one ninth of these died within a year of their arrival.

Once on St Dominigue they were taken to the market, paraded and auctioned. They were then branded with a red-hot iron bearing the first initial of their new owner's name. The men received this excruciating pain on their chest and back. For the women 'they were unconcerned to place this torture on their breasts, the most delicate and the most beautiful ornament of their sex'. (Métral)

On the plantations they were given into the charge of an experienced hand to guide and 'creolise' them. Families, tribes were separated since it was considered politic to divide those speaking the same language. In this new bewildering world there was little comfort, only the sympathy of eyes, the touch of hands, and the mercy of the night.

There were long hours of labour ahead, under the relentless sun, in the drenching rains that made the earth steam and in the cold early mornings that brought the ague, and always there was the knowledge that to pause in work, to attract the overseer's eye for any reason, could bring the whip or a sudden blow.

'Their labour begins at dawn, at 8 they eat. They work unremittingly till midday. At 2 they work again till the night, many times 10 or 11 in the evening. In this way during harvest they have hardly four or five hours' rest from their labours.

'Their food was given to them weekly, but they were unable to calcu-
late their needs and they had always run out by the end of the week.
They had no time to cook at all and ate most of their food raw.' (Yirod
Chantras – *Voyage d'une Suisse en différentes colonies*)

In spite of their weariness and wretchedness, they still found time to dance,
because it was in their nature and as essential to them as breathing. On Satur-
day nights they would gather, and to the sound of the guitars made from
calabash gourds and the drums they would dance till the dawn came.

On Sundays, their one free day, they were encouraged to tend their
own gardens to supplement their rations, but mainly in order to help
their master's pocket. Any surplus they sold at market. From this they
earned enough money to buy rum, perhaps clothes, and those who still
had hope saved for a lifetime to buy their freedom.

To forget the monotonous toil, the oppression, the privation, the slaves
did not only turn to music, rum and dancing, they had their religion –
not the religion of the white man – but their own, brought with them
from their own land. In the woods at night they worshipped Vaudoux,
the God of Dahomey, the god who ruled the sun, the stars, the moon and
earth, the supreme. To the sound of the drums they invoked the 'loa' –
the spirits – to come to them; they called on Legba – 'Papa Legba ouvrit
barrière pour nous', and the 'loa' came to bring them solace, as they had
come to them in Africa. Erzelie of the water, Damballa who brings the
rain, they recognized them as the spirits mounted them, and all were
united with one another and with Africa.

They knew that Vaudoux and the 'loa' would protect them when they
died, would carry them under the sea through the reefs where the conch
shells lay pink in the clear water, would carry them safely back to the
land of their fathers, and so, one way or the other, the time would come
when Vaudoux would free them.

Magic was a part of their religion too, though they did not consider it
magic. Spells and fetishes could protect you or point the finger at others.
There was another secret that some of those blessed with 'the science'
also knew, the draughts to heal or sicken: love potions, cures for fever,
for barrenness – and poison.

The masters knew of the dancing at night, of Vodun worship which
they considered childish superstition; they accepted it and dismissed it.
But they became increasingly aware of a startling increase in the cases of
poisoning which spread through the colony like a feverish epidemic, and
it occurred to them with some misgiving that they themselves might well
be the next victims. Poison was the black man's traditional weapon, at
least to white eyes; throughout the slave colonies he was believed to have

an instinctive skill in the mysteries of poison. It was hard to find the culprits, and in the ensuing panic many who were innocent were killed or tortured.

So yet another factor was added to the fear, mistrust and hate felt by both sides, black and white.

It is possible to sentimentalize the wretchedness of the slave's working life. Conditions of labour were no better for the common man in Europe, in factories, the mines and on the land, long after slavery had been abolished. But the men and women of Europe were not slaves and there lies the difference. It is impossible to comprehend a life which holds no freedom, and never will, except for those who live that life and there is one aspect of slavery in St Dominigue that cannot be sentimentalized or exaggerated.

As the slave force grew larger it became less controllable. The average slave population on a large estate would exceed 1000. The excuse for the whip was that it was essential in order to make the Negro work. In the Code Noir (decreed by Louis XIV) to the whip were added other punishments for various offences. The severance of ears, nose, a hand, a foot, and of course death. The Code Noir, it should be remembered, was issued in order to *protect* the slave, and was considered by many planters to be unnecessarily liberal. Fear of the ever-present potential black menace, the proximity of hundreds and thousands of 'savages' produced an increasing reaction of cruelty and subjugation. Fear and a subconscious envy of the black man's extrovert sexuality bred sadism. There can be no overstatement of the horrors that were perpetrated against the slaves, horrors that were regarded as commonplace. Eye witnesses reported hundreds of instances of cruelty and torture, many of which were recorded in the archives.

The most widely used deterrent was the lash: 'the victim was pegged to the ground by four stakes. He was repeatedly and violently lashed till the skin was torn from his back. The agony was increased by salt, or quicklime being rubbed into the wounds or flaming splinters of wood inserted.' The lash was not given only to men but to women, even pregnant women, too.

The tortures by fire were many: 'An unfortunate victim was thrown alive into the flames for spoiling a dish.' (Bousu, *Nouvelles Voyages Occidentales*) 'White-hot staves of wood were bound to the feet of some and replaced hour after hour in order to prolong their suffering.' (Peytraud, *Esclave aux Antilles*) Letters written in 1744 from Messieurs de Larnage and Mallait bear witness to 'the mutilation of arms, and legs and sex'.

Victims were thrown alive into cesspits, their heads forced under till they drowned; they were cast into boiling vats of sugar; they were

buried up to their necks in the ground, their heads and faces smeared with
molasses, and left there in the sun for the ants to find them, so that they
died slowly, unless their fellow slaves, who were forced to watch, stoned
them to death to end their agony.

In 1788 there was the notorious case of a planter named Le Jeune who,
suspecting that his slaves were poisoning him and in order to find out the
truth, put two Negresses to question by fire, slowly burning their feet,
legs and thighs. They were rescued by fellow slaves who fled with them
to the protection of a magistrate who found the women's limbs decom-
posing. Le Jeune defended himself by producing a box belonging to one
of them which contained a few leaves of tobacco and some rat droppings,
declaring this to be proof of poison. Fellow planters gave evidence and
petitioned on his behalf against expelling him from the Colony, and he
was absolved of all blame.

In 1736 a Monsieur Chapelle wrote a letter to the Minister in Paris of a
slave 'rammed with gunpowder, like a cannon and then made to explode
with the aid of a match'. Doubtless among the master's cronies this was
considered a good after-dinner joke.

The men who reported these horrors were not abolitionists or propa-
gandists; they were in most cases visitors, ordinary men protesting at
what they saw in this colony that on the surface seemed so fair and pleasant. 'Tortures inspired by the most base instincts, by frenzied imagination
. . . tortures in short in which the Colony became a wild beast that devoured human flesh, falling upon the slaves and tearing them to pieces.'
(Moreau de St Mery)

Female slaves were of course the property of the master to use as he
pleased; that all were reluctant when this included his bed goes against
the human average, as not all black women find white men repellent; in
fact it was an opportunity which was sought by many as a way of alle-
viating the hardship of their existence and gaining both privilege and
power over their fellow slaves. In some cases a lifetime relationship ensued,
as in the smaller, more parochial islands of the Caribbean, but in St
Dominigue this was rare; the size of the island, the frequent visits to
France of any men of substance, the pervasive atmosphere of decadence,
dissolution and accepted vice led to few natural relationships. It was far
more the general custom for women, and particularly the young girls, to
be used as sexual objects by the white masters, who thought of a slave
girl only as an animal and treated her as such. This thinking established a
precedent in the sex lives of black and white which has persisted to recent
times in the Caribbean. Even in the present century it was not unusual for
a planter to send his servant down to the village with instructions to
bring back a few girls.

This casual degradation was more scarring for the black man, rendered impotent to protest by his slavery, than for the woman, for if she had a mulatto child she gained stature, whereas he, even without personal involvement, felt a shame to his pride and manhood which he could never forget.

From this life, which was no life, it is not surprising that throughout the years thousands escaped from their bondage. If they were recaptured it meant death, but they had little to lose; hundreds of slaves a year committed suicide in order to seek another freedom; but others, more courageous, made their bid and escaped to the hills and to life. Here, in the high unreachable fastnesses which the contours of the island conceal, they built stockades within which they lived, hunting their food and growing a few provisions as they had in Africa. In 1720 alone over 1000 escaped to the hills. Women joined them or were taken in raids; they reproduced and so became a separate community living secretly within the island, a menacing intangible force who would sweep down on any plantation without warning, set it alight, murder the inhabitants, take weapons and supplies and vanish again into the hills. These bands of men were known as 'Marrons' (Maroons) from the Spanish 'Cimarron', a savage. As the century advanced there were many thousands of them existing within the Colony, creating a growing potential danger to the white planters.

The whole precarious social and economic structure of St Dominigue rested upon this foundation, upon this shifting, struggling mass of slaves. Although they were voiceless, the evil that was done to them and the corruption of those who did it spread like a creeping fungus throughout, penetrating and rotting the whole framework of society and tainting all, even the innocent.

The framework of the administration of the Colony was simple; representing France and the king was a Governor General who was always a military man; he commanded the troops, was responsible for the defence of the island, made the laws, was in charge of police and the administration and granting of land. Under him was the Administrator who controlled the finances, the civil service and public works.

The island was divided into three parts: the North – Cap Français (Le Cap); the West – Port au Prince; and the South – Les Cayes. In charge of each province was a Lieutenant General, also a soldier. The resident military forces consisted of 5000 men, the police force comprised white officers in command of mulattoes and freed Negroes. In 1788 there were on the island 42,000 white, 38,000 free mulattoes, 500,000 slaves and 8000 plantations and, to give some indication of the prosperity of the Colony, there were 80,000 sailors engaged in trade. St Dominigue, the 'Pearl of the Antilles', produced and exported more sugar then the entire British

West Indies put together. To be 'wealthy as a Creole' was a common saying in France, just as to be 'as rich as a Tobago planter' was in England. By saying 'Creole' the French were making no reference to colour. 'Creole' then, as now, refers to anyone who was born in the West Indian islands.

The strata of the society of St Dominigue were clearly defined: above the slaves came the freed blacks. They lived in general an urban existence, running small businesses or plying a trade. Then came the 'petits blancs' who worked as overseers and factory managers on the estates, were in the police or in business or were public servants.

Above all came the 'grands blancs', the proprietors, the administrators, often men of title, whose first loyalty was to the 'metropole' and, for the majority, to the king, men who aped the latest fads and the intellectual fashions that stemmed from Paris. In the chocolate houses and the fashionable 'English' clubs they discussed Rousseau and Voltaire – even if they did not read them. The favourite works of the time were *Paul et Virginie*, *Les Saisons* and *Manon Lescaut*. There was interest in the new sciences, chemistry, electricity and natural history, and in 1784 'a balloon was launched in Le Cap amongst scenes of incredible enthusiasm'. (Des Fosses) They were men who lived in 'the best of all possible worlds' – that they owed this to slavery hardly impinged upon their thinking.

The women's attitude towards their household slaves, with whom they lived most intimately, was also one of complete acceptance and equally complete dismissal. Perhaps this is best summed up by this quotation from Malenfant: 'Two young ladies, just arrived from France, inquired of their parents as to the nudity of the servants whilst waiting at table. "Why not?" they replied. "You will be demanding next that we clothe our cows, our mules and our dogs".'

Woven throughout the whole structure of society was another group that belonged to all classes and to none: the mulatto. There were 50,000 mulatto slaves but there were also mulattoes who were as rich as any man in St Dominigue. They existed in every stratum and were accepted by none. Among themselves, the gradations and permutations of their colour created unhealthy petty snobbery and social climbing. A true mulatto was of equal blood, both black and white. Then there were 'Sang Mêlées' 127 parts white to one black, 'Sacatras' eight white to 120 black, 'Griffes', 'Marabous', 'Mamelukes', 'Quarterons'. It was desirable to possess as much white blood as possible, this made you superior to the man who had less.

The whole system, the entire society of St Dominigue was based on colour, not on class or degree of achievement, not even on wealth or acres, but only on colour. It followed that to impute to any man black

blood was the greatest insult you could offer him. To whisper that a man
'had a grandmother on the coast' (Guinea) was to murder his reputation
and could cost him his livelihood. A young lieutenant was refused rank in
the militia because of this rumour, honour was satisfied when it was proved that his great-grandmother was a Carib from St Kitts. Indeed, this
was a ruse often used as an explanation for a dark skin; Indian ancestry
was produced, and coloured men would go to any lengths in order to
prove the purity of their blood.

All this may seem merely pathetic today, but the suffering that it
caused was immeasurable. The mulatto might possess 10,000 acres, be
master of 1000 slaves, but he had no rights, nothing. As far as the Colony
was concerned he did not exist. If he was in the military, serving his
country, he had to wear a different uniform from the whites; they wore
white and orange, he wore buff nankeen. A coloured man was forbidden
to carry a sword, sabre or side-arms, at one blow denying him the
traditional mark of a gentleman. In the theatre, in public vehicles, on
board ship he was given separate seating. Mulattoes could not be addressed as Monsieur or Madame, and when riding they had to dismount
before entering a town. More seriously they were not allowed to enter
the legal profession, as they might, in that way, have jurisdiction over a
white man; were not allowed to practise as a doctor or apothecary (lest
they caused the death or illness of a white man by poison); could not
serve as a priest for they might have to hear the confessions of a white
woman. Many mulattoes were brilliant, cultivated, well-educated men;
by way of compensation their fathers lavished money on them; they went
to the best schools and were sent to France where their pride was bolstered
by their acceptability, and in Paris they made a fashionable show, using
their money to gain them entrance into the highest society.

In St Dominigue their white father went to bed with their mother, but
neither they nor their mother could sit at the same table together with
their father, could not receive his guests, sit beside him in church or be
buried in the same tomb. 'Their fathers, half stifling the call of nature,
left them in this intermediate servitude which was no less shameful.'
(Métral) The psychological repercussions of this are obvious: the lack of
security, the envy, the aping of the white half-brothers, the mistrust and
shame for the mother.

As for the mulatto women, at least they had one weapon at their disposal – sex, which they did not hesitate to use on many levels. 'Like their
black grandmothers or mothers they knew well how to play upon the
passions they inspired in their masters; they became adept in the arts of
sensual delights; they had naturally naïve and touching grace, they mixed
this with caresses, tender refusals, in turn disdainful and with glances

full of lascivious languor. They used despair and the power of tears, without neglecting either adornment, or dancing or perfumed baths. They likewise covered their chains with flowers, but could only aspire to the rank of courtesan, never were they led to the altar . . . Love which can magnify everything could not break through the barriers of this slavery.' (Métral) Perhaps not, but it could be a powerful enough weapon to defeat the Assembly, who attempted to pass an edict forbidding mulatto women from wearing silks and colours in public – an order obviously inspired by jealous wives. When some mulatto women arrived at church in Cap Français wearing the banned silk, constables tore the clothes from their backs, leaving them 'with no other veil than their shame'. (Abbé Gregoire) The order was hastily rescinded, the Assembly had been naïve enough to underestimate the power of sex as a weapon, and the possibility that the women of colour would emulate the women of Athens and withhold their favours. Still, they could not fight their battle all the way to victory. In 1768 coloured women were forbidden by law to marry white men. White wives humiliated their husband's concubines whenever the opportunity arose, and were in their own turn equally humiliated in other ways. Jealousy and resentment infested the community. One governor is said to have reported to Paris that he found sexual jealousy to be the greatest cause of unrest in the Colony.

Colour prejudice, the pressure against the mulatto, increased; the more educated he became the more attempts were made to put him 'in his place'. The influential white planter element in France succeeded in making it difficult for coloured planters to travel free in the 'metropole'. Under Louis XV, the coloured man's rights, as stated in the Code of Louis XIV were slowly whittled away, both in France and in the Colony, until finally he had none. The passions that this aroused were only recognized as dangerous when it was already too late.

If this society was based upon gradations of colour it was also based upon envy and hate. The 'grands blancs' hated the mulattoes for the threat they implied, they despised the 'petits blancs' and they either ignored or loathed the blacks. The 'petits blancs' hated the 'grands blancs' for their unassailable privilege, they feared and yet looked down upon the mulattoes, the blacks they hated more fiercely than any. In their turn the freed blacks hated the 'petits blancs' for their overbearing attitude towards them, and for the same reason mistrusted and disliked the mulattoes, believing that the airs and privileges they aspired to were not theirs by right.

The first intimation of a crack in the established system came from the slaves, a warning sign which if it had been heeded might have forced the whites to realize the potential of those they oppressed.

A maroon chief, Mackandal, originally from Guinea, conceived a plan for rebellion on the grand scale: he planned to unite all the slaves as one under his leadership, eliminate the whites and take over the Colony. His plans were elaborately and carefully premeditated and his chosen weapon was poison. It seems that the whites' apprehensions about poison were certainly justified. For six years Mackandal had been perfecting his art as a poisoner. It is not known how many he murdered in his experiments, it should be remembered that many slaves killed themselves, but he claimed hundreds as his victims, not only whites but his own followers too.

The most commonly used poison was arsenic (which was easily come by as it was used as an insecticide in the cane fields), but other more sinister poisonous substances were also used; polluted earth, taken from the graves of the dead, was one of the commonest and most easily obtained poisons, but many roots and herbs, and more obvious killers such as ground glass, were also used.

The climax of Mackandal's years of plotting was to be the poisoning of the water supply of every house in the capital. Then, when the whites were helpless and dying in agony, his followers were to fall upon them and massacre them. The signal to massacre all the whites on the planta-tions was to be given to the insurgents across the island. It was hoped that the remaining whites would then flee .

Mackandal appears to have been a man with a hypnotic personality who may have well have taken hallucinogenic drugs.

Many of the local herbs and also the milky substance surrounding the raw cocoa bean were widely used as stimulating drugs. He saw visions and thought himself immortal. He was surrounded by a harem of women who believed him to be a god, a life-style not unlike that of some twentieth-century cult-figures. His weakness for drink, women and dancing led to his downfall. When visiting a dance at a plantation the jealous lover of one of his worshippers betrayed him to the overseer of the estate who secretly ordered that he should be plied with drink; he was captured, tried and burned at the stake. At the last moment he broke his bonds and leapt, flaming, from the fire. His followers believed that this proved he was indeed immortal, that although his body had burned he had trans-muted himself into a mosquito and would return as a man again. The skilful organization of this abortive plot (for the framework was cer-tainly well conceived) should have been a lesson to the whites that a cohesive underground movement existed, but they ignored it.

The blacks under Mackandal had made their effort and were now once more, so it was believed, reassuringly subjugated, but there was a wind of change blowing towards St Dominigue from the world outside, and from two quarters. In the north, the American War of Independence erupted with enormous impact upon the colonial islands of the Caribbean and many men enlisted to fight there under the French colours. In battle their inspiration had been colonial freedom and the rights of the common man against oppression, and when they returned to their own colony they did not forget. When England was forced in 1785 to acknowledge the independence of the United States there was general rejoicing in St Dominigue among all except the most hide-bound royalists. Those who were particularly heartened by the independence were the mulattoes and freed blacks who had formed a large proportion of the volunteers. They might have been less sanguine of this brave new country's future attitude towards their kind if they had heeded Thomas Jefferson's opinion of the black man: 'Civilization produces no changes in their behaviour, which proves that their stupidity is not in fact the result of slavery but of nature.'

To the east in France there was an even greater upheaval to come. Privilege, predominant for so many centuries, was losing its stranglehold upon the nation. The king of France, Louis XVI, was a wellintentioned, even virtuous man, but he could not govern; the nobles had ceased to perform any viable function, the church was corrupt and the 'parlements', the States-General and the Third Estate were divided. In this climate both the bourgeoisie and the man of radical thought were flexing their muscles ready to fill the vacuum. The mass of the people were short of food, particularly bread – the staple of their lives. The financial state of the country following the American war was chaotic. Louis called upon the States-General to form a council, but they were reactionary and failed, as Louis did, to realize that for privilege time was running out. Louis did not understand the depth of the political mood, the new aspirations of scientific thought and philosophy that were exciting the country, nor did he comprehend the heady effect of the doctrines of liberty, equality and the common man, or the strength which these hopes gave to men formerly unconsidered, once they were within their grasp.

Weary of waiting, the parliament of the Third Estate ousted the States-General and declared themselves to be the National Assembly, and their first task to draft a new constitution for the people. Louis, feeling his supreme powers were being denied, tried a show of force by mustering the troops at Versailles. The people of Paris replied and on 14 July 1789 the Bastille prison fell. Paris had made her gesture, France was to follow and the world believed that a new era of freedom had begun.

In St Dominigue a French sailor leapt from his ship to the quay to be the first to bring the news. He ran shouting through the streets that the

Bastille had fallen and the people were in revolt. In the divided colony the news was inflammatory, all seeing in the confusion that reigned in the 'metropole' a means to furthering their own ends. The whites hoped that in a revolution they might gain their independence from France and so achieve complete control of the Colony. The mulattoes, taking the brave words of the Declaration of the Rights of Man as gospel, felt the moment had come to press for their particular rights to be regained; the slaves heard the words 'Liberty and Equality' and pondered upon them.

In Paris in 1787 there had been founded 'La Societé des Amis des Noirs', a parallel to the abolitionist movement in England. This society repres-ented an attempt to fight back from the base in Paris the efforts of the whites in the Colony to erode the rights of the mulattoes both by legisla-tion on the island and by lobbying the National Assembly in Paris. Many radicals, such as Robespierre, Lafayette, Mirabeau and Abbé Gregoire, were members of the 'Amis des Noirs'.

In opposition to the 'Amis des Noirs', the landowners of the Colony formed in Paris the 'Club de Massiac'; the object of this 'club' was to protect the interests of the white planters and landowners on the island by using the influence of its noble members within the Assembly to demand independent dominion status and also to block the attempts of the coloured people to obtain political rights. To a certain extent they succeeded; the National Assembly passed a resolution which, true to the 'Rights of Man', granted the coloured their rights but ambiguously left the decision, whether to enforce the law, to each colonial authority to decide for itself.

A brilliant young mulatto from St Dominigue, Ogé, who had been educated in France and lived there, was a keen spokesman for the 'Amis des Noirs'; he considered that the time was ripe to bring the news of the Assembly's decision to the Colony and to force its ratification upon the legislators of his homeland, and he put his plan before the society. They encouraged him, so he made his way to England where he secretly met the abolitionists. Clarkson financed him and, full of hope and idealism, he sailed for America where he purchased arms before landing on the island, accompanied by his brother and a friend, Chavannes. His arrival in the Colony was meant to be kept secret, but one of the British aboli-tionists had betrayed him to the Club de Massiac, and the whites were prepared for him. He marched with a band of 200 mulattoes against 800 troops at Le Cap and was defeated. He was captured and made to confess his sins before being hideously tortured outside the cathedral. He was only thirty years old; it is said that he wept as he died, crying for mercy, surely as much for his hopes and his people, as for himself. But he did not die for nothing; the coloured in the Colony became more steeled against the whites than ever. The Jacobins in Paris were incensed with righteous fury. Ogé became a martyr and the 'Amis des Noirs' prepared themselves for an outright attack upon the Assembly to clarify the mulatto position once and for all and without equivocation.

Abbé Gregoire rose and spoke with fervour upon the double standard of the white planters: 'It is *we* who at a distance of 2000 leagues from you have constrained to protect *your* children against neglect, contempt and the unnatural cruelty of their fathers . . . by what strange perversion of reason can it be deemed disgraceful in a white man to marry a black or mulatto woman when it is not thought dishonourable in him to be connected with her in the most licentious familiarity?' He also reminded the mulattoes present of the situation of their slaves. 'Do not forget that they, like yourselves, are born free and remain free as all men do. It is you who are accused even more than the white men of cruelty to the Negroes.'

Robespierre as always commanded silence as he rose; he spoke scathingly and with passion: 'You urge the "Rights of Man" but you believe in them so little yourselves that you have sanctified slavery . . . Let the colonies perish,' he called, 'if we are to sacrifice our freedom and our glory in order to preserve them.'

The day was won, at least in France. In St Dominigue as the news was received, chaos reigned. The whites, humiliated and enraged by the granting of political equality to the mulattoes, turned upon them with animal savagery, but before a white–mulatto confrontation could explode an event occurred that none had looked for. The Negro slaves revolted.

In this colony at this time against this background of violence, and inheritance of every kind of greed, hatred and cruelty, a man had been born and lived, who changed the destiny of the people not only in his own nation but for the generations that followed in other lands, too, where men were black. His name was Toussaint and he was a slave.

2 Young Toussaint: Plantation Slave

Two leagues from Le Cap there lay the sugar estate L'habitation Breda, owned by the Comte de Noé. The estate was as large and prosperous as any on the island, it spread from the fertile northern plain over the foot-hills of the mountain range. A broad river snaked its way over the lower-lying land, and streams under gothic arches of bamboo brought cool mountain water through mile after mile of the sugar cane, that stood twice the height of a tall man.

The great house at Breda would have followed the style of plantation houses throughout the West Indies in the eighteenth century, only differing according to the affluence of the owner. An avenue of Royal palms led up to the house which stood on an eminence, both to catch the slightest breeze and so that the whole working estate could be viewed from the pillared gallery. It was built of small red ballast bricks and square-hewn stone, and like the houses of Le Cap had a slate roof. The house was surrounded by lawns and spreading shade trees whose branches were made feathery by parasitic ferns and bird-sown orchids. Beside the house there was a small garden of tea-roses in square beds with formal brick paths. The roses were a reminder of France, but here in the heat their colour was bleached by the fierce sun, their scent only a pale echo of the roses of Malmaison. Jasmine and stephanotis twined the pillars of the gallery. In a corner of the pleasant garden there was a stone tower with a large bell that tolled before dawn to summon the slaves to labour. Not far from the house stood the factory with its boiler rooms, warehouses and tall chimney stack. To the leeward of the house and factory lay the barracks and the crowded wattle and palm-thatched huts of the slaves.

On the outskirts of this compound there lived, among the 1000 slaves who worked the estate, a man who was privileged above the rest, a man who had been singled out by his master and who in a world of uniform obscurity retained his own identity. He was the second son of an African king, King Goau-Guinou of the Aradas tribe. As a young man he had been taken in tribal battle and sold by his captors at the market in Wydah, Dahomey, to a Portuguese slave trader. From there he was pressed on board a slave ship bound for Cap Français, St Dominigue, where he was sold in the market in the centre of town to the Comte de Noé.

The young prince's inherent authority must have made a disturbing impression on the Comte, a man with a reputation for humanity and liberal thought. Perhaps he felt ashamed when he confronted his new purchase whom he had bought like an animal, but who stood before him with the assured pride and innate dignity of a king. Whatever the reason, the Comte's reaction was unusual. He granted him immediately the 'liberté de savanne', a partial freedom that allowed the slave, although still the property of his master, liberty within the confines of the estate to live his own life. The young prince was apportioned a parcel of land and given five slaves of his own to work for him. In the enclosed world of the sugar estate he was a man of some position.

The prince accepted his new life and, with the encouragement of his master, decided to take a wife. He chose a girl from his own tribe, who was, according to contemporary reports, beautiful, lively and intelligent. He had been married before in Dahomey to Affiba, the daughter of the king of a neighbouring tribe, the Aggas. As the Aradas practised polygamy, to take another wife was of no concern to the prince. Affiba was, like him, a warrior, for Badou the overlord of Dahomey had fighting troops of young women chosen from the Aradas and Agga tribes. 'The women of Aradas were renowned for their large and magnificent breasts, and the sight of their bodies gave not only an impression of strength but of beauty.' (Moreau de Saint Mery) Unknown to her husband, Affiba had also been captured and was now a slave, together with their two children, a boy and a girl, on a neighbouring estate to Breda. Market gossip brought the news of a coming wedding, a wedding which, because of the master's regard for the bridegroom, was to be a big event, creating a precedent in the slaves' world of monotonous labour: a day's holiday was to be granted, with feasting and dancing to mark the occasion. Affiba heard that the bridegroom was her husband and for her it was the ultimate despair. It is said she gave up the will to live and died before the marriage. The story of Affiba of Africa became a legend among the local slaves, a tale to be told in the short hour of leisure between dusk and weary sleep.

The new bride Pauline bore her husband five children, all of whom (except one who died young) lived to follow the warrior tradition of their ancestors: Pierre, the eldest, became a colonel in the army of the king of Spain; Paul served as a general in the French colonial army; and Marie Jean, the only girl, married a colonel. The boy who died was called Goau-Guinou after his grandfather the king, to whom he bore a striking resemblance, and then there was Toussaint: François Dominique Toussaint à Breda was born on 20 May perhaps in 1743 or 1746, for the birth of slaves was as casually recorded as that of any animal on the estates.

Although he was born into slavery, from the first he profited from the privileges granted to his father.

His home was larger than most of the slave cabins, but was still made of mud and wattle with a thatched roof of plaited palm. It was surrounded by plantain trees, cassava, sweet potato, yam and the giant fanned leaves of tannia. Chickens pecked and complained round the door and under the loofah vine, and tied to a stake by its back leg, the family's prized possession, the pig, grunted heavily in the heat. Toussaint, like all the children, would have to bring water for the pig from the stream, carrying the water in a clay pot on his head. He would have to help his mother feed the chickens and sweep the yard with a bunch of twigs held in his hand. Every morning his mother would wash the children, emptying the water over their heads with a calabash gourd. She would rub their arms and legs vigorously to make them hard and strong, stretching each finger and wriggling toe till it cracked while they shivered in the cool morning air, the water caught in sparkling drops on the black wool of their hair.

His mother grew vivid flowers and herbs in pots round the house, herbs that could cure the fevers that came when the rains fell: the fleshy leaves of 'wonder of the world' to bind on an aching head or tooth; 'jump up and kiss me' to make a man or woman strong in love; aloe whose spiked spears concealed a jelly that when laid warm on a wound drew out the poison; bitter-bush which the children hated to drink when they were dosed against the dysentery that swept through the plantations like a plague.

Toussaint loved the flowers and the herbs and quickly became knowledgeable about their properties for both humans and animals. His father taught him the lores of simple medicine remembered from his homeland, and as he grew older Toussaint became known on the plantation for his skill in curing the sick.

At home the family spoke their own tribal tongue. Their father would sing to them the songs of their ancestors, and when he had drunk the strong, sweet rum from the cane, he would dance, his body shiny with sweat; and with a long stick in his hand instead of a spear he would tread the dance of the warriors in mounting rhythm, the dance of the brothers of his tribe, now so far away that the memory was fading and only now and then remembered. The smell, the dust, the wind of Africa were becoming forgotten in this new green home, where life was so different; where a man was no longer a warrior, a hunter, but had to work the land like a woman to grow his food, or work like a beast to grow the white man's sugar, his cotton and indigo.

Toussaint would sit on the pounded mud floor and listen to the stories of his grandfather, the King, to tales of battles and prowess, the arts of fighting and the tactics of war, of stealthy attacks which struck suddenly and savagely, of how a few men with cunning could defeat many; and how without even using a spear an enemy could be brought low by the strategy of the mind.

Toussaint was born a slave in St Dominigue, but Africa was in his blood. He listened and dreamed of being a warrior like his father, of being a wise man who ruled justly and was renowned like his grandfather. He dreamed the dreams of many small boys, particularly boys who are smaller than their friends, whose arms and legs are puny and who in the scuffles of childhood are always defeated by the pack. Toussaint was slow to grow and he was nicknamed 'Fatras Baton' – thrashing stick. Like many who are small he resented defeat. From an early age he was determined to overcome his physical disadvantage, refusing to accept his lack of strength and recognizing it only as a challenge, something to be overcome. He was considered to be aloof, a solitary boy, for he climbed the hillsides alone and crawled up the rocky crags on the mountains above Breda until he was confident that when he stood on the peak he was no longer breathless. He swam in the fast-flowing rivers, fighting the currents like an enemy. He learned to ride early, spurring his horse up perilous stony banks and galloping day after day, mile after mile across the savannahs.

By the time he was twelve 'thrashing stick' was already famous for his horsemanship. He could leap on a galloping horse, instilling in the animal the confidence that would make it ford a dangerous river. His compatibility, his genuine love of horseflesh lasted all his life. On a horse the short jockey's body with its slightly bowed legs became both graceful and powerful. He was to become known throughout the colony as the 'Centaur of the Savannahs'. He rode tirelessly, at one with his mount, and even in middle age he would ride 125 miles and more a day and dismount with the same light agility as he had when he leapt into the saddle.

During his formative years Toussaint came under the influence of an old and respected man upon the estate, his godfather, Pierre Baptiste. A godfather then, as today in the West Indies, possessed far more importance and power in a child's life than is usual elsewhere. There is no doubt that Pierre Baptiste more than anyone shaped the future destiny of Toussaint. Baptiste worked in the hospital run by the Fathers of Charity. One of the priests, a Father Luxembourg, was impressed by his intelligence and encouraged him to learn to read and write, thereby breaking an unwritten law in the colony, where it was thought not only sensible but essential to maintain a slave's ignorance. Baptiste was also given books by the Father, taught French (rather than Creole), Latin and the rudiments of geometry.

The priest also instilled in him a devout belief in Christianity. Baptiste in his turn passed on his knowledge to Toussaint who quickly learned to read, although he never learned to write pure French, writing to the end of his life in phonetic Creole. He devoured any book available, and when he had exhausted the library of the Fathers he turned to the manager of the estate, Beagué, who, being a tolerant man and impressed by the boy's intelligence, lent him books from his shelves – unusual behaviour for the manager of a sugar plantation in St Dominigue. Toussaint read Roman history and philosophy as well as the religious books of the Fathers. His library in later life and listed after his death, included Caesar's *Commentaries*, de Claison's *History of Alexander and Caesar*, Guiselhard's *Military Memories of the Greeks and Romans*, Herodotus, Socrates and Plutarch as well as many books on military strategy. The most well-thumbed book was Epicetus, who was also born a slave. It is not too fanciful to believe that the stoic's philosophy was readily understood and absorbed by Toussaint and helped to form his character. Certainly he believed like Epicetus that endurance, abstinence and discipline were the foundations of virtue.

Baptiste laid the foundations of Toussaint's religious faith which never deserted him, and whose tenets he attempted, and succeeded more than most men, to live by all his life. His religion was not only a solace but an inspiration to him. It is difficult to comprehend that a slave could believe in God's mercy when surrounded by so much evidence to the contrary, but Toussaint's faith was simple and unquestioning. He believed, and therefore he did not doubt.

Beagué made use of the boy's intelligence, industry and interest in animals by making him husbandman to the animals on the estate. His affinity with them was such that the only times when he was recorded as losing his temper, animals were involved. When he saw another slave ill-treating an animal he would grow beside himself with rage and attack with fury those twice the size of himself.

His anger in these circumstances was not only confined to his equals. When he was eighteen, in a dispute over one of the horses, Toussaint struck Beagué. To strike a white man under the Code Noir was the gravest of offences, to draw blood meant death. It proves Toussaint's value to his master as well as the manager's exceptional indulgence that the incident was overlooked.

We know that Toussaint was never ill-treated by the owners of Breda. But there is a story that he was set upon by a white man when leaving church. Toussaint was wearing his Sunday clothes and was reading his prayer book. The man, infuriated by the presumption of a 'nigger' actually reading, struck the book from Toussaint's hand and beat him

about the head with his cudgel until his coat was spattered with blood.
Toussaint offered no resistance, but it is said he kept the coat untouched as
the reminder of a wrong. He remembered wrongs, storing them away
until the moment seemed apt to equal the score.

In Toussaint's late twenties, Bayon de Libertas – a cousin of the Comte
de Noé from the Languedoc – took over the running of the estate. He,
like his wife and his two young daughters, was a kindly, gentle man whose
attitude towards his slaves was paternal. Toussaint quickly became a
favourite with his new master and his family who treated him with easy
familiarity and trust.

He was now at the height of his manhood but he was still 'Fatras Baton',
only five feet two inches tall, but his body was strong and wiry with the
suppleness and agility of an athlete. He was not handsome, even allowing
for the fact that contemporary European observers could find no merit
at all in a black face. His face was oval, his nose rather long, his mouth
large and thick-lipped, but his eyes were remarkable, with a disquieting,
almost hypnotic magnetism. It was said of him in later life that 'nobody
can approach Toussaint without fear, or leave him without emotion'.
(General Vincent)

As a slave he learned to conceal the development of his personality.
His reputation was one of mildness. 'He was proverbial for his patience,
in so much that it was a favourite amusement of the young and incon-
siderate on the same estate to endeavour to provoke him by wanton
tricks. But so perfectly had he regulated his temper that he constantly
answered with a meek smile.' (Marcus Rainsford)

His ability to cloak his feelings was the badge of his slavery. His
stoicism was not only gleaned from books: he concealed his pride, his
ambition, the extent of his intelligence, above all he concealed the passion that was to make him lead a whole nation in rebellion. Through the
long years of adolescence, manhood and early middle age he remained
'old Toussaint', the perfect servant. Submissive, obliging, a quiet man with
a conciliatory, passive disposition, the very opposite of the man he was to
become. His other self, his true character, was carefully and deliberately
concealed behind the quick ever-ready smile, the deferential manner.
Toussaint in later years was often accused of being deceitful. If he was,
then he had been forced to learn deceit early. Dissimulation is the necessary characteristic of the slave. Toussaint turned the years of practised
duplicity to good use when he found it expedient.

In Toussaint's late thirties, Bayon de Libertas promoted him to postilion
in charge of the stables and to head stockman. He would drive his master
into Le Cap or accompany him on social visits to neighbouring
plantations, riding the leading horse in front of the shining carriage with

its crested doors. He would wait outside the assembly rooms or the newly fashionable 'English clubs' where the planters met to discuss the latest news from the 'metropole', the price of sugar, and the rumours of the disturbing new political movements that were the talk of the Colony. Toussaint, as he curried his horses till they gleamed, would also learn of the new philosophies and the hopes of the common man in the faraway world that existed outside island life. He would stand patiently in the shade beside the milliners and dressmakers where his mistress and the young ladies were being shown the latest importations from Paris. After loading their purchases he would conduct them safely home along the dusty roads between the sugar cane smelling of molasses in the heat of the sinking sun. In the evening's cool he would escort the family when they went visiting and as they sat on their host's gallery sipping 'sangaree' and travelled sherry, he would be entertained in the kitchen quarters, given a measure of rum flavoured with lime and grated nutmeg, and he would hear on the grapevine the news, whose tendrils threaded their way through all the estates, of the treatments meted out to his fellow slaves, less fortunate than himself: a whipping for burning a dish, bestial punishments for small offences, men, women and children separated and sold away. He would see the maidservant pregnant by a passing fancy of the master or the sons of the household; and he would always be aware that if he himself did not behave with effacing circumspection he would be liable to abuse by any overseer who crossed his path, simply because he was there, he was black and a slave.

Some nights he would travel with the family to balls and assemblies given when the crop had been cut, and he with the rest of the servants would watch through the jalousies the dancing, the gavotte, the minuet under the candlelit chandeliers, would observe the kaleidoscope of human emotions, intensified by claustrophobic island society. Outside in the dark he would talk in whispers to other men like him who had also heard rumours of hope, men who had lived for so long with none. Then in the palest light before dawn he would drive the family safely home, and as he rode he thought of what he had seen and heard.

Toussaint was an exemplary and trusted servant, but his personal life as a young man caused his master increasing concern. His privileged position, his smart livery with breeches, buttoned coat and cockaded hat, his superior intelligence, his manner and his eloquent eyes attracted the women on the estate, a fact of which Toussaint did not hesitate to take advantage. Finding that a climate of too noticeable sexuality was disturbing his ordered household, his master suggested that it was time his womanizing stopped and that he settle down and take a wife. De Libertas found for his slave a girl he considered suitable. Toussaint calmly replied,

'I will choose my own wife.' As he wrote afterwards: 'After many years of wandering my master wished me to marry a young and lively Negress. I resisted their suggestions which went against the ideas that I had already formed of what consituted a happy marriage.' Toussaint wanted a wife who had 'the expertise and knowledge necessary to run a household'. The wife he eventually chose, for he did not, in spite of pressure from his master, marry until he was around forty, was Suzanne Simone Baptiste. She was the daughter of his godfather Pierre Baptiste, and was five years younger than Toussaint. She was a gentle, comfortable woman, who was already pregnant when Toussaint married her. The child was by a mulatto called Seraphim Le Clerc. It has been suggested that the child, a boy named Placide, was in fact Toussaint's, but Placide was certainly a mulatto and both Toussaint and Suzanne were of pure Negro blood. Toussaint loved children and Placide, be he stepson or not, was the child of his heart. Isaac was born a year after Placide and St Jean ten years later, but Placide was always his favourite. Later Placide's wife was to write, 'Toussaint had particular affection for Placide.' And asking for news of his family, Toussaint added 'especially Placide'. He treated his children fairly, loving them all with a demonstrative and deep emotion. His love for Suzanne lasted all his life; although he was not faithful to her he loved her tenderly. She was an abiding anchor in his life; her calm, her simplicity and lack of pretension sustained and satisfied him. He looked back on his early years of marriage with nostalgia and wrote: 'We went, Suzanne and I, to work on our land hand in hand and we returned the same way. We hardly noticed the weariness of the day's work. The Almighty blessed our labour. We reaped abundantly so that not only did we have enough for ourselves but had the pleasure of giving to those blacks who were lacking. On Sundays and feast days we went to Mass, and after a pleasant meal we passed the rest of the day with our family, finishing the day with our prayers.'

Did he romanticize those years, concealing the degradation of total servitude? Or did he accept it, creating for himself and his family an illusion of quiet contentment? He had bought the freedom of the woman who looked after his mother before she died, when Toussaint was still only a child, and yet he never attempted to buy his own freedom or that of his own family. It is incongruous from all we know of slavery that he was by the efforts of his labours a comparatively rich man. He wrote 'the revolution found me with about 648,000 francs'. There seems no reason why he should have exaggerated or lied about this fact. But then why did he not buy his freedom and that of his children?

Perhaps he preferred his land, his master's horses, the security of protection rather than making his way as a free-black in an urban existence.

On many occasions in his life Toussaint became curiously reluctant to take decisions, yet at other times his actions were swift and decisive. Perhaps he felt labels did not matter. Whether free or a slave he was still black, and in St Dominigue that was the shackle. He wrote in retrospect in August 1797: 'I was born a slave, but nature gave me a soul of a free man. Every day I raised up my hands in prayer to God to implore him to come to the aid of my brethren and to shed the light of his mercy upon them.' He recognized that he was more fortunate than most. His passion for liberty was objective, almost academic, it was not exacerbated by his personal experience but by a pure knowledge of what was right. His passion was not spurred by vengeance or hatred for the white man, he never showed any sense of racism at all. His mind was clear of cant and self-pity. History showed him that millions of white men had been slaves and suffered, like him and his brothers, and would probably do so again. He remained unswervingly objective all his life. He genuinely believed that all men were equal in the sight of God. Equal in virtue and in sin, whatever their colour. It was not a popular view during his lifetime, any more than it is today. His prowess in battle is remembered with pride in modern Haiti, but his attempts to create national unity are still regarded as a regrettable sign of weakness. To Toussaint the fury of the battlefield was a means to an end, the end being peace. Once over and the victory won, it was time for tolerance and humanity.

We know he possessed a book by Abbé Raynal, as it was found among the books in his library. He had read 'Natural liberty is the right which is given to all men to dispose of himself according to his will . . . If self-interest alone prevails with nations and their masters there is another power. Nature speaks louder than self-interest . . . A man of courage, a leader only is wanted . . . Where is he? He will appear, we cannot doubt it. He will come and raise the sacred standard of liberty and gather round it the companions of his misfortune, more impetuous than mountain torrents they will leave behind them on all sides the indelible signs of their just resentment. The old world and the new will applaud him and the name of the hero who will have established the rights of the human race will be blessed by all.'

So he read the words of hope and he waited, he listened to the underground murmurings of resistance, he listened to the news from France that the sailors brought into Le Cap and he passed it all on to others. He met those who like himself were waiting, seeking them out in the secret tangle of the forest, and he spoke to them of freedom, and year after year he waited and prayed.

3   1791: The Slave Rebellion

On Sunday night, 14 August 1791, on the Leonormand plantation in the Bois Caiman a group of people met, walking together as silently and stealthily as cats through the thick dark night. Their masters with their families, sweating a little and fanning themselves in their prickly lace jabots and high collars, sat in happy ignorance. Those who served them their wine and their dinner knew, as they bent over them with kindly servitude, answering each order with attention. In the nurseries the wet-nurse knew, as she held the baby, its small bobbing head so fair against her black breast.

They gathered in a clearing, their bodies darker than their own shadows under the fitful moon. They carried flambeaux with them, rags soaked in oil on rough sticks. It was a murky night, there was thunder and sudden drenching rain with a high wind, a 'blow' which comes over the hills with such force that it is like standing against a presence.

They had planned this for many months. Two responsible men from each plantation represented their fellows. They had come from Limonade, Limbé, Port Margot and from the Plaine du Nord.

There were well over 200 men who knew, like Toussaint, that the time had now come. It is not known with certainty whether Toussaint was there, but as the leader of the slaves of Breda, and one of the chief planners and instigators of the rebellion, he surely must have been. He never revealed the fact, nor did those who were later forced to confess and tell the story of that night ever reveal his name.

The leader of the meeting was Boukman, a giant of a man of herculean strength. He was a Jamaican, a maroon who lived in the dense forest of Morne Rouge, making sudden forays on plantations and carrying off what he needed to live by, as his Jamaican ancestors had done. He was a grotesque-looking man according to contemporary views, with a 'terrible countenance', a face like an exaggerated African carving. He was not only a man of great physical stature, but with the presence essential in a leader. He was also a killer. It was necessary. He was the right man to rouse his people from their long years of apathy, for only by the stimulus of violence could they hope to gain their freedom.

Boukman was a houngan, a priest of Vodun (Voodoo), who practised the religion of his ancestors of Dahomey. He stood in front of a rough altar surrounded by the silent crowd, ready to dedicate the cause to the old gods and to ask their help. There was a woman priest there too, a 'mambu', massive, rock-like, dressed in white, and young girls who were a necessary part of the ceremony who swayed among the unmoving men, clasped to each other, a snake coiling and uncoiling in the orange light of the torches.

The wind rose, branches cracked off the high forest trees. The mambu took the white cockerel and bit off its head, then spurted the blood on the faces and breasts of the men nearest to her in the circle. Those behind swayed and moaned very deep in their throats. The houngan, Boukman, killed a gazelle and a goat with his machete, then a peccary; as the pig shrieked and gurgled a young man fell to the ground, his back arched, writhing as the priest straddled him as if in an act of love. One of the girls screamed shrilly again and again then staggered in circles speaking in the gruff voice of a man before she too fell to the ground, her body flexing in orgasm. Four men carried her away tenderly into the bushes and did not return.

In a high voice Boukman chanted a prayer to Vaudoux, his body shaking from head to foot, his voice that of a priest rather than a man. He spoke in Creole – 'Bon dié qui fait soleil clairé nous en haut . . . good god who made the sun to shine above us, who rouses the waves and makes the storm, who watches us though hidden in the clouds. Who knows all that the white man does. The god of the white man inspires him to crime, our god leads us to do good. Our god demands vengeance, he will direct our arms and help us. Throw away the symbol of the god of the whites who has caused us so many tears. Good god, give us the liberty which is in all our hearts.'

There was a mulatto there who spoke of the wrongs of the white man, of how the king of France wished to help them, to give them two days a week for their gardens, but how the white man was preventing this. The king of France had created laws to protect them, but the white man ignored the law. The white man sat alone on his pinnacle and cared nothing for their suffering.

Jeannot was there, Jean François and Biassou.

Jean François was a strange man to find at such a meeting, an unlikely instigator of revolution. The driving force that motivated him was his hatred of his former master for, like Boukman, he had fled to a secret life in the hills. He was ambitious, volatile, frivolous and charming, and he was also highly intelligent. He was not a brave man but hated violence and could only bring himself to it when drunk, at which time his normal sexual feelings turned to brutality. His dedication to the cause seems to have sprung as much from a desire for his own aggrandizement as from conviction. But in spite of something lightweight in his character he had the magnetism of a leader. Biassou worked for the Fathers of Charity at Le Cap. He was the very opposite of Jean François, brusque, quick-tempered and reckless. He was intolerant of those less dependable than himself and suspicious of their motives. He was a man of tireless vitality and his dedication towards the cause was deep and sincere. His weakness, like Jean François', was for women and drink. Jeannot, a slave from the Bullet plantation, was a small, thin man with a forbidding manner and a veiled crafty face. He was utterly remorseless not only towards the whites whom he hated with an overpowering passion but even towards his own kind. He was of the stuff that many a leader is made. He would stop at nothing to gain his own ends, he was daring, seizing quickly on chances, quick-witted and capable of total hypocrisy. He feared no one and nothing: unfortunately he found inspiration in cruelty, a sadist without the refinements that so-called civilization brings.

These men had been born slaves and yet they were no different from many free men who have ruled nations and led their people to war: energetic, ambitious and ruthless men who at times are capable of treachery and conscienceless mendacity, since the desire to conquer does not necessarily breed virtue. Boukman, Jeannot, Biassou, Jean François and Toussaint may have displayed many of the faults of free men of the past who were leaders; but they were not free men. The fact that they were born into slavery emphasized any faults they might have possessed and created others that originally they did not have. Their cause was just, and for those who fight for the freedom of their fellow men, our judgement is moderated.

They had gathered, they had pledged themselves in blood and together they sang a song of war:

> Eh! Eh! Bomba! Heu! Heu!
> Canga, bafio Té.
> Canga, moune de lé
> Canga, do ki la!
> Canga, li!

> We swear to destroy the whites
> and all they possess.
> Let us die rather than fail
> to keep this vow.

Nature seemed to encourage them that night, in the wind, the thunder and the dark. Later, in the rain they filed back on the narrow winding tracks that were unknown to white men. They returned to homes that had never been a home, to their huts and crowded barracks and they gave the message to those who had waited behind. It is decided. Net yet. But soon.

The plan was organized and clear. The slaves in Le Cap were to rise first and massacre their masters, something that could be easily accomplished as there were 10,000 slaves in the town alone and only 3600 whites. Simultaneously, the plantation slaves were to rise and massacre everyone who stood in their way, mulatto or black and, following the plan in Le Cap, eliminate all whites. But something went wrong with the timing and the slaves in Le Cap missed their opportunity, then it was too late.

Eight days later on 22 August 1791 the field slaves arose. Led by Jean François, Biassou, Boukman and Jeannot they fell upon every plantation on the northern plain, Galliflet, Limonade, Noé, Clément. Noé in the parish of Acul was the first to go, although there they did not harm the doctor or his wife. Throughout the holocaust the slaves, perhaps remembering past kindnesses, spared the doctors. From Noé on, everything was put to the flame, not a tree was left.

They had no weapons but fury, vengeance and fire; they strangled their masters with their bare hands and raped their mistresses upon the bodies of their sons and husbands, before gouging out their eyes and leaving them to die in their burning houses. They mass raped the young girls and carried them off with them, priggish little aristocrats, educated in France, who sat in the shade to protect their skins, and knew no world except fashion and fêtes. They nailed children to the gate posts of their fathers' plantations, and a white baby with a spike through his body was their banner.

They picked up weapons as they went, their masters' guns and iron pieces from the wrecked factories. They tore the clothes from their victims' bodies and pranced and laughed in satin breeches and blood-stained chemises. Loving servants were the first to turn upon those they had seemed to care for most. Slaves who tried to shield their 'families' were in their turn killed by the mobs or fled to the hills.

The order was complete destruction, factories were torn down, the great iron boiling vats overturned, the machinery wrecked and everything that could burn was burned.

Through the flames, with the sugar blazing like a torch and the air thick with sweet smoke, some escaped. Distraught women in silk dresses and thin shoes stumbled frantically along roads they had never walked before to Le Cap. Fortunate men, who had seen the flames and heard the noise of the mob, rode off to carry the news. Some reached Le Cap with the dawn. The news that the slaves had risen and all in the north was lost

was given to the Governor, de Blanchelande. At ten that morning the
alarm was sounded and the troops called out.

In Le Cap the population smelt the smoke and saw the sky turned red by
the flames. It is said it resembled a volcanic eruption. They knew without
any doubt what had happened. The underlying dread of centuries had at
last come to pass. As the few survivors crawled into the town panic
turned to fury. The 'petits blancs' turned not only upon the free blacks
but upon the mulattoes also with a savagery which equalled anything the
slaves had done. Servants were dragged out of houses and hacked to
pieces in the streets. A carpenter was placed between two of his boards
and sawn in half. Blacks were chased through the town and, when
cornered, were strung up on the nearest tree or tortured before a jeering
populace.

De Blanchelande was desperate; he ordered the militia and all able-
bodied men to put up fortifications round the town. The cannon was
turned from the sea to the land where the enemy now lay. He was helpless
and ineffective in stopping the mob rule and hatred within the town
itself. 'The whites in their fury regarded all who were black as enemies,
they massacred indiscriminately even those who had remained faithful to
them.' (Malenfant)

The once elegant little town, with its symmetrical streets and whitewashed houses with the central courtyards planted with oranges and
bananas, was fast being abandoned. The bathing establishments, the
ballroom, the clubs stood empty and looted.

Frantic men pleaded with the captains of already overcrowded ships to
take their wives and children to safety – anywhere. The more fortunate
sailed to France, Jamaica, the United States or Trinidad. Some took a
handful of house slaves with them. Mulatto mistresses and their children
sailed with white wives and their half-brothers and sisters. Some hatreds
were healed by the mutual terror.

Under the scarlet blossom of the poincianas swayed the stiff black
bodies of hanged men. On the Quai de St Louis where every Sunday the
'grand blancs' paraded after Mass piles of unburied bodies lay on the neat
pavé, the sated flies crawling on the blood-caked stones which once were
watered every day to cool and freshen the air. A pall of smoke choked the
town; everything was covered with a layer of sticky sugary ash which
floated down day and night like black snow.

One hundred thousand slaves were free and 4000 were marching on
Le Cap. They sang and beat their drums as they came. Their houngans
dancing in front called on Ogun, the god of war. The women exhorted
the men onwards with shouts and high-pitched demoniacal cries, their
children running between their legs, ignoring death. As they came within

range of the gunfire they were eerily silent and still. When fire opened they rushed forward and threw themselves on the cannon, trying to overturn them with their bare hands, trying to stifle the firing with their own bodies. Wave after wave of them attacked and attacked again, clambering and leaping over the bodies of their fallen comrades. It was useless. They had no weapons but those they had plundered from the estates – and they did not know how to use them.

When it was over, it was said that 'absolute silence succeeded the dreadful uproar; this was replaced by the pathetic cries of dying prisoners . . . the transition from silence to noise and from noise to cries of anguish and misery.'

The first attack on Le Cap lasted all night. The town was defended by a small band of 400 regular troops and the militia, volunteers with some degree of training. Monsieur de Touzard was in command; a soldier of experience, he had fought in the War for Independence in the United States. As the onslaught ended he managed to drive off the rebels before him, inflicting many losses. But the situation had become so serious within the town itself that de Blanchelande recalled him, fearing a general massacre.

The leaders of the rebels realized there was no course of action open to them but retreat, and to re-form in some sort of order. Their army was only a mob and Jean François' and Biassou's natural intelligence made them see that their situation was for the moment hopeless. They withdrew towards the hills using the only weapon left to them – fire – burning all behind them as they went.

The Jamaican planter, Bryan Edwards, wrote: 'We arrived in the harbour of Le Cap at evening on September 26th and the first sight which arrested our attention as we approached was a dreadful scene of devastation by fire. The noble plain adjoining Le Cap was covered with ashes, and the surrounding hills, as far as the eye could reach, everywhere presented to us ruins, still smoking houses and plantations at that moment in flames.' The fire, the scorching heat, the clouds of ash-filled smoke had by then continued for over a month.

Neither side took prisoners, there was no mercy, it was not the time for mercy. Both sides killed their captives with equal savagery. Prisoners were disembowelled and left to die, their limbs cut off before, mercifully, their head was severed from their body.

Jeannot was one of the instigators of the more horrific acts of savagery. He hanged those he had captured by hooks stuck under their chins. He himself put out their eyes with red-hot pincers. He cut the throat of a prisoner and lapped at the blood as it flowed, encouraging those around him to join him: 'Ah, my friends, how good, how sweet is the blood of the whites. Drink it deep and swear revenge against our oppressors, never peace, never surrender, I swear by God.' There is no doubt that as he became more steeped in the blood of his enemies his naturally violent and sadistic nature overbalanced from plain savagery into insanity. That his hatred was genuine there is also no doubt, as was his passion for freedom, for the revolution. As Schoelcher says, 'The barbarous behaviour of the masters was responsible for the barbarous behaviour of the slaves.'

Boukman was killed in either this attack or a later skirmish. His head was cut off and placed upon a spike where it stood in the Place d'Armes in Le Cap, with a placard stating 'This is the head of Boukman, Chief of the Rebels.' 'He preserved the horrifying expression of body and atrocity of soul which he had always possessed.' In fact, he was a sad loss to men who needed at this time leaders of strength, direction and courage.

Thousands of men and women died in a few days. In one month 2000 whites and 10,000 blacks had died or vanished without trace. Ex-slaves who were themselves afraid of the rebels fled to the hills. Mulattoes and whites made their way, frightened every moment for their lives, up the steep passes and across the Spanish border to safety. In Le Cap, boatloads sailed every day for anywhere that would give them shelter.

The first holocaust was over, the next phase was slow to begin. Each faction was in a state of shock; in the confusion no one, from the Governor to the simplest slave, knew which way to turn.

On the plantation of Breda, Madame de Libertas was alone except for her two young daughters. She must have been a woman of exceptional courage and strength of character, for she must have been well aware of the terror and horror that had destroyed her neighbours and the adjoining plantations. She remained, unharmed. Her husband had left her in Toussaint's care as he always did when away on business. Madame de Libertas must have trusted him implicitly, even with her life, and, a more difficult trust for a mother, her children's.

When the uprising came, Bayon de Libertas and some fellow planters who were also in Le Cap made their way back to Breda. For he wrote afterwards, 'It was with inexpressible joy that I saw Toussaint among the slaves', and, 'Toussaint, it was he alone who protected us.' Seeing his family safe, he made his way to the coast to try and get a passage on one of the schooners to the United States of America, again leaving his wife and children with Toussaint.

It was a grave responsibility. Toussaint, being Toussaint, could only honour the trust and faith that had been placed in him; realizing as the days went by that the temper of the slaves of Breda was changing and that he could no longer contain 1000 slaves who had freedom within their grasp in order to protect one white woman and her two children, he told her that it was time to go. He packed the family's valuables and loaded the mules with produce from the estate so that they would have saleable goods for their journey and for their arrival in a foreign land. At night, for the last time, he helped Madame de Libertas into the carriage he had driven for so many years and had kept with such care and pride, then, putting them in the charge of his brother, he watched them drive away.

It was over, forty-odd years were finished and could never return. Toussaint's affection for the family was genuine and, like all true affection, practical. He sent money to them in Baltimore where they had settled, in order that they might continue to live in style as he had remembered them. His concern led him to write later to the Corps Législatif on their behalf: 'Recognition being the finest perquisite to a virtuous and sympathetic man I realize that I must make it my first duty to listen to its voice. The place to which chance and great events, from which I was far from seeing, have raised me . . . has not made me forget that 20-odd years ago the burden of slavery was lifted from me by one of those men who place more importance on the duties to be fulfilled towards suffering humanity than on the product of work of a miserable being. I speak here of my old master the virtuous Bayon now aged sixty.' Toussaint pleaded with the Corps Législatif for permission for de Libertas to reside once more in the Colony 'where the former slaves gave his subsistence to recompense him for the fact that he had once treated them with humanity'. De Libertas' daughters too remembered Toussaint with gratitude and affection and kept in touch with the L'Ouverture family after Toussaint's death and wrote a letter of condolence to Isaac asking for 'a memento of your honoured and respected father'.

Toussaint left everything in order at Breda in his usual methodical way. He sent his own family in the care of Pierre Baptiste over the San Raphael mountains to the Spanish border and safety; then, taking his horses and the most reliable of the slaves of Breda with him, he rode off to join the rebels. As he rode towards the rebels' camp, he himself described his feelings: 'those first moments were one of a beautiful delirium, born of a great love of freedom', . . . then he added 'the only objects of my conduct were mankind, the love of country and of my brethren'.

Jean François, Biassou and Jeannot had retreated to the Galliflet plantation at Grand Rivière and there set up camp. The camp was roughly surrounded by cannon seized from various outposts. The heads of slaughtered prisoners were impaled on spikes which formed a grisly fence around it. Toussaint passed the sentries two months after the insurrection. His first reaction must have been one of disgust and shame at the degradation and disorder that confronted him. The soldiers were a bizarre sight, dressed in the rags and tatters of the finery of their former masters: plumed hats over women's bodices, embroidered taffeta coats over loin-cloths, and many were naked. The cavalry was mounted on mules and horses stolen from the estates and the factories, the animals by now exhausted from continuous travel over precipitous and rock-filled roads. The soldiers' only weapons were iron staves and bars, table legs and sticks from the bush. They shouldered a paucity of plundered arms, which they had simply used as clubs, not knowing how to use them properly. They had no ammunition or powder and little food.

Their elation was gone, their triumph over; the vengeance and the bloodlust that had carried them on to impossible feats of courage had faded. To take Le Cap, to kill again, to plunder a town and set it on fire was not as easy as falling upon a plantation or gutting a great house. They were weary, and all that remained from their triumph was a self-sickness. Some were dying from festering wounds, many succumbing to the virulent fevers that were endemic to the island. Shelter was inadequate and it was a time for 'the rains' which fell on half-clothed bodies and unprotected heads. Any West Indian of African descent can be struck down with cold and fever within a few hours of getting soaked.

Toussaint's first reaction was a practical one. He made immediate use of his knowledge of herbs and medicines by taking over the tending of the wounded and the sick. Quietly walking on his rounds among the men he talked to them, instilling confidence as he went. He heard their experiences, listened to their needs, and in this way he assessed the situation far better than by conferences with the officers. Many a general in the past has discovered this truth.

The camp had been divided into three commands under Jean François, who was 'Grand Admiral and Commander in Chief', Biassou, who called himself 'Generalissimo of the Conquered Territories', and Jeannot, who had chosen the title 'Grand Judge'. Toussaint on his arrival was made 'Chief Physician to the Army'.

The contrast between the leaders and their men was notable. They had endeavoured to dress themselves in the most theatrical flamboyance, copying the officers they had seen in Le Cap but adding carnival touches of their own. From the estates, from the prisoners they had captured, they had taken a mixture of uniforms and put them together with that particular stylishness that only a black man possesses. Jean François, always a dandy, wore a handsome grey uniform with golden epaulettes and cordons and yellow facings. He had also discovered in some drawer in a great house press, the cross of the 'Order of St Louis' which he wore pinned to his breast. All the officers sported plumed hats, swords and top boots, which they must have found very uncomfortable. There were colonels, commanders, marshals, whatever rank they felt most suitable for their personality.

It is easy to scoff at such posturings, self-decoration and grandiose titles; but even in a ragged army such as this it was still necessary for officers to dress differently from their men and in the eighteenth century this difference was even more pronounced than today. It is essential, on and off the field, for an officer and his authority to be immediately recognizable. Armies, even revolutionary ones, are not democratic institutions.

Jean François' task, that of keeping in check an undisciplined mob of thousands, who had just tasted freedom, was not an easy one. He cannot be blamed for using every ruse available to him. If he aped the 'old master', perhaps there was wisdom in his thinking. In the end old habits die hard. Jean François was a commander with a touch of greatness, as his subsequent career was to prove. With an iron hand he enforced discipline, by death if necessary – human life in the early days of the rebellion had become expendably cheap – but he also employed the velvet glove of charm of manner, gaiety and good looks which made those who served under him his willing followers. Biassou and Jeannot managed to keep their sections under control by making brutal examples of those who were recalcitrant, but the rebel army was still a long way from being a force to be reckoned with.

There were four priests attached to the camp: Fathers Delahaye, Sulpice, Boucher and Bienvenu who, either from a belief in the cause, a desire to save souls or for political reasons, had elected to side with the rebels. There were a few mulattoes, many black freed men and, later, many whites. There is one incongruous fact that is hard to comprehend: the rebel army had mustered under the standard of the House of Bourbon, the Royal Standard of the King of France. They called their army the 'King's Army'. 'Vive le Roi' and 'Ancien Régime' were their mottoes.

Many knew of the Code Noir and of its instigator, King Louis XIV; it was at least an attempt in a barbarous age to guard against some of the worst aspects of slavery. They also knew that many of the more humanitarian edicts of the code had been ignored by the planters. So, they thought that it followed that this king was on their side against the planters and the Assembly. They had also learned from mulatto agents, anxious to secure the black support against the whites, of the local Assembly's reversal of the decree from Paris giving freed men of colour their rights. They believed with naïve romanticism that the king had been imprisoned by the whites in Paris because he had endeavoured to liberate the slaves of St Dominigue. It has been said that Toussaint was himself a Royalist agent and that he had been heavily bribed by the Royalist factor. He is supposed to have overheard a conversation between Bayon de Libertas and a Royalist concerning a plan for relieving the slave gangs. 'He had the boldness to interrupt and approve the plan, adding that there should be a promise of three days' freedom and an end to flogging. Later he said it would be only right to guarantee liberty to those slaves who might stir up the others, which was tantamount to offering himself for the job!' (Sannon)

It is doubtful if any white (the man was unlikely to be both a mulatto and a guest at a white planter's house), however strongly Royalist, would have been insane enough to bring the slaves out in revolt with the obvious risk of his family, his friends, his associates being murdered, losing all his property and possessions and his own life, simply for the lost cause of the king or a political association such as the Club de Massiac. It is also extremely unlikely that Toussaint would have gone along with such confused ideological thinking – he was far too pragmatic.

Many strange fidelities spring up in revolutions, but for rebellious slaves to be fighting for the same cause as those whom they had murdered in their thousands, was, to say the least, inconsistent.

If indeed the counter-revolutionary 'grand blancs' – inspired from Paris – did incite the slaves to revolt they certainly made a grave mistake.

The slaves, of course, were in reality fighting for their freedom, though perhaps they were secondarily fighting the Assembly and the 'establishment' that had made them slaves and had extinguished that freedom. They were also fighting the men they knew to be responsible for their misery, the whites and, it should not be forgotten, the mulattoes. They were too uninformed or misinformed to comprehend that the Assembly in Paris was very different from the Assembly in St Dominigue, to realize that Robespierre and the Jacobins were the men who had fought for the rights of the coloured man. Politically bewildered, unable to read or write, they believed that it was the king alone who defended them against all Assemblies, and perhaps they saw in him the leader they craved. They were to find another.

4 The Insurrection Continued: The French Intervention

Toussaint's influence was soon apparent in the rebel camp: a humanitarian throughout his life, it was obvious that he would be incapable of tolerating Jeannot's paranoiac behaviour. Jean François only needed his support to tip the balance of his own feelings, feelings which were not entirely those of righteous indignation, since he was jealous of Jeannot's bravery in battle and his growing hold upon his men. Jeannot appealed to their worst side and led them, by his example, to commit diabolical acts of cruelty which they never would have without his influence.

Toussaint and Jean François waited for him to make a mistake that defied general orders. Jeannot made it. He killed a white civilian, a Monsieur Paradole, in front of his four young children, who vainly tried to protect his body with their own. Jean François was infuriated, put Jeannot on trial and by mutual agreement of all officers he was condemned to death. He died badly; cruelty is often the weapon of a coward. He screamed for mercy, crawled on his knees to the priest, Father Bienvenu, who offered him the Last Sacrament, and sobbed against the hem of his robe. 'He clutched the father with so much force that the violence must have caused pain when tearing him away.' (Raynal) He fought the men who tried to blindfold him and screamed hysterically until the moment he was shot, bound to the same tree which he had ordered to be embedded with iron hooks to impale the bodies of his many victims. He had never shown mercy and Jean François, Biassou and Toussaint showed none to him.

With Jeannot gone the mood in the camp at Galliflet became more rational. The wild excesses of the first months were curbed. Indiscriminate slaughter was confined to brief bursts of fury against prisoners of war. Toussaint served under Biassou. He was raised in fighting rank, but still continued in his post as Chief Physician to the army. He went to work quietly and methodically. He looked around him at the land of the fertile north which had once been the pride of St Dominigue, and saw only the twisted skeletons of blackened trees, the tumbled and charred factories and the eyeless sockets of windowless houses. He also saw in the waste land the green sprouts of the cane pushing through the earth beside the uneven burnt stubble which the rain had soaked and brought out again, bringing new hope. Agriculture, husbandry had been and was to remain one of the chief concerns and pleasures of Toussaint's life. He knew it had been necessary to destroy in order to build, but now the destruction was over. His army needed food, and to pay for that food, for uniforms, for arms, it needed the sugar cane. Anarchy had never been for him the easy solution and with relief he returned to order. His men were told to plant, to grow provisions, something not many of them cared to do, for an African's hands have little sympathy with the soil and Toussaint's directives came too late to solve the problem of lack of food for the army.

His next concern was for the hygiene of the camp, which must have been appalling. In the eighteenth century any army camp was a scene of disgusting squalor and a constant source of infection and re-infection. Toussaint was well aware, unlike many of his contemporaries, that dirt breeds disease. Perhaps it was that Toussaint was an exceptionally fastidious man, perhaps it was his close link with his forebears in Africa which gave him the instinctive knowledge that in the tropics certain rules of cleanliness are essential to survival. It is noticeable to this day in the West Indies that on the remoter islands, where the African traditions still survive, the people are careful to observe the basic rules of hygiene.

So, in the most practical ways, the force of his small, compelling presence began to be felt. The treatment of the prisoners in rebel hands was his next concern. His over-protectiveness of the white man has often been criticized in his own time and since. It is hard to know whether his compassion sprang from the habit of slave and master or from natural humanity, but, whichever may have been the case, he meted out punishment to those under his command who were discovered committing flagrant acts of cruelty.

He was, in the same way, troubled by any disrespect or liberty taken by his men towards women. Under him rape became a punishable offence and later, as he gained more power, it became punishable by death. Toussaint was not sexually a puritan, he loved too many women too much in his early years for that to be possible, but his love of women also made him protective. Throughout his life there are many recorded instances of this attitude. In any revolution women are the sufferers, made expendable by their men with a cause. Toussaint never ignored them, but would find time, however great his urgency, to stop by the wayside and give his concern and his protection to the victims of war. He wrote of finding a group of white women without clothing, or food, having been raped by British soldiers: he gave one of them his cloak and ordered his men to cover the rest with their coats and shirts. He also ordered his victuallers to give them a barrel of wine, meat and bread and to conduct them into town. His virility, his physical strength and his intelligence produced in him the natural attitude of any male to a female – tenderness. His respect for women was misconstrued by the more sophisticated and cynical French, but it was simply the normal reaction of the natural male.

Jean-François recognized Toussaint's steady worth and raised him to the rank of Commander in control of a section of the army. Under Toussaint's growing military influence the army's assaults increased their penetration and the rebels consolidated their position, taking many of the forward outposts round Le Cap. It was noted by the whites that these attacks were becoming more cohesive and were also becoming alarmingly unpredictable. De Blanchelande's troops, listless with fever, waited in their poorly-fortified earthworks. Straining their ears in the eerie buzzing twilight, when the frogs croak and small animals chatter and creak their way through the bush, they waited for other, more menacing sounds that might herald an attack by men without uniforms whose very colour turned them into shadows. They sat, musket in hand, easing the sweat of fear from the back of their soaked coats, knowing their enemy might be only a few yards away. Before there had been warning, they had heard the clamour, the drums, the bird-like shrieks, but now there was a disquieting change.

'The manner of their approach', says Des Fosses, proved they were directed by a superior intelligence; 'they did not expose themselves *en masse* with the former fury, they formed groups, hiding in thickets before falling on their enemy. They even withdrew swiftly into the undergrowth. One was dealing with an enemy who, instead of making a concerted attack on the colours, [the insurgents] were disposed in small groups so that they were able to surround or wipe out isolated or small detachments. It was a new type of warfare more dangerous because it was unknown.' It was Toussaint who first brought guerrilla warfare to the notice of military historians. The maroons in Jamaica under Cudjoe used a similar African-inspired type of attack, but no one before or for many years to follow was to combine strict discipline and precision with athletic prowess among his troops as did Toussaint.

The orange-coated forces of de Touzard and de Blanchelande were helpless against the oiled and writhing bodies that leapt upon them out of nowhere, leaving them no time to set their cannon; it was noted that whereas they once had used machetes, spears of sharpened bamboo and iron cudgels, now they were learning to shoot.

The cries of the houngan which had carried warning to the enemy were no longer heard. Toussaint was deliberately trying to eliminate the power of Vodun over the section of the army which he commanded. His men's faith in their houngans and in the power of fetishes led them to believe they were invulnerable. Madiou, a Haitian historian, says that when they went into combat 'they threw themselves against the French with pro- digious intrepidity crying that the bullets were but dust . . . they died without regret believing that they would be returning to Africa'. Tous- saint could ill afford heavy losses among the men he was training so care- fully and he constantly exhorted his men to deny superstition, telling them that the victory lay within themselves and not with their gods. In the same way, he attempted to forbid the ritual dances that lasted all night and would leave his men sluggish when they assembled for their morning drill. The other commanders were less concerned because they were themselves less disciplined.

There was another side to Toussaint's fight against Vodun: his firmly- held Christian beliefs instilled in him by his godfather Pierre Baptiste, and by the French priests who had first given him the sacrament and who still surrounded him. He recognized both free will and conscience and with his usual far-sighted objectivity realized that a religion whose emphasis is upon fatalism and superstition builds not only a poor fighting force but a weak nation. A people who are prepared to accept the death of a child from neglect as the evil eye, or the loss of a crop which has been carelessly planted and left untended as the 'bad turn of the moon' were, he knew, not going to survive in this world of new philosophies and sciences, where balloons could take off into the sky. Toussaint was determined that his people were going to survive; single handed, if necessary, he was going to build from a conglomerate mass of African tribes not just an army but a nation.

His own self-discipline was monastically strict – although later when power and more time came his way his fondness for women reasserted itself. Most Creoles eat and drink prodigiously but Toussaint was content to exist, even after a hard day in the field, on a plantain, a piece of cassava bread or a bowl of soup. He would toy with a glass of wine in company, but rather for its taste than for its effect. Although hard on others his first discipline was directed towards himself and next towards his officers: 'You must maintain the strictest order among your troops. These are the two foremost virtues of military command.' He reminded them that these were the qualities which brought success to the Romans. To the majority of his officers Rome must have meant little but to Toussaint it meant a great deal. Caesar lived with him in his mind and in the long sleepless nights – for he was a man who found only two or three hours of sleep a night necessary to maintain energy – he read and re-read the plans and directives for battle and the philosophies of war of the great soldier, Julius Caesar.

Pamphile Lacroix who was a chief of staff of Napoleon wrote, 'No

European army was subjected to severer discipline than Toussaint's . . . officers have the power of life and death over those under their command with pistol in hand.' He noted that the control over looting was particularly severe and was punishable by death. When one considers the behaviour of Wellington's troops in the Peninsula wars when looting and raping were considered the perquisite of the common soldier, this certainly shows a remarkable command and an astonishing hold over an army which most Europeans wrote off as savages. Marcus Rainsford (an English officer whom Toussaint later befriended) wrote, 'such promptitude and dexterity prevailed the whole time as would have astonished any European officer who had the smallest idea of their previous situation'.

This obsession with discipline and order did not at first bring him the same easy popularity enjoyed by the flamboyant Jean François, who was beloved by the Negroes in his command, or by Biassou. Although exceptionally wiry and fit he was, of course, an older man; he spoke quietly and his manner was often reserved, but he combined an almost stiff dignity with sudden warmth. Rainsford says of him, 'his countenance was terrible to an enemy' and yet, he adds, 'full of the most prepossessing suavity to the object of his friendship or love. His manners and deportment were elegant when occasion required but easy and familiar in common.' Lacroix says 'his men learned to worship him', but these were early days when he was still subordinate to Biassou, at least in rank, although becoming increasingly and, to Biassou, menacingly powerful.

Faced with this growing opposition Governor de Blanchelande, who was virtually a prisoner in Le Cap, became increasingly bewildered and confused. He endeavoured to contain the insurrection by permitting no communication between the north, now lost, and the west and south. His ill-trained troops tried vainly to stop the passage of ex-slaves from the north to the rest of the island, but they were helpless against the drums which passed on the message from mountain top to mountain top, against the voice that cried the news in passing, against men who walked by night over secret passes and along river beds.

He appealed to the rest of the world, scratching out letters which to this day sound frantic in their despair. 'The flames have devastated our possessions, the arms of our Negro army are coloured with the blood of our brothers. Immediate help is needed . . . before all is lost.' He had expected help from Jamaica, it was not forthcoming; his plea was politely and diplomatically pushed aside. Lord Effingham, the Governor General of Jamaica, was not prepared to become involved in any war directly against the blacks, since the slaves of Jamaica, the self-freed maroons in the hills, were already a constant concern to him. The non-conformist churches on the island were preaching equality, backed by the abolitionists in Britain. The last thing Effingham wanted to do was to rock the boat. The planters of Jamaica talked of nothing but the 'terror of St Dominigue'; but for the time being, until the situation changed itself, Jamaica was prepared to take no overt action.

De Blanchelande then appealed to General Washington. The Assembly sent an envoy, a Monsieur Rousteau, to plead for aid. Although Washington tactfully declared himself sympathetic towards St Dominigue's problems he, at the same time, found it unfortunate that he had no suitably trained troops available, and his colleagues did not wish to involve his new country in such a confused enterprise, involving a foreign power. All that Washington was prepared to do was to send, at a mutually agreed price, arms and supplies.

De Blanchelande was probably not aware that the rebels were also negotiating with private factions in the southern part of the United States and had agreed to exchange sugar, rum and molasses for shipments of supplies. This business arrangement clearly smacks of Toussaint's practical mind. It followed a trading pattern that has always existed between the Caribbean and North America. The islands, geographically and historically, are vulnerable targets for commercialism, a free-for-all for astute foreign businessmen and politicians whether under the guise of trade or aid.

De Blanchelande's appeals to France brought slow reaction. William Pitt in England was so unconcerned that he merely remarked with ironic wit that 'it seems that the French prefer burnt sugar with their coffee'.

It was left for Spain to be the opportunist. As old colonial enemies of France they seized the chance of gaining control of the whole island. Through the medium of Father Bienvenu they approached the rebel leaders; then a flood of supplies from Spain were brought on mules, or on the backs of men, over the dusty rock-strewn road that leads from the mountain border to Galliflet.

Proof of this aid was found in a letter which read:

I am annoyed that you did not warn me earlier that you were short of ammunition. Had I known it I would have sent you some, and you would receive increasing help as well as everything you asked me for when you defended the interests of the King.

Don Alonzo

This letter is certainly ambiguous; it is unlikely that Don Alonzo referred to the French king, so it would seem that the rebels had embraced all royalist causes, expedience being their guide. They needed all the aid they could obtain from any source and were not particular from whom or under what guise they obtained it.

France at last acted. Three Civil Commissioners were known to be on their way from Paris, much to de Blanchelande's relief. His term of duty was nearly at an end. The Assembly could not deal with the situation, nor could he. He made another attempt to put his house in order and demanded the rebels' submission. He received a letter back which must have greatly surprised him and given him pause for thought.

Galliflet Camp
Sir,

We have never sought to deviate from the duty and from the respect we owe to the King's representative, nor indeed, to His Majesty. We have proof of it in our possession. But you, General, who are a just man, come among us and see this land which we have sprinkled with our sweat or, rather, with our blood; these buildings which we have raised, and that in the hope of a just reward. Have we obtained it, General? The King, the universe, have bemoaned our fate and have broken the chains we bear. And we, humble victims, we were ready for anything, not wishing at all to abandon our masters. What am I saying? I am wrong! Those who should have been as fathers to us, after God, they were tyrants, monsters unworthy of the fruits of our labours, and you wish, brave General, that we should be like sheep and should go and throw ourselves into the wolf's mouth? No, it is too late. God, who fights for the innocent, is our guide. He will never abandon us. This is our motto – Conquer or Die.

To prove to you, worthy General, that we are not as cruel as you may believe, we wish, with all our hearts, to make peace. BUT on condition that all the whites, whether from the plains or the hills, retreat in your presence and return to their homes and so leave Le Cap, without any exception, and take with them their gold and jewels. We only seek after that so precious thing, beloved liberty.

There, General, our profession of faith which we will uphold until the last drop of our blood. Then will all our vows have been fulfilled and, believe me, it costs our hearts dear that we have taken this course.

But, alas! I finish by assuring you that the entire contents of this is as sincere as if we were before you. The respect which we have for you, and which we swear to maintain, will not disappoint you, think that it is weakness, as we shall never have another motto: Conquer or Die for Liberty.

Your humble and obedient servants
The Generals and Chiefs who make up our Army

Not unnaturally de Blanchelande on receiving this concluded that there were whites involved with the rebel cause. A lawyer, a Procurator Gros, had joined them and, together with Fathers Bienvenu and Delahaye, was guiding their diplomacy. The flowery, unctuous lack of sincerity shown in this letter hardly bears the mark of simple men. It would be gratifying to believe that the priests who had joined the rebels were impartial and were inspired only by godly concern for their flock; but according to Malouet (in *Collections of Memories of the Colonies*) who was a contemporary observer, if a prejudiced one, the priesthood was corrupt before the revolution and even more corrupt after it. He wrote: 'What pierced the heart with pain was the thought that most of the parish priests had only remained among them to profit by their ignorance or to place it at the mercy of a wild fantasy.' Even the holiest men in St Dominigue's history seemed capable of ignoring the most blatant cruelties and injustices as a means to an end. To this day in parts of South America this can still be found to be true.

An unsavoury example of the dual role played by the priests of St Dominigue was recorded at the time and has often been quoted. The whites under the command of Monsieur de Touzard attacked the town of Limbé. 'M. de Touzard was fairly glad in this expedition to seize from black hands in the Limbé church a large number of white children and eighty white and coloured women.' The women told de Touzard that the priest 'had played the infamous part of deciding on the wretches to prostitute to Biassou'. De Touzard set up a gallows and hanged him in front of his church. Jeannot the murderer was encouraged to take Mass by his confessor at La Rivière, a service which Jeannot attended regularly in a carriage drawn by six horses.

Every year 40,000 slaves were imported and they died in the same numbers. For the baptism, birth or death of these the priests received at least one piastre a head or about 440,000 francs. The revenue of the clergy of St Dominigue amounted to 1,920,000 francs which was shared by the forty or fifty priests in charge of the island. For this, little was done to help the lot of the slaves or to guide them spiritually. To the slave Christianity and Vodun were simply a double insurance against the 'mals yeux' and a double passport to a world of freedom after death.

The priests in the rebels' camp took their place with the leaders and Father Bienvenu's negotiations with the Spanish were likely to be as beneficial to him as to the other parties involved.

For de Blanchelande the situation grew worse and worse. Not only did the rebels continue to resist, but now two violently opposing factions were splitting the whole structure of society. The 'grands blancs', the proprietors, the pro-royalist counter-revolutionaries (that is, counter-revolutionaries to the Jacobins of France), sported the 'white cockade' on their hats. The 'petits blancs', the followers of the revolution in France, wore the 'red cockade', and street fighting broke out for the most trivial cause. The Red Cockades also made any excuse to attack their old enemies, the mulattoes. To add to the confusion, in the west the mulattoes made their throw and rose against the 'petits blancs', who now had control of the municipalities and local governments. Wearied of the constant persecution which even led to lynchings of mulattoes by the ignorant whites, they turned. Under their flag the mulattoes saw a real hope of gaining predominance over both 'petits blancs' and the more reactionary 'grands blancs', although at this time many White Cockades were joining their cause in opposition to the Red Cockades, the followers of the Republic in France.

Such were the fragmented loyalties that formed the mulatto force. Their leaders were men of stature and substance, mulattoes who were in every way superior to the 'petits blancs' who had lorded it over them for so long simply because their skin was whiter. The main leader of the movement was Anoré Rigaud, a pure mulatto, the son of a rich planter father and a Negress called Rose Bossy. His life had been a privileged one, his father had sent him to Bordeaux to be educated and there he had learnt the trade of silversmith. He had money in his own right, but his inclinations had never been towards trade but towards the army. He had joined the colours in France, and had fought in Guadeloupe and for the rebels in the American War of Independence. His experience together with a natural flair were to make him a brilliant soldier. Schoelcher says of him: 'Rigaud was one of those men whose worth is somewhat incomplete and who are unable to reach the heights. A participant in a revolution of helots who were breaking their chains, his great courage and his intelligence from a military point of view made him powerful, but devoid of the qualities of a leader he could do nothing with that power. Furthermore, he did not have sufficient will-power to overcome the extreme violence in his character which never enabled him to be master of himself. Narrow-minded, he never succeeded either in stifling the feelings of prejudice against the Negroes, whom he did not forgive, or of the whites for having the same feeling towards him and towards his class. He attributed, it seems, his distress at having in him something of the Negro to an almost incredible childhood. "He was" says Madiou, "the son of a black and a white. He was very dark with crinkly hair. He always wore a wig of smooth hair." Perhaps, it is true, the smooth-haired wig was connected with his immoderate love of pleasure. Madiou shows him as several times leaving his army at the beginning of the southern war to go to the coral islands and amuse himself by giving balls.'

The other military leader of the mulatto revolt was Louis Jacques Beauvais. He came from the mulatto aristocracy and, like Rigaud, was educated in France and had known service in America. He was a man of great personal glamour, charming and so good-looking that he was known as the handsomest man in St Dominigue; and, physical beauty carrying its own passport, he was even accepted by the whites. In spite of this he was of a quiet and serious disposition. As a leader he was charismatic, loved and blindly followed by all who served under him or came into contact with him.

The political leader of the mulatto movement was Pierre Pinchinat, a very different type from his colleagues, an unprincipled but brilliant man who combined the aspirations of power with sexual licence. His vicious personal life in no way prevented him from being a near genius, it simply created animosities and lack of faith among those who would otherwise have admired him wholeheartedly for his quick grasp and control of the situation and for his adept diplomacy.

The following of these men was strong, for under their flag the mulattoes saw a real hope of gaining predominance over both the 'petits blancs' and the more reactionary of the 'grands blancs'. To swell their numbers, Rigaud and Beauvais recruited a body of 300 former slaves who had abandoned their estates on hearing of the rebel insurrection in the north, and who were known for some reason as the 'Swiss'.

The mulattoes won their first encounter decisively, totally routing the municipalities of the west which were dominated by the 'Red Cockades', the 'petits blancs'. Peace was hastily declared. In the public square of Port au Prince vows of brotherhood were exchanged. The church bells rang and all colours went to church and sang the Te Deum together.

There seemed to be only one remaining problem: the 'Swiss'. All agreed that it was bad policy to return these ex-slaves to their former plantations where they might foment trouble, and so it was callously agreed to ship them away from the island and dump them in Honduras, on some deserted beach, to fend for themselves. They never reached Honduras. The captain of the ship, after pocketing the money for the journey, found the haul to Jamaica easier. There the Governor refused to accept them. The ship sailed back to St Dominigue where it anchored for the night off the Môle de Nicholas. The 'Swiss' slept, crammed in the hold.

In the early hours of the morning, boats filled with armed men rowed stealthily through the calm water, the water drops splashing softly off their oars as they came alongside. The men in the hold slept on. The heavy hatches were quietly lifted and before the men were awake they were seized, their throats were cut and they were pitched overboard into the water. Their shark-torn bodies were washed up on the shore, and there the people found them; and so they knew. It is said that Rigaud and Beauvais protested vehemently against the plan, but not vehemently enough. It is also said that the slaughter was a deliberate anti-mulatto plot contrived by the whites to split the mulattoes and the blacks further apart; it could very easily have been expedience, a solution for both white and mulatto factions. Although Rigaud later denied any part in it, this treachery was never forgotten or forgiven by the Negro population, and is remembered to this day.

In Le Cap the Assembly were still unable to come to any decision on rebel, mulatto or white uprisings. Tentative promises were made to the mulattoes in an attempt to placate them: they were told that they would receive their rights once the troubles were over; but the mulattoes were not impressed by promises which had been broken so many times before. They were no longer prepared to wait. Port au Prince was soon in flames, the fire set, it is said, by mulatto women. The houses, their wood dried for years by the heat of the sun, blazed up like tinder and the conflagration spread so rapidly that even those who had set the fire were trapped. Frantic women and children tried to escape, crowding the boats in the harbour, trampling each other underfoot as they fought their way on to the small craft and causing them to overturn. Few could swim, so hundreds drowned. Amid the flames, once again natural enemies turned upon each other, the vows of brotherhood and peace soon forgotten. The slaves of the west rose with the mulattoes, and all the horrors of the north were repeated.

In the south the whites came out strongly against the mulattoes, and they in turn raised the slaves. In this conflict the whites perpetrated acts of barbarism equal to any that Jeannot committed out of fear, revenge or simply blood-lust. No mulatto was safe; a young pregnent woman who was discovered by whites cowering in the protection of her mother's arms was seized, slit open by the sword and her unborn baby torn from her and thrown in the flames 'so that there should not be another mulatto'. Women and children were burnt alive and, it is said, mulattoes were deliberately infected with smallpox. In their tortures the whites used the ingenuity that civilization brings, as well as returning to barbarism.

The Colony of St Dominigue was now a blood bath from the north to the south and west. The populace appeared to be hurtling headlong down a path of self-destruction. Massacre had become a commonplace, mercy was forgotten, the hatreds that had eaten away at the hearts of all for so many years now reigned. White killed white, mulatto turned on mulatto, black upon black. Vengeance was the cry of all, vengeance for everything known and unknown that each had perpetrated against all. Rigaud's brother wrote 'Long Live Liberty, Long Live Equality, Long Live Love'. But love had long since been vanquished and now terror reigned.

The slaves had risen and with their rising the social and economic foundations of the island had shifted and split open and now the whole structure tottered, was crumbling and falling. There seemed no way in November 1791 that the great edifice that had once been St Dominigue, 'the Pearl of the Antilles', could ever be built anew.

On 29 November 1791 three Commissioners appointed by the National Assembly in Paris landed on the island of St Dominigue. They were Roume, St Leger and Mirbeck. Both Roume and St Leger had come to St Dominigue from posts on another Caribbean island. Roume, a Grenadian, was Commissioner in Tobago. St Leger also lived on Tobago where he was a doctor and an interpreter of English. They were, in fact, colonial men. On their arrival they announced to the Assembly that they were expecting the imminent arrival of a large body of trained troops. They must have been fully aware that this promise was at best a prevarication and at worst a lie. The Assembly however took them at their word and received them with enthusiastic relief.

At Galliflet, Jean François, Biassou and Toussaint still held their ground by guerilla attacks, but they had made no dramatic progress and now they were faced with a new enemy, the threat of famine, a threat which grew daily nearer. Already some of their army had weakened and died through lack of proper nourishment. It had always been a danger they anticipated and now it was upon them. Listless through lack of food and the absence of positive action, the troops were becoming restive. The leaders held council and decided to attempt negotiation.

Their demands were liberty for 400 of the principal leaders; in return for this they guaranteed that they would lead the slaves back to the plantations, with the proviso that an extra free day a week would be granted, and the use of the whip as a punishment be banned. None of their consciences can have been clear about these terms. They knew their men, they themselves had led them to freedom, a freedom that had been hard won and would not now be given easily away. They also knew that a negotiation of this kind would be considered by the slaves nothing more nor less than treachery. Jean François was only too aware of this – he wrote: 'False principles will make the slaves intractable, they will believe they have been betrayed.'

Toussaint as one of the most powerful of the leaders must also have agreed to the terms of the negotiations. He was as culpable as any. Perhaps it was a fault, perhaps it was part of his strength, that his ideals throughout his life were tailored by pragmatic considerations. His heroism remained firmly anchored in practicality.

At this point the leaders could see little hope ahead, but if there was an escape route they were going to attempt to find it. That they were prepared to sacrifice brothers they had fought for and alongside in order to save their own skins does them little credit, but it is no more than human.

They sent as emissaries to the Assembly two Negroes who carried a letter with them to open the negotiations. There is no doubt that this letter was composed by Toussaint, his style is unmistakable. We know that Toussaint could write only phonetic Creole, but he dictated painstakingly, speaking, then listening carefully as his draft was read back to him, then altering and re-dictating until the end result satisfied his perfectionist mind. Many of his letters are small masterpieces of punctilious effort, many of them deliberately and cleverly ambivalent.

6 December 1791

Great misfortunes have beset this rich and important colony – we were involved in it and there is nothing more for us to say to justify ourselves. One day you will give us back all the justice that our position merits. The mother country demands a completely separate form of government from the colonies; but the feelings of clemency and goodness, which are not laws, but affections of the heart, should cross the seas and we should be understood in the general pardon which the king granted to everyone indiscriminately.

We see from the law of the 28th September [1791] that the National Assembly and the king grant you leave to pronounce finally on the status of non-free persons and the political status of coloured men. We defend the decrees of the National Assembly and your own, invested with all the necessary formalities, to the last drop of our blood. A large population which submits with confidence to the orders of the monarch and the legislative body which it invests with its power definitely merits some consideration. It would, in fact, be interesting if you declared, by a decree sanctioned by the general Assembly, that your intention is to take an interest in the fate of slaves. Knowing that they are the object of your concern and knowing it through their leaders, to whom you would send this work, they would be satisfied and that would help restore the broken equilibrium, without loss and in a short time.

Jean François, General.   Biassou, Field-Marshal.
Desprez, Manzeau, Toussaint and Aubert, ad hoc Commissioners.

The whole tone of this precariously balanced epistle is very different from that of the effusive letter sent to de Blanchelande before Toussaint had gained influence in the rebel camp. This later letter bears the sure stamp of the diplomat. Diplomacy is not necessarily admirable and can

too often be a politer term for mendacity and this letter, however
smoothly couched in its language, is nevertheless a betrayal.

The Assembly were unimpressed; indeed, they were outraged that any
ex-slave should attempt to dictate to them or to advise any course of
conduct for them to follow. It is a clever letter, it presupposes a mutual
interest in 'this rich and important colony', nudging the proprietors to
consider their financial interests. It reminds them firmly of the law passed
by the National Assembly regarding the rights of free men. It skates
gracefully over the leaders' agreement to assist in sending their own men
back into slavery, accepting the fact that they would be responsible for
'this work', and refers to the restoration of slavery with nicety as helping
to restore the 'broken equilibrium'.

The Assembly may have been capable of understanding the subtle
inferences of all this, but to the slaves it would have meant nothing; the
results of such an agreement, however, would have been only too clear
to them.

The Assembly's answer was 'Get out'. They dismissed the emissaries
humiliatingly. However, as the two men prepared to leave they were
told that the new Commissioners wished to see them. They were received
with unfamiliar courtesy and it was proposed that a meeting between
the Commissioners and Jean François should be held at St Michel, a plantation near Le Cap.

When the news was brought back to the rebel camp Toussaint and
Jean François were hopeful. Biassou, a blunter, more straightforward and
emotional character, reacted against any further parley, and infuriated
by the treatment of his emissaries by the Assembly, threatened to shoot
all the white prisoners who still remained in rebel hands. Toussaint, whose
principles toward prisoners of war were as ethical, if not more so, as
soldiers of this century, prevailed upon him to be patient a little longer
and Jean François, as Commander in Chief, agreed to meet the new
Commissioners.

He rode to the St Michel plantation on the appointed day accompanied
by a uniformed guard of cavalry officers. An impressive and handsome
figure he was, as usual, elegantly if a little too magnificently attired. As the
small band of rebels clattered through the plantation's pillared gates a
most unfortunate incident occurred. A white man rushed forward, his
purple face distorted with hatred and his eyes bloodshot with fury (and
probably too much rum). He seized the bridle of Jean François' horse and,
brandishing his whip, he slashed wildy at Jean François, striking him in the
face. The horse reared and Jean François wheeled the animal round and,
shouting to his men, made for the gate. The man was Jean François'
former master, the man whom Jean François had so detested that the

intensity of his hatred had inspired him to lead 12,000 slaves into rebellion.

Jean François was trembling with rage, and his men, equally incensed, would have drawn swords if at that moment St Leger had not walked calmly into their midst, courageously going up to Jean François and greeting him with respect. He spoke graciously and quietly to all the rebels and with his Irish charm, for he was of Irish origin, placated them. Jean François showed an emotional reaction after the scene of unpleasantness and responded to such warm and unprecedented behaviour by falling on one knee before him.

The terms of the agreement were repeated by the blacks. In exchange for their freedom the 400 principal leaders would persuade the thousands of other slaves to return to their plantations and to slavery. The Commissioners asked for an exchange of prisoners and Jean François replied by asking for the return of his wife, still held prisoner in Le Cap. (It is not known whether she was released or what became of her. His mother, however, who was also a prisoner, was granted her freedom.) Amid mutual expressions of goodwill Jean François bowed his departure, assuring the Commissioners that he wished to acknowledge the 'only white man whom he had ever met who showed humanity'.

Jean François returned to Galliflet, bringing back the news of his meeting and of what he probably considered to be his success. Toussaint and Biassou were unconvinced, they had not confronted St Leger and been beguiled by his charm. Even if they had it is doubtful if either of them would have sunk to their knees before him. The Commissioners were, after all, white men, and were they to be trusted?

Toussaint was often slow in coming to the major decisions of his life, needing some small spur to make him act, or like so many of his race waiting for some signal, some omen to guide him. He was a Catholic but Dahomey lurked behind his back, and there the sun, the moon, the stars, the spirits control man's destiny. It was necessary for him consciously or unconsciously to hear their voice and to heed it. Since he had written the letter to the Commissioners he had had time to think, time to walk among his men and talk to those whom he knew he was about to betray. There were old friends among them, men from Breda, men from the Aradas tribe to whom he would stop and talk in their own tongue. They trusted him, to them he was considered their chieftain. It was a time to search his heart to come to the decision that only he could make, not Jean François, not Biassou. He went through the motions of complying with the proposed agreement, but he came to his own decision when the moment was right and his mind was clear and resolved. Throughout his life, once he had made up his mind all hesitation was gone; he acted fearlessly and decisively, never looking back with regret; what he had to do he did, what was done was done.

Jean François had agreed with the Commissioners to the exchange of
200 prisoners. Toussaint was put in charge of their safe conduct to Le Cap
under an armed guard, a necessary precaution bearing in mind the restless
mood of the rebels. The prisoners were led into Le Cap where they testi-
fied that their treatment had been fair, a state of affairs they owed solely
to Toussaint. There can be no doubt that they were telling the truth
since, once safely out of rebel hands, there was no cause for them to lie.

Jean François and Biassou had written a letter to the Commissioners, a
letter which makes sad reading. They reiterated their offer to help the
Commissioners to re-enslave their fellow rebels. They referred disloyally
to their men's ignorance, to the fact that as Africans they were still controlled by their tribal chieftains which would make the handling of them
difficult in the circumstances, but if the chieftains (in other words the
leaders of the rebels) could be assured of their freedom, then the Commissioners could rely upon them to seek out any 'obstinate blacks who might
take to the woods'. Treachery can go no further and it is more than
likely that this cold-blooded letter setting out in detail the terms of the
betrayal helped Toussaint to come to his decision.

Having delivered his prisoners Toussaint presented himself before the
Assembly. The President would not even deign to speak to him or to the
delegation but merely handed them a note demanding 400 more prisoners
and 'further proof of your repentance'. Toussaint refused, insisting that
he could agree to the return of no more than sixty. The Assembly in
their turn refused to consider this and made it clear that any negotiation
or decision the Commissioners might have made was subsidiary to the
Assembly's final word. The game was finally over. The negotiations were
abandoned.

It is hard to comprehend the blindness of the men who made up the
Assembly, the conditioned minds that could only see standing before
them a few inconsiderable black men, slaves, not men who commanded
tens of thousands of potential soldiers, and hard to accept the stupidity
that led them to believe that their pale skins were enough to make them
invulnerably superior. In their unthinking arrogance they would not give
their time or thought to a small black man who they believed could not
even read the note they handed him. That he had any significance or
merited any consideration at all was beyond their comprehension. That
one day he would wield supreme power over them, that they would
bow before him, await audience with him, and treat him not as an equal
but as a superior was unthinkable.

Toussaint left the Assembly chamber and rode back through the devastated streets of Le Cap which he knew so well, passing through the now

neglected square opposite the cathedral, along the promenade which hedged the harbour, once full of ships but where now only brigantines from America were moored. He left the town and took the road that climbed up the hill towards Galliflet. Perhaps he was relieved, perhaps he was for the moment spent. It was over. Now his mind was clear and calm. The spur he needed he had found in those shuttered white faces. Now he could ride through the gates of the camp and meet the eyes of those who greeted him as he passed, and in his own eyes they would read nothing of which he need any longer feel ashamed.

He informed Jean François and Biassou that there was no hope of further negotiation with either the Commissioners or the Assembly.

For him there was now only one road and, no matter where it led, he was committed. He now had only one goal: the complete abolition of slavery and the freedom of his people for ever.

5   1793: Alliance with Spain

On 17 September 1792 the former Commissioners Roume, St Leger and Mirbeck left the Colony thankfully. They had caused the deterioration rather than the improvement of the situation for not only was the rebel army still harassing the north but throughout the south and west bands of maroons and roaming slaves left the life of no one safe. To replace these Commissioners, three more were sent from Paris: Sonthonax, Polverel and Ailhaud. Sonthonax and Polverel were dedicated Jacobins, but Ailhaud appears to have had no particular views upon anything. Leger Félicité Sonthonax was a former deputy of the national convention, a briefless barrister who came from a rich bourgeois family and had an inborn hatred of aristocrats and what is nowadays called in the West Indies the 'Plantocracy'. He was a dedicated, if rather over-emotional man and a great follower of the new thought. These three men were convinced they were carrying the flag of liberty overseas to France's richest colony; but that they were also accompanied by 6000 troops must have considerably increased their feeling of confidence.

The situation which confronted them when they landed on St Dominigue was enough, however, to daunt the most dedicated idealist. They were welcomed by no one. The landowners were infuriated by their liberal attitudes; the mulattoes, whom they had come to befriend, were, to their astonishment, equally infuriated by their rumoured intention to bring about the abolition of slavery; and even the freed blacks, who considered themselves mulattoes, were antagonistic. The President of the Assembly spoke for all when he welcomed the new Commissioners: 'the colonists have not imported half a million Negroes into St Dominigue in order to make them French citizens'. Surrounded by such open hostility, Sonthonax said that there had never been any such intention.

Whilst Sonthonax and Polverel tried to reach some kind of agreement with all the whites and the coloureds, they had a much more pressing task on their hands, that of defeating the slave army; the 6000 men they had brought with them were despatched to make an immediate attack. This force was commanded by a very remarkable man, Étienne Maynaud

Bizefranc, Comte de Laveaux, a man who was not only a brave soldier, but possessed a disarmingly attractive personality and that quality known as charm. He was unusually sensitive, a man who was to become one of the greatest friends that Toussaint would ever have; but now they were enemies in the field, and Laveaux certainly did not endear himself initially to Toussaint by soundly defeating him. During this thrust by Laveaux there was a particularly fierce encounter. The Chevalier d'Assas, Commander of the National Guard, attempted to take Mont Pelée, an important position held by Toussaint which commanded the entrance to Dondon and Grande Rivière. He stormed the height with a large body of men and inflicted severe losses on Toussaint; during the mêlée Toussaint and d'Assas faced each other, and they fought hand to hand with desperate ferocity until d'Assas wounded Toussaint in the arm. Fearing encirclement, Toussaint withdrew to his second line of defence at Tannerie, but a few days later he attacked again, leading his men with his arm in a sling, and reoccupied the 'Morne' which he held until he was finally driven off by Laveaux back to Tannerie.

During this battle there fought by his side a young officer called Jean Jacques Dessalines, a handsome 'red-skinned' Negro from Senegal, fearless in the field and unscrupulous off it. After this battle Toussaint created him Captain. He was to play an equal part with Toussaint in the destiny of St Dominigue and also in the destiny of Toussaint himself.

Toussaint's losses had been heavy, he had lost half of his men and so he withdrew from Tannerie. Thousands of Biassou's troops were deserting to the French or taking to the mountains in panic. Toussaint led 600 men up into the mountains too, and waited. It was a cruel blow to him but a good lesson, his first resounding defeat.

In spite of their troops' victory the Commissioners were as confused as ever and, harassed on every side, they made the decision to turn against the whites and to arm the mulattoes under Rigaud and Beauvais. In the Assembly in Port au Prince there were scenes of vituperation and near hysteria (the climate does not help men to remain calm or rational under stress) and then from Paris came the news that the people of France had beheaded their King. This was the final straw. Officers from the Commissioner's army deserted, fleeing over the border to Spain, or joining up with the rebel slave army to side with Jean François, Biassou and Toussaint and, to Sonthonax' total bewilderment, swore loyalty to a king who no longer existed. Any slaves who had returned to the estates again took to the mountains. The tangled skein of loyalties was impossible for the Commissioners to comprehend.

To make matters worse for Sonthonax, France was now at war with both Britain (and British Jamaica was only a hundred miles away) and

Spain (and San Domingo sat on his shoulder). He appealed for help to
France and General Galbaud was sent out in order to resolve the situation
in case of a dual attack. He could not have been a more unfortunate
choice. He owned property on the island and, acting from his pocket, he
immediately sided with the French planters against the mulattoes whom
Sonthonax had armed and encouraged. The Commissioners were forced
to order him to leave the island, which he pretended to be willing to do
but, seizing Polverel's son as a hostage, in exchange for his own brother,
he threatened to attack Le Cap. Polverel replied: 'I adore my son, but
he cannot be exchanged for the life of a traitor. Please do not refer to
this matter again.' Galbaud then attacked Le Cap, so Sonthonax and
Polverel turned to the black army for help and in order to enlist their aid
promised them their freedom from slavery. Persuaded by this promise a
force under Macaya fell upon Galbaud's men – 3000 sailors he had enlisted
from his warships – and once more Le Cap was set on fire. Ten thousand
refugees scrambled on to seventeen warships and sailed for the United
States where the lucky ones landed at Chesapeake, while hundreds were
drowned trying to escape the flames.

Toussaint was up in the hills playing his own game and it was a Spanish
one. As early as 1791 he had been negotiating with the Spanish independently of Jean François. A letter written from Grande Rivière in October
1791 (only a few months after the original slave rebellion) reads:

Mon cher ami,
    I receive your letter with pleasure, I am not able to satisfy your
wishes, we do not wish to leave our side and remove all to Spain. If
the Spanish have something to say to us then they must come to us, as
for me I do not have the time at my disposal; I wish you good health
and best wishes for your life,
your friend,
                                                        Médecin Général.
    Good wishes to the Secretary and also to Monsieur le Général.

He was still only 'Médecin Général', but this letter was not signed by
the other leaders.

He wrote again two weeks later to the same unidentified 'Cher Ami'.

Grande Rivière, October 15th 1791
My very dear Friend,
    While I am waiting from day to day an answer to the requests I have
made to the Spaniard several times, I beg of you to wait for a more
suitable time to do what you have confided to me out of friendship. I

wish I could go, provided I could have crowbars in every house to knock down rock from the mountain Haut de Cap to prevent them from reaching us, because I believe there are no other means, unless we are prepared to expose our people to the massacre. Please make sure that the information given to you by the spy who has been sent, gives the exact location of the powder keg of the Haut de Cap, so that we shall be able to seize it; thus my dear friend, you can realize the precautions I have taken about this particular affair; and you can inform Boukman. As for Jean François, let him carry on driving with his ladies, he has not even honoured me with a few lines for the last few days.

This surprises me very much. If you need rum, I will send you some whenever you wish but try to use it sparingly; for you know that you must not give them too much or it will drive them mad. Send me several carts which I need to transport wood for mounting the huts which are at Tannerie to house my people.

Please give my humble respects to your mother and sister.

I have the honour, my very great friend, to be your very humble and obedient servant,

Signed: General Doctor.

This letter from the archives of Haiti shows that there was a very early link with the slave rebellion and Spain, which was probably priest-inspired. But this letter was written very early on in the rebellion and proves that although Toussaint has often not been considered one of the primary instigators he most certainly must have been. Boukman died in or soon after the first attack on Le Cap.

Toussaint's role involving his dear friends across the border has always been a mystifying one, often skated over by his admirers. Of course his family were there and the road to St Raphael was the rebels' escape route if the worst came to the worst. Also the Spanish had been supplying them with arms. It was the news of the guillotining of the King of France which finally made up the rebel leaders' minds and convinced them to go over to Spain, to join with the Spanish forces against the Commissioners. Toussaint saw the opportunity of more arms and ammunition but, even more important, the help of experienced officers in furthering the training of his men. Jean François, Biassou and Toussaint ignored the pleas for amnesty and cooperation from Sonthonax and Laveaux. Toussaint went to meet Laveaux as an emissary of the rebels. He was quiet, soberly dressed and polite, and both men spoke without heat but the interview failed.

Jean François wrote to Laveaux saying that he had issued a manifesto to his 'compatriots, in which I plainly show them the destiny that awaits them if they let themselves be beguiled by your fine words of liberty and equality, etc. When I see that M. Laveaux and other French gentlemen of his quality are granting their daughters in marriage to Negroes then I shall be able to believe in this so called equality.'

Toussaint stated that 'the blacks wished to serve under a king and the Spanish king offered them his protection'. The word of the Spanish was more acceptable to him than the word of the French. Sonthonax had already stated to the Assembly that he had no intention of freeing the slaves, and the rebel leaders did not trust the Commissioners nor did they as yet trust Laveaux.

It has been suggested that Toussaint, coming from a line of kings, held some mystical belief in the power and divine right of kingship – if he ever had he was soon to disabuse himself of it. Certainly some of his fellow chiefs did hold such ideas. Macaya wrote: 'I am the subject of three kings: the King of the Congo, Lord of all the Blacks; the King of France who represents the father, the King of Spain who represents the mother. The three Kings are the descendants of those who, led by a star, went to adore the Man-God. I can therefore not serve the Republic, as I do not wish to be drawn into conflict with my brothers who are the subject of these three Kings.' It is obvious that this reference to the Magi was priest-inspired, and Toussaint too was very much under the influence of the priests who surrounded him. Certainly they would have denounced the killing of the French king by atheists and the suppressing of religion by the new Republic, all of which added an emotional reason for his decision to choose Spain rather than the Commissioners' offers.

In the meantime after Galbaud's defeat Sonthonax had 15,000 slaves on his hands to whom he had promised freedom. He had no alternative; on 29 August 1793 he declared the emancipation of the slaves of St Dominigue. He cried out to the crowd that gathered to hear the proclamation that he had 'a white skin but the soul of a black man'. The crowds knelt with joy in front of him and Sonthonax was reduced to tears, but he was a man much given to tears and wept both in victory and in defeat.

Four days before Sonthonax's declaration of freedom Toussaint sent out a proclamation of his own. 'Having been the first to champion liberty it is my duty to continue to work for it. I cannot permit another to remove my power and to take the lead. As I have begun so will I end. Join me and you will enjoy the rights of free men sooner than by any other means. Neither whites or mulattoes have influenced my plans, only the Supreme Being has inspired me. We have begun and so we will carry on; we know how to achieve our purpose.'

Toussaint had for the first time turned politician rather than soldier. His informers had told him of Sonthonax's decision to free the slaves and he was quick to react, fearing the effect of that decision not only among the blacks as a whole but among his own men. He was already involved with Spain and at this juncture he certainly could not risk desertion by his men for promises which he felt to be empty. On the same day as the proclamation of emancipation was issued by Sonthonax, Toussaint sent out another appeal to his people.

Brothers and Friends

I am Toussaint L'Ouverture. My name is perhaps not unknown to you. I have undertaken vengeance. I want Liberty and Equality to reign in Saint Dominigue. I am working to put them into existence. Brothers, unite with us and fight by our side for the same cause.

Your very humble and very obedient servant
Toussaint L'Ouverture
General of the Army of the King for the Public Good

This was the first time that Toussaint had signed himself with the new name he had taken. It is not known why he chose the name Louverture or L'Ouverture. It has been suggested that perhaps it was associated with Vodun. In Vodun there is a prayer to Legba to 'open the gates'. But knowing Toussaint's views on Vodun this seems unlikely. It is also said that Polverel made the jest 'this man seems to find the openings everywhere', but that was later when he was already known as L'Ouverture. Although most historians refer to him as L'Ouverture he always, after this first letter with the signature of his new name, signed himself Louverture. He said to Laveaux once laughingly, 'I thought it was a good name for bravery.' With his new name he finally abandoned the badge of slavery, the label of plantation slave at Breda, the estate where he had been born; from now on he was to be known forever as Toussaint L'Ouverture.

Together with Jean François and Biassou he now went over to Spain. He was clearly impressed by the Spanish, both in their way of life and their arts of warfare, and he learned and learned quickly all that he could from them. The lack of ammunition and arms which had always bedevilled him was temporarily over. The Spanish officers treated him as an equal, even the French ex-royalist officers who had joined his army treated him with respect. The Spanish offered his army 'Liberty for all now and forever. The rights of Spanish citizenship and valuable land grants for all

both in French and Spanish territories.' This was to be the loophole by
which Toussaint could abandon his new allies if and when he might find
this necessary, for he was obdurate in his belief that 'Liberty for all' meant
all, not just the officers of his army or his men.

Toussaint was made a Colonel, Jean François and Biassou Lieutenant
Generals in the service of the King of Spain. Toussaint accepted his lower
rank but no longer considered himself subordinate to Biassou. He wrote
to Laveaux: 'The Spanish have offered me their protection and liberty
for all who fight for the King and having always fought for that same
liberty I adhere to their offer.'

The leaders were treated with courtesy by Governor Joaquin Garcia
and the Marques da Hermonas.

The rebels intensified their attacks upon the Commissioners' army and
more rebels, royalists, whites and mulattoes joined their ranks. Toussaint
swept down from the heights of the Spanish border and took, in amazingly quick succession, Dondon, Gros Morne, Marmalade, Plaisance, Acul,
Limbé, Port Magot and Petit St Louis. He had then achieved mastery
over the whole of the north of the northern province. When he took
Port Dauphin he attacked for eight days, commanding the central sector
on foot. On the ninth day he seized a horse and, galloping up and down
the ranks, ordered his men to attack 'to storm the town or die in the
attempt', then led charge after charge himself. In the evening the town
fell. This is the more astonishing if one can comprehend the terrain
involved. The roads were – and still are – more like river beds than roads,
which when the rains come do indeed revert to rivers, and the rivers
themselves are only forded with great difficulty and previous experience.
Toussaint had no ordinance or any kind of maps for his campaign, but
by searching questioning of men who knew various sections of each area
he managed to create rough maps of his own, and discovered the passes
that existed through the mountains, mountains so pleated that in order to
scale them it is necessary to descend and then climb over and over again,
achieving only a few feet after hours of exhausting effort. On the plains
by the sea there are salt lakes and swamps in which a man can sink up to
his knees once off a narrow and previously known track. The undergrowth is a tangle of lianas, cactus and thorny bushes, the humidity
makes it hard to move swiftly, the heat from the afternoon sun is merciless
and the rain when it comes stalks through the land like a moving bead
curtain, bringing in its wake fever and lassitude. It is no wonder General
LeClerc who later experienced this wrote wearily to Napoleon that it
was impossible to imagine such a country to fight over unless one had
experienced it and that it was 'worse than Switzerland'.

As Toussaint took the towns he did not put them to the fire and did not permit looting; when the whites and mulattoes realized they had no atrocities to fear from him and that their women were protected they surrendered to him almost eagerly. Literally thousands joined his forces in a matter of months. The French officers in command of Le Cap (de Nully and de Lafeuille) deserted and joined Toussaint, so General de Brandicourt was put in command in their place. Toussaint who liked to play games in war set an ambush for Brandicourt in a ravine, and leaving his nephew Moïse in command of the major force which surrounded the General, Toussaint urged his horse up a rocky cliff face and dropped down quietly behind Brandicourt himself. Brandicourt ordered his men to charge, but Toussaint rode up to the General without fear. When he was face to face with him he said, 'Quite useless, my dear General, I admire your courage, but I would admire your intelligence more if you were to order your column to surrender and thus avoid a battle which can bring you no profit whatsoever.' He then commanded Brandicourt to write a letter to his second-in-command Pacot, ordering him also to surrender. Brandicourt with tears of rage and impotence was forced to agree, and so with their drums beating and still bearing their colours 1500 men, mostly whites, marched formally into Toussaint's camp; his startled men, on seeing such numbers turned to flee, then they saw Toussaint riding at their head and smiling his crooked, rather toothless smile. Where he had once had 600 troops under his command he had during a matter of months now accrued in all 5000.

It was during this campaign that a spent bullet had hit him in the mouth and he lost two teeth, a fact he tried to conceal with understandable and rather endearing vanity.

By early 1794 the Spaniards had controlled and isolated (apart from Le Cap) the entire north, entirely due to Toussaint.

The Commissioners and Laveaux not only had the problem of Toussaint and the Spanish on their hands, they had another difficulty which was equally menacing: the landowners had appealed to the British for aid and the Marquis de Charmilly was sent to open negotiations in London. This time Pitt was more willing to cooperate, since Britain was at war with France, and he saw a rich prize within his grasp. The British had already opened their campaign in the West Indies and having taken Tobago with ease they felt that, with the support of the planters of St Dominigue and the proximity of their forces and their ships in Jamaica, they could achieve the same easy victory there; and at first this hopeful supposition proved to be correct. Major General Sir Adam Williamson, commanding the troops in Jamaica, was directed to occupy St Dominigue and on 20 September 1793, 500 troops landed on the southern tip of the island and took Jeremie. The British flag was hoisted and the French inhabitants greeted the event with cries of 'God Save King George'. Two days later, another 900 troops entered Môle St Nicholas and Leogane surrendered. The force was commanded by an unscrupulous character, Colonel John Whitelocke, who was later cashiered when in command in Buenos Aires for being 'deficient in zeal, judgment and personal exertion'. Whilst in St Dominigue he certainly displayed a lack of integrity which does not fit in with the popular image of the British officer.

The British swept on without opposition, they took Port au Prince, the capital of the south and in a year two-thirds of the Colony was occupied by either the British or the Spanish. Whitelocke had a novel method of making war. If any French officer made a show of resistance, which in the circumstances it was foolhardy to do, Whitelocke offered him a considerable bribe; it does neither side any credit that the majority accepted his offer. Laveaux was the exception; the British offered him 15 million écus, but Laveaux replied: 'Permit me to make it plain to you the indignity to which you have subjected me in believing that I would be so base, villainous and vile as to accept 15 million écus. I am a General, the commander of an army, you have sought to dishonour me in the eyes of my comrades in arms . . . It is an outrage for which you must give me personal satisfaction, I demand it in the name of honour which exists between nations . . . you may have your choice of arms . . . your position as an enemy does not give you the right to offer me a personal insult and so I demand satisfaction.' He received no reply and, infuriated, Laveaux instructed his officers to 'reply to any such offer that is made to you with lead, that sort of reply is never compromising'.

The British, through the offices of Whitelocke, also offered Rigaud the less attractive financial inducement of 3 million écus, explaining to Whitelocke it was necessary to offer more to Laveaux because he was white. In fact Laveaux was at the end of his tether. He wrote to the Commissioners that 'during the last six months I have had to reduce the rations of officers and men to six ounces of bread a day'; his forces were reduced by disease and he was running out of ammunition: both officers and men were suffering the greatest privations; 'we have no shoes, no soap, no shirts, no tobacco, the majority of my men are as barefooted as Africans, we have not even a flint to give to the men'. But he added with resigned heroism, 'In spite of this you can be assured in the name of the army and of the Republic that I shall never surrender.'

It was under these conditions that Laveaux made up his mind to contact Toussaint once more and through the office of Abbé Delahaye he opened secret negotiations with him.

6   1794: Toussaint Alone and Amity with the French

In spite of his triumphs Toussaint was well aware that the British were marching through the south and west with ease and, ignoring the fact that there had been any attempt at emancipation, they restored slavery in every territory which came under their control. The pleas of Wilberforce to Pitt were disregarded by both Pitt and the commanders of the conquering army, whose views in any case were influenced by Jamaica.

Toussaint was also growing increasingly disillusioned with his Spanish allies when he saw no attempt on their part to abolish slavery. The promises of freedom for all were becoming increasingly hollow; the Spanish still traded slaves, often refugees from the French side, with Puerto Rico and Cuba. He became outwardly defiant by taking matters as far as he could into his own hands. Every town he took, every 'habitation' he passed through he assembled the slaves and proclaimed to them in stirring words that the Spanish king and he, Toussaint L'Ouverture, were giving them their freedom. Sonthonax' fine words had been largely ignored by the landowners and had hardly penetrated to the plantation slaves but, hearing Toussaint, a black man like themselves, they believed him.

His discontent was not only Spanish-inspired: his relationship with both Jean François and Biassou was deteriorating, there were constant irritating pinpricks born of jealousy. Toussaint, although officially still subordinate to Biassou, was clearly not considered so either by the Spanish or by Toussaint himself. Knowing this Biassou became, in self-defence, increasingly arrogant and aggressive, his self-importance growing as his military success diminished; always a drinker and a womanizer, his self-indulgence was now affecting his skill as a soldier, and for all this he blamed Toussaint.

In a clumsy attempt to remove the opposition, through his mulatto secretary he wrote a letter to Don Garcia the Governor, in which amid protestations of loyalty and self-justification he denounced Toussaint's attitude towards the slaves: 'He raises and arms all the slaves . . . he preaches disobedience and insurrection and declares himself to be head of the rebels. We demand the head of this guilty man who against the sacred decree of the King is promising liberty to all.' This from Biassou, one of the prime instigators of the rebellion – if it were not so tragic in its evidence of human frailty, it would be laughable. The secret meeting in the Bois Caiman, the vows were all forgotten now Biassou was a general in the Spanish army.

Toussaint was too valuable to Don Garcia and da Hermonas for them to take any action, so the letter was ignored, but Toussaint on hearing of it acted in a manner particularly in character: he told Jean François of Biassou's treachery, which might not have concerned Jean François at all had not Toussaint had the machiavellian guile to add that he felt Jean François should know, Biassou was also plotting against Jean François. He also pointed out that apart from this Biassou's lack of military prowess in the field did not merit his position, so why not remove him from his post, which would, of course, leave Jean François in sole command. Jean François was both deceived and flattered and agreed with Toussaint. Before he could change his mind, and while Biassou was inspecting Toussaint's troops Toussaint had Biassou seized and thrown into jail. 'An order from General François', he told him calmly. But the Spanish and French officers pleaded with Jean François on Biassou's behalf; they too were becoming more and more disquieted about Toussaint freeing the slaves and were beginning to have an uneasy feeling that this quiet man but daring soldier's ambition for his people was implacable. Toussaint wrote protestations of loyalty to Don Garcia but he knew the time of his alliance with Spain was running out; he knew himself to have been duped and that he had deceived himself in believing that Spain would lightly abandon slavery any more than would the British.

Then, in February 1794, the news came to him of the French National Assembly's confirmation of the freedom of the slaves in St Dominigue, and his mind was made up. He sent an emissary, one of his French officers, to treat with Laveaux who did not hesitate – he could hardly afford to in the circumstances – but sent an immediate reply, urging Toussaint to hasten to the aid of the Republic and promising to make him a Brigadier General.

The decision had been agreed on both sides, but Toussaint's family were behind the Spanish border and if he undertook any precipitate action without first ensuring their safety he was well aware that he could not guarantee their security in Spanish hands. He moved fast. Boldly, brazenly, he took the offensive and went into Spain. Accompanied by his adopted nephew Moïse, Dessalines, Maurepas and his younger brother Jean Pierre and almost a hundred dragoons he took the steep mountainous road past the rush-fringed lakes and through the forests of stunted pine and so back into San Domingo.

To pass the border into San Domingo was like stepping into another world; here was ancient Spain, not a French sugar colony. On the great plains, instead of waving cane there were thousands of heads of long-horned cattle controlled by rancheros in flat cowhide hats nearly all of whom were mulatto or white. The people were generally poor and almost entirely agricultural, a peasant class which did not exist in St Dominigue; on the whole of this Spanish side of the island there were only 15,000 slaves, who helped their masters grow a few acres of tobacco for their personal use. These slaves were used mostly as an export trade and were sold (especially refugees from the French side) to Puerto Rico and Cuba. The people were too poor to possess more than one or two slaves who lived with the family. Raynal says that 'they appeared to spend the majority of their time swinging hammocks'.

The small towns were dominated by old whitewashed stone churches whose dark interiors sheltered strange wooden crucifixes of primitive agony which centuries before had made the long journey over the sea from Spain. The low houses were also whitewashed with wide arched entrances and doors of iron-studded wood which were kept closed throughout the day; their only furniture was hammocks or low wooden chairs on which the women sat stiffly in their rusty black dresses. The only light came from a central courtyard where they cooked their staple diet – strips of dried meat – on a 'boucan'. Pomegranate trees made a small shade and straggling small-budded roses clung to the walls. In most of the larger towns there was an ancient and crumbling fort and a bull-ring to which the whole population crowded, and when the church bells rang for Mass everyone attended. It was a society of humble people dominated by the priest, the soldier and the administrator.

Toussaint was greeted in San Domingo as a conquering hero, and was created General, presented with an ornamental sword and had pinned to his breast by the Marquis da Hermonas the medal of the order of Queen Isabella and the gold medal of Charles IV inscribed 'El Merito'. A banquet was given in his honour and a bullfight staged for his entertainment. Te Deums were sung and it was noticed that he spent a great deal of his time in devout prayer. Da Hermonas, carried away by such a combination of bravery and religious devotion, exclaimed 'If God descended upon earth he could find no one with a purer heart than Toussaint L'Ouverture.' In this instance he might have heeded Biassou's less generous comment: 'He says a thousand rosaries a day in order to deceive everyone the better.' Don Garcia began to have the same idea and to suspect that all did not ring quite true.

Toussaint's happiness at being reunited with his family once more was genuine and Suzanne's shy joy and pride in her husband, her gentle acknowledgement that the man who had worked side by side with her in the fields was now a great man, was pure and true. But Toussaint's happiness was clouded by his anxiety for his family; with his ever-alert eye and perceptiveness he sensed that his family was being watched and he was right. Don Garcia acted swiftly and suddenly, removed da Hermonas from his post, feeling him to be too much under Toussaint's influence, and replaced him by General Cabrera, threw Moïse into prison and placed Toussaint's entire family under house arrest. Toussaint who rarely showed anger was beside himself with rage but, controlling it, he protested to Don Garcia in most formal terms, merely saying that he was 'disturbed and distressed at this action'. Don Garcia ordered their release, Toussaint thanked him, with murder in his heart, for his 'just and generous action'. Don Garcia replied that perhaps it was time for him to return to his campaign. Toussaint was most certainly going to do that, but in rather a different way from the one Don Garcia had expected!

Toussaint held a secret meeting with Moïse, Dessalines and Maurepas, telling them to be ready for anything. He warned his family to be prepared to leave at an instant's notice.

On 6 May 1794 he took Mass with Cabrera, arriving at the church with his guard of ninety dragoons, who waited for him outside, but his family did not accompany him. He prayed with his usual devotion and left the church with Cabrera; outside they spoke, in after-church voices, pleasantly and quietly together, then suddenly Toussaint gave a signal, leapt on his horse and spurred it to a gallop; he and his men thundered out of the town knocking the astounded citizens out of the way as they left. During the long incense-laden Mass his family had already left. Toussaint and his men stormed away down the stony track and back across the mountain into St Dominigue to his camp at Marmalade where his men were waiting for him.

Once there, he heard that Biassou with the connivance of Jean François had captured some of his officers who were being held at Biassou's camp at Ennery. Impulsively he immediately set off with his young brother Jean Pierre. It was a trap. Biassou ambushed them and in the skirmish Jean Pierre was shot and fell dead from his horse. Toussaint wheeled, spurred his horse and escaped, leaving his brother; it was not a time for sentiment. But he avenged him. He picked a group of hardened men and then set off for Biassou's camp at Ennery where he found Biassou, elated by his triumph, on his palliasse making love to one of his many camp followers. Biassou with more agility than dignity took to his heels and then crawled to Dondon on foot. Toussaint showed no mercy but sacked the camp, killing with cold and ruthless energy all Biassou's supporters. In his panic Biassou had left behind his carriage and horses, a gold watch and a diamond-encrusted snuff box; it gave Toussaint the greatest satisfaction to return them to him, with the manners of a gentleman, accompanied by his most gracious compliments.

The war was now on, not only with his old commander, but now he had declared open rebellion against the Spanish. On 18 May 1794 he wrote to Laveaux: 'It is true, General, that I was deceived by the enemies of the Republic, but what man can boast of being able to escape every pitfall. In truth I was ensnared by them.

'You will recollect that before the disaster of Cap Français I made certain overtures to you in the sole hope that we might be able to fight against the enemies of France. Unfortunately for everyone concerned the conciliatory means I proposed – recognition of the Negroes' freedom – was rejected. It was at this juncture that the Spaniards offered me their protection and freedom for all who would fight in the service of the King. I accepted their offers finding myself abandoned by my right brothers, the French. I have seen the decree of the National Convention dated 4 February 1794 declaring the abolition of slavery; this is the most comforting news for all friends of the human race. Let us therefore occupy ourselves solely with the defeating of our enemies.'

This he proceeded to do: first he took Dondon and then, the same day, rode on towards Gonaîves, riding at the head of his men and waving his sword above his head. He was wounded in the hip in the engagement but simply ignored it. Then, with superhuman energy and relentless determination, he took all the major ports in the former Spanish field. Jean François, now his chief opponent, tried to rally his forces but they had become superstitious, so that when they saw Toussaint's small grim figure leading his men against them they threw down their arms and fled, and spoke of him as one possessed – their bullets were only made of lead not silver.

Toussaint's nephew Moïse was at one point forced to retreat by Jean François whose ability as a general was never in doubt. Toussaint came to his aid, cutting across country with a swiftness that Jean François could not have expected and making a surprise attack. He wrote to Laveaux: 'I came very near to capturing Jean François himself, he owes his escape to the thickness of the undergrowth, he made away but he abandoned all his personal belongings. His baggage, his correspondence are all in my hands. He saved his shirt and breeches, nothing more.' For the moment Jean François and Biassou retreated behind the Spanish border.

Toussaint established order wherever he went, a policy he was always to pursue, persuading the people to go back to work and to resume their normal lives. Even the white planters began to believe that it might be possible to leave the comparative safety of the towns and to return to

their homes and estates in the countryside. But their hopes were premature for Toussaint's troops massacred over 200 white men, women and
children. Toussaint wrote to Laveaux: 'I am heartbroken by the event
that has befallen so many unfortunate whites who are the victims of this
affair, I am not like many who can view scenes of horror with composure.'
He believed that battles were between soldiers and that the civilian
population of whatever colour must be protected; it was not merely sentiment or softheartedness, they were the future of his country and he had
already made up his mind that the whites were as necessary and as
important to that future as the blacks.

Jean François' slaughter of 800 whites at Port Dauphin filled him with
nauseated fury and he wrote to Laveaux: 'I have always had a horror of
leaders who find satisfaction in shedding blood. My religion whose
beliefs I intend to observe forbids it.'

Toussaint's army swept on but they were often hungry, poorly clad
and always, always in need of ammunition. He wrote to Laveaux that
they had no shirts or trousers, 'only a few rags that barely cover'. This
was to be true of his whole campaign. He wrote constantly, throughout
the years that were to follow, always thinking of his men: 'My soldiers
are naked, they have no bread and see no priest'; again: 'I am completely
out of powder, I beg you to send me some flints.' But in spite of this and
the gruelling pace which Toussaint set them their spirits were high. He
marched his men sixty-four kilometres in a single day over the worst
possible terrain. Toussaint was often stern and unbending to his officers.
Towards them he was very much the general, the slightest deviation from
orders received a sharp reprimand and he was not open to any form of
argument; but as far as his men were concerned it was a different story, to
them he was a genial father, and when they were downhearted he would
encourage them to sing with 'Fatras Baton':

> La poudre c' de l'eau, ping! Pandang!
> Canon ce bambou! Ping Pang-dang!

If a man near him was wounded he was the first to come to his aid. He
never acted the part of general in the field except to lead them and, if
necessary, he would not hesitate to perform the manual task of the humblest soldier. He wrote to Laveaux that whilst helping his men heave a
cannon into place 'the gun barrel was dropped while being placed into its
carriage and all five fingers of my left (fortunately) hand were almost
severed'. Characteristically on this occasion he ignored the injury which
must have been agonizing, jumped up on his horse and rode into the
attack. When he briefed his men before battle he was straightforward and

simple – he wrote to Laveaux: 'I stated the position of the enemy and told them it was absolutely necessary to drive him off.' If he told his men it was 'absolutely necessary' they believed him and drove off the enemy, whatever the cost.

On 27 July 1794 he went to Dondon to be received by Laveaux and be given his formal expressions of gratitude. Toussaint was not dressed in uniform but was wearing a white silk coat with a lace and cambric shirt with white plumes in his hat. Laveaux removed one of the scarlet plumes from his own hat and placed it between the white of Toussaint's. Toussaint presented his staff to him, Moïse, Dessalines, Dumesnil, Clairveaux and Belair, and his two white aides, Birotte and Dubuisson, and then Laveaux created Toussaint Commander of the West Cordon.

The two soldiers stood and looked into each other's eyes; it was a strange confrontation: the aristocrat, familiar with the salons of Paris, fresh-complexioned with years of privilege and good living, and the black ex-slave, his skin already bearing the greyish bloom of age, the eyes of one so blue the other's so mulberry black; they knew in that instant that there were no barriers between them. Laveaux felt a natural affinity towards the Negro; he had no sentimentality born of guilt, he just liked the black race. This immediate bond which they felt grew into a deep and mutual affection which was to last all their lives; however later events may have divided them, they retained a tenderness and respect for each other which is a rare thing between men.

Toussaint was to say and reiterate many times: 'After God, it was Laveaux.' He meant it, he trusted him utterly, perhaps the first man and the last in his life he had ever trusted. He wrote him emotional letters of adulation and love which read almost like the letters of a boy. 'Undoubtedly there are perfect friendships, but I cannot believe that there is a friendship more ideal than that which I feel towards you. Yes, the affection General Toussaint feels for you is like that of a son for a father. Your tomb will be his. He would gladly die for you. His arms and his spirit will always be at your service, if I should die I will take into my grave the honour of having defended a friend and father of virtue as well as liberty itself . . . I embrace you a million times.'

They sent each other touching little gifts, Laveaux sent Toussaint some truffles noting 'it is something important that I send you, be so kind as to accept it from one who wishes you the best of health, who embraces you with all his heart.' He addressed his letters to Toussaint 'To my most intimate friend' and Toussaint referred to himself as 'your son' – 'be sure that your son is your sincere friend' and 'how happy I am to have such a good father who loves me as much as you do'. It was an age when men were permitted to love each other without embarrassment or the implication of sex. But this love carried with it the usual problem – jealousy. Love encloses those who share it, and those who do not share it wish to divide it. It did not take the island long to realize that Laveaux listened only to Toussaint and that Toussaint would defend Laveaux, a white man, with his life.

7   1794-5: The British Campaign

Although Toussaint had temporarily routed the Spanish in the north there were still the British in the south and west to contend with.

Sonthonax and Polverel had been forced out of Port au Prince by the British in order to save their skins. Sonthonax had made an attempt at defiance saying to Commodore Ford, the Commander of the British Squadron, 'if we were ever forced to leave this place nothing would be left of your ships but smoke and the rest would be at the bottom of the sea', and when Ford sent an ultimatum to him to surrender the town Sonthonax replied: 'Our gunners, Monsieur le Comte, are at their posts,' but both he and Polverel were forced to flee, accompanied only by a small group of Negroes, and the British took the town. Sonthonax' position was hopeless and on 15 June 1794 he was recalled to France to face trial for treason. His patron Brissot had been guillotined and the Club de Massiac, incensed by his freeing of the slaves, were determined to get him. Laveaux was now in charge of the Colony together with Villatte, a mulatto whom he created Commandant of Le Cap and his second in command.

The future of the French republic in St Dominigue now rested upon the shoulders of Laveaux and Toussaint. The armies of Rigaud and Beauvais were attempting to hold off the British, but the British had a navy, and also money which they were only too happy to hand out to anyone prepared to join them. The white émigrés flocked to their side and many mulattoes joined their forces, partly because of the British attitude towards the continuation of slavery, and partly because it is always safer to be on the winning side.

The advantage of possessing a navy, of course, was that the British were able to ship in continuous reinforcements and arms with their money, and to keep the Spanish supplied with arms, who with this assistance were valuable allies. Although Rigaud and Beauvais had managed to retake Tiburon, the British encroachment was steady and, in spite of yellow fever devastating their troops, replacements were always quickly available; besides yellow fever was also attacking the mulatto army who had no reinforcements.

Toussaint had to be everywhere at once attacking the Spanish, holding back the British and miraculously he succeeded. 'Never', says Pamphile Lacroix, 'did one know where he was, nor what he was doing, if he was leaving, if he was staying, where he was going, from where he was coming.' Colonel Vincent in a note to Bonaparte said: 'At the head of all is the most active and indefatigable man one can imagine. One can definitely say that he is everywhere and above all in the place where sound judgement and danger lead him to believe that his presence is the most essential. His great sobriety and the ability given only to him of never resting, the advantage he has of going back to office work after a tiresome journey, of replying to a hundred letters a day and of habitually exhausting five secretaries.' His first confrontation with British troops was at Camp Fonche on the river Artibonite; he drove them across the river and back to St Marc to which he laid siege. To his chagrin he lost the engagement, due partly to the British heavy artillery and partly to the defection of a whole regiment of mulattoes to the enemy side. He wrote bitterly to Laveaux: 'I shall deal differently with them in the future, I have treated them like a father and they have repaid me with this dastardly attempt to betray me to the enemy.' He never trusted them again; whatever later declarations of brotherhood he may have made, from now on he watched them like a hawk.

Toussaint's dealings with the British army were punctilious and gentlemanly, which is more than can be said of the way the British waged the war in St Dominigue; however, as far as prisoners were concerned both sides showed equal graciousness. Whitelocke wrote to Toussaint on 18 April 1794 thanking him for his 'generous conduct to the prisoners you have taken' and later the British Commissioner of Prisoners of War in St Dominigue wrote to Toussaint: 'I hope that the prisoners you have received gave you an account of the gentleness and the respect with which they have been treated by me.' The *London Gazette* was to write of Toussaint in 1798: 'Toussaint is a Negro and in the jargon of war he is also called a brigand. But we would like to say that this Negro who was born to avenge the outrage to his race has proved that the character of a man has nothing to do with his colour.'

Toussaint took the offensive against the British and carried the war into the western plain, advancing to the Mirebelais Valley. He took Petite Rivière and Verrettes at the point of the bayonet, but they were retaken by the British, the mulattoes from both the countryside and his own army enlisting with the Redcoats. Toussaint became more and more embittered with the mulattoes but he managed to take the town of Mirebelais – an important prize – and then again was driven off. He attacked once more, opposite Mirebelais he faced a large combined force of British, Spanish and 800 French émigrés under the command of the Marquis d'Espinville. After five months of fighting in and around Mirebelais Toussaint took the town in June 1795. 'I served the enemy in true Republican fashion . . . And when the enemy saw himself taken both from in front and from the rear and surrounded on all sides the gallant and impertinent Dessources jumped from his horse and rushed into a thicket with the debris of his army, crying "Every man for himself". The rain and the night prevented me from pursuing them. This battle could have lasted from eleven in the morning till six in the evening and cost me only six men and as many wounded. I have strewn the road with corpses for the space of more than a league. My victory has been most complete and if the famous Dessources has the good luck to re-enter St Marc it will be without cannon, without baggage, in short what is called without drum or trumpet. He has lost all, including his honour – if the vile Royalists are capable of having any. He will remember for a long time the Republican lesson which I taught him.' Beauvais, the mulatto commander, wrote 'I have heard of the prodigious valour which Toussaint showed at Mirebelais.'

The British and Spanish retired but d'Espinville and his 800 men had retreated inside the fort where Toussaint surrounded them. D'Espinville, realizing there was no hope, asked to parley with Toussaint. They faced each other, both battle-stained, the black man the victor with the white marquis at his mercy. The marquis, elegant in his perfectly tailored French uniform, clung to the shreds of his dignity in front of this small man in his ill-fitting coat, his leggings stained white with horse-sweat and his large round hat placed firmly upon the cotton bandana which he always wore in battle. The marquis said defiantly that he and his men were prepared to die fighting as he realized that if they surrendered they could expect no clemency. Toussaint looked at him coolly, he was clearly offended by the implication that as a 'brigand' he would not adhere to the rules of war. 'I do not shoot my prisoners,' he said, adding, 'I give you my word and also if you wish to join my forces you may do so.'

The marquis showed by his eyes that he did not believe him, a fact which was quite clear to Toussaint who raised his voice and, placing his right hand upon the hilt of his sword as if he too had been born an aristocrat, he said, 'I swear it upon my sword.' He was true to his word. Although Laveaux' committee demanded a court martial Toussaint obstinately refused this and Laveaux had no recourse but to support his friend.

After the town had surrendered a band of about twenty planters with their wives and children, accompanied by their household slaves and about 200 pack-mules all heavily laden with gold, silver and all the valuable effects they could manage to take with them, were surrounded by

Toussaint's soldiers as they tried to escape to the coast and were brought in front of the General, who could present, when he liked, a formidably alarming presence. The men were desperately apprehensive not only for themselves but for their families, the women clutched their children to them and all stared at this man who had become a myth and, by rumour, a monstrous one; they had no comparisons by which to judge him, to them he was a black savage, one of the instigators of a rebellion which had pitched them all into a new world of fear and insecurity; the tales of horror had passed from one white mouth to another, from plantation to plantation, tales which were not imaginary but true, accounts which told of no mercy for anyone who was white, whatever their sex or age from the oldest to the youngest. Surrounded by black soldiers they faced the man whom they felt to be the symbol of all they dreaded. Toussaint bowed to them and then asked his men sharply if they had taken anything from the baggage. They quickly answered 'no', knowing his stern views on looting. He then turned to the planters and said that they had his permission to go on their way with all their belongings to wherever they wished to go, but that he thought it wiser to give them an armed escort to ensure their safety. Their slaves also would be free to accompany them – a few of the slaves asked permission to join his army but the majority wished to go with their old masters. Toussaint nodded, he understood, he had once been a slave to a good master, had once packed his master's valuables onto pack-mules. They were escorted to Port au Prince where they arrived without harm.

The gold and silver and the lifetime wealth of twenty such planters could have helped both him and his men, always short of money, but he was a merciful man and the pleading eyes of a woman or the bewildered face of a child always played upon his emotions, but there were always two motivations to his actions, the heart and the head, and he was looking to the future – he needed the whites.

The town of Mirebelais lay in a vale of great beauty and fertility, surrounded by mountains and traced by little streams that made their way across the lush cane fields and savannahs to the river Artibonite. To Toussaint, coming from the scorched earth of the north it seemed like paradise; as a dedicated agriculturalist he saw the richness of the earth and the strength of the cane, and it gave him pleasure; as a lover of beauty he looked at all around him and was soothed and refreshed. For a few brief weeks he forgot the rigours of battle, the constant strain and discomfort and never-ending responsibility. He moved into the old Administrator's quarters in Mirebelais, an elegant old house built of mahogany with a wide veranda all round it and broad shading eaves, the garden well-established and from contemporary reports considered exceptionally beautiful. Toussaint walked through the high-ceilinged rooms with their panelled walls and floors of gleaming patina; he sat on the gilt and tapestry chairs, and saw his reflection in the long looking glasses. He ate off linen and lace, drank wine from crystal glasses and slept in a soft and curtained bed. His valet brought jugs of hot water to fill his bath and at night the scent of roses and stephanotis filled his room.

The tailors and dressmakers of Mirebelais must have been busy, for Toussaint entertained every night and the noblest white émigrés were only too glad to accept his invitation. So, for the first time in St Dominigue, white, mulatto and black met together for the purposes of pleasure; mulatto women who until this moment had only lived half a life in the shadows of a great house now danced under the candles in the full brilliance of their beauty with Viscomtes and Marquis who before would only have entertained them in their beds. His black officers moved among the guests, offered their snuff box to the men and talked politely to the Frenchwomen who smiled at them nervously and looked at them sideways over their fans, realizing that they were men, not animals. Mulattoes offered them their arm and they could not refuse. Men of colour, who had thought it beneath their dignity to speak to a black man except in commerce, talked politics or gossiped with the officers. Toussaint, whose only salon had been the battlefield, amazed the whites by his air of natural confidence, his easy manners and his elegant turn of wit. He had indeed opened the door to a new world. The company strolled in the moonlit garden and it was noticed that Toussaint led many of the more beautiful of the white women out among the roses, talking intimately to them, and that they seemed charmed by his attentions. Sometimes he would pluck a rose for them and it was said 'he seemed to prefer white roses and white women'.

Lacroix states that he and General Boudet found a box among Toussaint's personal effects with a false bottom and that in it were many tresses of hair of all colours, rings, hearts of gold crossed with arrows, little keys, souvenirs and an infinity of love-letters which left no doubt of the successes achieved by Toussaint. Predictably Lacroix adds 'notwithstanding his repulsive physique' (doubtless he meant his colour, although nobody ever said Toussaint was handsome), 'he was in control of their fortunes and they were in his power'. A very low estimation of Toussaint's character and a very male one, probably promoted by envy; to Lacroix it seemed impossible that any white woman would lower herself, unless under duress, to share Toussaint's bed, but even men admitted that Toussaint had charm, and power of itself can be sexually attractive. For the first time it was permissible for these high-born French ladies to experience sex with a man of another colour, something heretofore forbidden which made it more exciting, something which, being women, they surely must have conjectured upon. It is said that two of his white mistresses were a mother and daughter. Ah well, why not? Toussaint, too, was enjoying new experiences.

Lacroix praises Boudet for his decision to burn the letters and to throw the rest in the sea where they could not be found, in order to protect the rich and ancient families of these ladies from 'shame and sickness of heart'.

Whatever he may have done in the privacy of his bedroom, Toussaint's behaviour in public was the reverse of lewd and his attitude towards the sex lives of others was puritanical. He once told the mother of a girl whose bodice he considered too revealing to take her home, and before she left the ballroom he took out his handkerchief and covered her bosom. He told his generals that 'immorality in high places leads to a decline in public morals'. He ordered his own nephew to prison for having an open affair with a married woman. His officers were forced to marry their mistresses. His standards perhaps were double, they were French and they were Catholic. Under the influence of the priests who surrounded him he forbade divorce. His constant companions were Father Martini, an Italian, and Father Lanthenure who never left his side on his travels throughout the island. He was discretion itself about his private life. He loved his wife, he wished neither to hurt her nor humiliate her in front of others.

The gaiety and relaxation in Mirebelais was short-lived. Toussaint was informed that the cultivators had risen against the whites in the north, that they were armed and that they were murdering them. He rode all night with a body of 400 to 500 men and faced their chief, Dotty. 'I assembled the men', he wrote to Laveaux, 'and told them that if they had anything to complain about murder was not the best way to solve it. One of them said "Our life is a misery. Alas, General, there is no doubt they want to make us slaves again, there is no equality here like on your side. We are badly thought of, we don't want much . . . but we are forced to give our pigs and chickens which we could sell in the market and if we protest they throw us in prison." I replied "All the reasons you have given me seem just, but if you had a cabin full of them you have made yourself guilty in the sight of God." '

He mustered all the blacks in the district and called upon them to work hard and to give no trouble, making Dotty their official leader and responsible for them. The men surrounded him shouting 'Long live Toussaint, long live Laveaux, long live the Republic'. But there was another uprising, Toussaint was shot in the leg 'for my pains' and suffered great discomfort, and Dotty was condemned to death. Toussaint was enraged when he discovered that it was the British who were distributing arms among the cultivators. It was a disheartening time for Toussaint and a difficult one for his people. The transition from slave to 'cultivator' was not an easy one. They had been promised their freedom and for them freedom meant the end of work, yet here they were still being expected to work; admittedly they were paid, they received a percentage of the profit of the estates, but they did not want to work. They wanted to return to the old life of Africa which many of them recalled, not to cut cane, sweat in the sun, get drenched by the rain or toil in the sugar factories. They could exist from their own provision-gardens and work for an hour or two in their own time; their requirements were few: they did not need shoes, barely wore clothes, they were accustomed to little food, for they were so used to existing on the barest necessities of life that they needed little else. There was no longer the fear of the whip but there was still the boss, the white man.

Toussaint realized this, but he was obsessed by the necessity for agriculture and he could not convince his people that the provision-garden was all very well, but it was also vital to export. He tried to explain to them that for the Republic to survive it must produce, but they knew nothing of economics; life was lived from dawn to sunset, and the future, their children's future, was intangible. They had been told they were free, but free to do what? Not apparently what they wanted, so they felt cheated. British and mulatto agents, as well as arming them, told them that Toussaint who urged them to work was only trying to enslave them again. Bewildered, they did not know whom to believe but there was no escaping the fact that they were being ordered to return to the plantations.

Toussaint fought on; he issued a proclamation: 'O You Africans, my brothers, you who have cost me so many battles, so much labour and so much concern, you whose liberty was created with your own blood. How long will I have the shame of seeing my deluded children turn from the advice of a father who loves them.' He told them 'work is a virtue, it is a necessity. It is the general dignity of the State. All vagrant and idle men will be arrested and punished under the law' . . . firm words and firm intentions.

It was not only the cultivators who were the problem: he had to cajole and even bribe the landowners to return to their properties. He hoped that the cultivators might learn from them, might glean what they could from the old civilization and use it for their own advancement and their country's. This is one of the reasons he knew the whites to be necessary. His people could not read, write or add figures. They knew nothing of management or organization. How could they? They had never been allowed to learn. It was only the very exceptional men among them, like

Toussaint and the other leaders of the revolution, who had the qualities of leadership, a sense of direction and order, and an understanding of cause and effect.

Toussaint persisted: 'Liberty cannot exist without work.'

He wrote to Laveaux that he had installed five agricultural officers for the district, adding 'I hope you do not mind but I think it is necessary'.

Later on he was to treat the cultivators in the same way that he treated his army. He issued a decree that made it the responsibility of each owner of property to render an account of the conduct of his cultivators to the military commander of his area. If they had any complaint about a worker he was to be arrested immediately and punished if a case was proven against him. If anyone was unemployed he had to register for employment and work would be found for him; if he failed to register then he had to pay retribution to the state or face imprisonment. Toussaint said: 'Agriculture is the support of stable government, it is by this we procure commerce, ease and plenty and from it are born both the arts and industry. It employs the arms of all, encourages techniques on every level and for all the people, and the result is the end of unrest among the general public, trouble disappears with the end of idleness which is its mother and when all can see the fruit of their labours.' Toussaint would certainly not have agreed with Faulkner that 'idleness breeds all our virtues'.

Whilst in Mirebelais he found relief from the problems of the cultivator by turning to physical activity himself – something too many of his countrymen rejected but which he craved.

The British had made a breach in the river-bank in order to flood the crops. Sudden, heavy rain had aggravated the situation and the gap was now nearly 200 feet wide. He wrote to Laveaux: 'I closed the breach with trunks of trees and with rocks. More than 800 people were occupied on this project and after eight days I have only just finished.' This was the kind of thing he loved to do; he enjoyed manual labour, moving a cannon, unsaddling and rubbing down the horses and now, knee-deep in the fast flowing river, he helped and directed the men, heaving stones and backing the tree trunks into place. He found comradeship in the mutual effort and it satisfied him; achievement of any kind, however simple, gave him pleasure.

One day in Mirebelais a deputation of maroons from the mountains of Le Trou who were known locally as the 'd'occos' or 'dockos' came down from the heights where they had lived for generations, making forays on neighbouring villages and the houses of both black and white. They were much feared, but the Administration had found it impossible to subjugate what had grown into an army of robbers. They presented themselves to

Toussaint and their chief Mamzelle offered him their service and their loyalty. Toussaint welcomed them and accepted their offer. He gave them clothes, arms and ammunition. Among them were many men of the Aradas tribe to whom he spoke in their own tongue, and when they heard him they wept and threw themselves on the ground at his feet, swearing fealty to him as their king. For Toussaint it must have been a moving moment.

The British were a constant thorn in Toussaint's side, not because he was at this time fighting them but because of their method of making war. Not only were they arming the cultivators but they were infiltrating his army dressed in rebel uniforms and trying to persuade his men to join their forces. Toussaint discovered two of his own officers who he was informed had accepted the bribes, one white and one mulatto. He wrote to Viscomte de Bruges who was in command under the British:

Sir,

The cowards you sent with directions to the citizens of Petite Montagne to try to drag them with them, in the worst treachery, by joining up with them and the English to, so to speak, bring the conquest of St Dominigue totally to an end by using the worst means of seduction under the guise of humanitarian principles, were arrested by the worthy citizens who preferred death to being cowardly and treacherous. I am keeping these villains and will punish them for their treacherous cowardice. Make war with honour and the force of arms – why use treachery! – to try and seduce Republicans. It is in vain! The Republican is free.

In order to frighten them perhaps you say in your addresses to these brave and worthy Republicans of Petite Montagne that you prefer conciliatory means before taking up again the campaign which must bring to an end the conquest of St Dominigue? Chase this fancy from your ideas. Your menaces cannot frighten us. We await you and will prove to you that the conquest you hope to make is only a fancy.

Farewell.
Toussaint L'Ouverture.

Yet he could be forgiving to those who turned traitor; a white officer who had deserted to the British was captured by Toussaint's men and brought before him. Toussaint looked long at him and then said, his mouth concealing laughter, 'Ah, I see that we are too good friends for fate to keep us long apart.' The officer's command was restored to him and nothing more was said.

There was one heartening factor for Toussaint and Laveaux to cling to.

By the Treaty of Basle in 1795 the Spanish government ceded to France the Spanish side of Hispaniola. The transfer did not take place immediately but it put an end to the Spanish attack upon St Dominigue. The Spanish troops who had fought with the British returned to Spain and Jean François' and Biassou's armies were disbanded and many of their soldiers joined Toussaint.

Jean François remained in the service of Spain, he was made lieutenant general and retired to Cadiz, later becoming Governor of Orun. He was rich and popular with the Spanish court, particularly with the women, his remarkable good looks and fine physique were considered exotic and he made a most favourable and successful impression. He forgot St Dominigue and revolutions as quickly as he could, never setting foot on the island again, but living a life of luxurious carefree pleasure until he died in 1820.

Biassou went to St Augustine in Florida where he bought a large plantation, farmed, ironically, by slaves, but he drank both his land and his money away and died in a brawl when drunk. Toussaint with his usual kindness to women in distress granted his widow a pension.

It was essential to remove the British from the island as quickly as possible. With Sonthonax gone Toussaint saw the moment in sight when St Dominigue might at last become a nation on its own, not dominated by those who did not comprehend the complicated amalgam of its people, their way of life and their customs.

The British firmly retained slavery and far away in Paris the members of the Chamber, men who had never seen his land, squabbled over the destiny of his people. Whatever their fine words of Equality, Brotherhood and Liberty, in their hearts a mulatto remained a mulatto, and a black a black, and inferior to the white man. All that Toussaint was striving for was freedom and only that, but he sensed that the contest was far from over, and in the fight to come there might well be no victory for his people.

If the French, as he suspected, were to restore slavery again it would be a fight to the death, the years of insurrection, slaughter and horror would return and the misery that had drained his land would sear it with scars which might never heal. He dreamed of a country where black, coloured and white no longer hated each other but worked together for prosperity and peace. It was a dream far beyond his time and one that is still, in most countries of the world, only a dream to this day. Toussaint possessed none of the resentment to be expected in the ex-slave, to him all men were equal in the sight of God; he had many complexities, but in this he had none, he was 'as a child'.

He had come, reluctantly, to the conclusion that St Dominigue must control her own fate. Independence was the only way to combat the factions in the Chamber in Paris who were pressing for the return of slavery. Vaublanc, a member of the Chamber, had recently made an impassioned speech there in defence of slavery, which was much acclaimed, which proved there existed a strong faction who thought as he did, and whose intention was to restore slavery throughout the French possessions in the West Indies as quickly as possible

But first there was the more pressing problem of the British. He prepared for the attack and contacted Rigaud and Beauvais in the south to tell them of his plans. The assault was to be simultaneous.

He reorganized his army, forming ten regiments of infantry, each consisting of 1600 men, and two of cavalry. The regiments were all commanded by blacks or mulattoes, with the single exception of Brigadier General Rodrigues who was white. His Chief of Staff was also white – General Agé. Among his commanding officers were Dessalines, Paul Louverture, Maurepas, Gabart and Moïse.

The British under General White had an army of 20,000 men, consisting of 5000 British regulars and 8000 Negroes, and the rest were made up of mixed nationalities, all white or mulatto. These Negroes were not rebels or freed slaves but slaves who had been sold by their masters to the British, to swell their forces. As far as equipment was concerned the British had far superior artillery and an unlimited supply of arms.

On 3 February 1795 Toussaint attacked. The British forces held a line stretching from Jeremie at the far point in the south to Môle St Nicholas in the north. Toussaint was well aware that their army was superior in numbers; because of this superior strength, his plan of campaign was never to attack on a broad front, but to make spearhead attacks at strategic points on one part of the line at a time. At each point of contact he broke through and routed the enemy. His mobility was his secret – as it always had been – the speed of his attack and the swiftness with which he moved his men from one point to the next. They moved by night, marching like dancers with rhythmic grace, eating what little food they had also at night, no smoke plumes giving away their position or the direction they were travelling. When they halted they rested by streams with one relaxed hand lying in the water, cooling their head ties before they marched again. They sprawled on the ground, their bodies as limp as rag dolls, or sat with their heads on their knees and fell asleep in an instant, and then rapidly on, their drums of goatskin and wood playing a soft insistent beat which removed all fatigue. Toussaint first surprised Mirebelais, and at the same time Rigaud and Beauvais attacked in the south. In seven days Toussaint had won seven victories and Rigaud and Beauvais had scored a brilliant victory at Jeremie.

The British had completely underestimated the strength and military prowess of the army they were fighting. They had not an inkling of what was about to fall upon them, but had been misled both by their ingrained prejudice ('how could a black army defeat a British army?') also by the fact that up to then they had had no major encounters with Toussaint's troops, except at Mirebelais. They had met in a few skirmishes of a guerilla kind, but nothing like this. Too late, they realized that they were not fighting a band of black bandits but highly-trained, disciplined soldiers, with military leaders who were assured and experienced in making war; and they had more than underestimated Toussaint L'Ouverture.

Rainsford, a British officer, wrote: 'Each general had a demi brigade which went through the manual exercise with a degree of experience seldom witnessed, and performed equally well several manoeuvres applicable to their method of fighting. At a whistle the whole brigade ran 300 or 400 yards then separating threw themselves flat on the ground changing to their back or sides keeping up a strong fire the whole time till they were recalled, then they formed again and in an instant into their wonted regularity. This single manoeuvre was executed with such facility and precision as totally to prevent cavalry from charging them.'

Apart from the discipline of his men, apart from being a great leader, apart from efficiency and tireless energy the main reason for Toussaint's victory was the emotional bond he shared with his troops: a black man like them.

On the eve of the assault Toussaint issued a proclamation, his words as stirring as any general's before or since: 'That my hopes for you, my friends, will not prove to be in vain, show yourselves to be men who know what liberty means and are prepared to defend it. The army is about to march, take, my friends, the resolution not to return home until you have chased from the Colony the English and the Émigrés, only then can you enjoy the sweetness of liberty, the justice of the Republic and of our country, which you know cannot be possible if your enemies still occupy this land of freedom. Let not fatigue, the mountains nor the cliffs prevent you, we must conquer and it is now the time . . . It is not for fortune or for riches that we fight, there will be time to think of that when we have chased these enemies from our shores, it is for liberty which is the most precious of all earthly possessions, which we must preserve for our children, our brothers and our comrades. God who created all to be free has made it clear that it is our duty to preserve it for all who come after us.

'It is my intention and my resolve not to cease the fight until I have driven the English and the Emigrés entirely from our shores. Let us leave them nothing which they once possessed. We will make our land flourish once more for this is the foundation and the structure of our liberty.'

They were going into battle against soldiers who had no common cause to inspire them, men who were virtually mercenaries. The British commanders who came and went were only too glad to leave when recalled; they were simply doing their job in charge of an expeditionary force which, far away in London, Pitt and Dundas for political reasons and for gain had made a part of their duties, and as professional soldiers they did their duty. There were only 5000 British regular troops who were also under orders and doing their duty, but no one was attacking their country, they were not defending their own land or freedom and they would have been only too glad to leave St Dominigue and never see it again. Thousands upon thousands of them did, but not alive. They fought alongside a hotch-potch of races, French, Spanish, Irish and mulatto, all with different axes to grind, none of which the British soldiers understood or with which they had any sympathy. They fought side by side with 8000 Negroes whom they considered savages, and all the time there was the climate and the dread of yellow fever. Their red coats were soaked by the drenching rain and did not dry out for hours, their bodies ran with cold sweat beneath the soaking wool, the close humidity was worse than the clear sky and blazing sun. Even in the dry season, in February, it can rain. Toussaint was skilful in timing his attacks to use the weather as his ally. The black troops attached to the British can hardly have had their heart in their job, bearing in mind that they were fighting to preserve the very system which they had rebelled against.

The British officers in command also made another mistake in their consideration of Toussaint, 'the bandit'; they discovered that he fought like a gentleman. He gave his officers a strict briefing to 'treat prisoners humanely and to receive deserters from the enemy ranks as friends and brothers. I will hold you personally responsible for any act contrary to these orders that remains unpunished.'

He assured General White of his intentions towards prisoners: 'the mutual consideration which civilized men owe to each other has prompted me to take all necessary steps to ensure their safety.' When he found this civilized behaviour was not reciprocated he despatched to White one of his more stinging communications. 'You have demeaned yourself in the eyes of this and future generations, you have allowed one of your commanders (La Pointe the coward) to issue this order which it is not possible could have been issued without your knowledge: "Give the Brigands no quarter! Take no prisoners!" . . . I feel that although I am a Negro, though I have not received as fine an education as you and the officers of his Britannic Majesty, I feel that if I were to be guilty of such infamy it would reflect upon the honour of my country and I would have tarnished its glory.'

Nor did he only protect the prisoners, he protected the civilians. He told the proprietors who had remained under the British and supported them, 'Your property will be safe,' and that if they were loyal to the Republic full rights of French citizenship would be granted to them and 'the veil of forgetfulness will be drawn over your past acts, your lives will be protected.'

Seven victories in seven days, the front line was broken and the main towns at his mercy. General Maitland took over command. He was an able if unscrupulous man, an experienced and crafty soldier who later became Governor of Malta. He proved his good sense by realizing at once that the situation was hopeless. The attack had now continued for one month and in that time the British had only 2500 men out of 20,000 remaining to defend their garrisons, and half of these were sick. His force was in danger of total destruction. The British government, who were not present to judge the situation, offered him more troops if he felt he could continue the occupation, but the condition of his men and the superiority of Toussaint's army made him come to the conclusion that he was beaten.

The military historian Fortescue writes that 'the British Campaign in the West Indies . . . cost England in army and navy little fewer than 100,000 men, half of them dead and half permanently unfit for service.' He added: 'the secret of England's impotence for the six years of the war may be said to be in the two fatal words St Dominigue.' The cost in money in St Dominigue alone had been £300,000 in 1794, £800,000 in 1795 and £600,000 in 1796, and all for nothing.

Many historians have found it convenient to make yellow fever the main cause of the British defeat in St Dominigue, but it was only contributory; Maitland himself conceded that Toussaint would have won even without the ravages of this terrible disease. Yellow fever killed in three days, few recovered. The old proprietor families had become almost immune, it was the newcomers to the islands whom it cut down in swathes as though Death with his scythe walked in their midst. Strong men, realizing they had contracted the disease, went into paroxysms of terror and died on the spot. It came in epidemics, an island might be free of it for several years before it struck again. The pain was appalling and all knew there was no hope, the soldiers had no nursing and no medical skill, as Albert de Lattre who wrote an account of LeClerc's campaign in St Dominigue states: 'there was a mulattress Cotin who was the bene-factor of the human race, she overcame the yellow fever (the fever of Siam): three glasses of red wine, a walnut of nutmeg and the yolk of an egg well cooked over coals and then powdered, which produced sweating

Christophe's Palace
COURTESY OF MARY EVANS PICTURE LIBRARY

J. J. Dessalines
COURTESY OF THE MANSELL COLLECTION

Henri Christophe 1767–1820
COURTESY OF THE MANSELL COLLECTION

Lt General The Right Honourable Sir Thomas Maitland, GCMG, KCB

Général Leclerc
COURTESY OF MUSÉE DE L'ARMÉE, PARIS

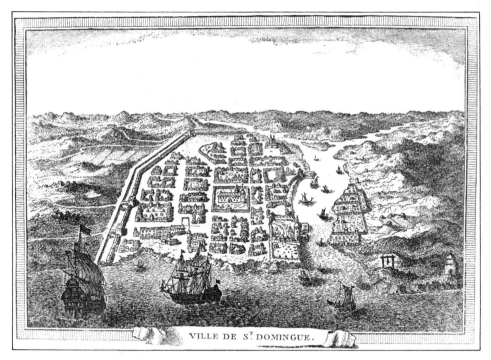

St Dominigue
COURTESY OF THE MANSELL COLLECTION

Landing at Jacmel, Haiti
COURTESY OF THE MANSELL COLLECTION

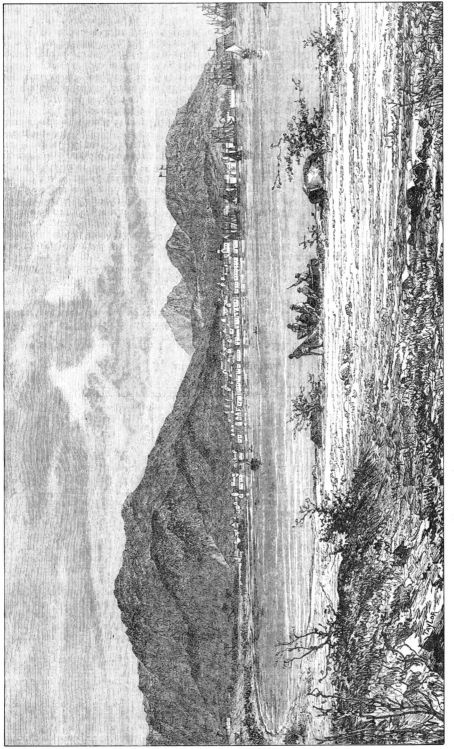

The Bay of Port-au-Prince, Haiti
COURTESY OF THE MANSELL COLLECTION

Toussaint's guerillas harry the French troops
COURTESY OF MARY EVANS PICTURE LIBRARY

Napoleon on the rocks of St Helena by Delarocho

and so saved the sufferers.' Wine, egg and nutmeg could not save them, nothing could. And no one guessed what caused it, no one could have known that it was the little mosquito which buzzed around their heads at night as they slept, that stung them on their elbows and knuckles, not just one more irritation to be borne in this terrible climate, but a killer.

Maitland sent a despatch to Toussaint asking for armistice, and offering in return to evacuate Port au Prince, Croix des Bouquets, St Marc and L'Archaye, and Toussaint agreed.

The British were to retain only Jeremie in the south and Môle St Nicholas in the north. These were to be considered ports of disembarkment. Cunningly Maitland tried to drive a rift between Rigaud and Toussaint, but Toussaint would have none of it, quickly saying 'we serve the same cause'. Maitland insisted that there should be amnesty for all proprietors who had lived in the British territory; Toussaint countered by saying that this would have been his own first requisite for peace terms. Sir Spencer St John wrote later: 'Toussaint with a greatness of mind which was remarkable agreed to allow those French colonists who had sided with us to remain and promised to respect their properties; as it was known that this magnanimous black ever kept his word, no important exodus followed our retreat.' Only for the émigrés who had actually fought with the British was there to be no amnesty. All forts formerly held by the British were to be handed over to Toussaint undamaged and complete with cannon. Maitland cavilled at this but was forced to agree.

The British campaign was virtually over and Toussaint must surely have had a sense of relief. He knew he could have continued the battle and obliterated the enemy, but his victory had been so speedy that his army had suffered few losses; to have continued might have caused unnecessary bloodshed, and his men were always his first concern. If the British were prepared to plead for a truce that was victory enough.

If he was justly pleased with himself he was equally proud of his generals who had behaved with fearless bravery. Des Fourneaux, Dessalines and Christophe had especially distinguished themselves, Christophe in particular. This was the first time that the future King of Haiti was to make his mark in history.

The British withdrew to Jeremie and Môle St Nicholas and Toussaint's troops occupied the now evacuated territory. The black troops under the British joined Toussaint's force, swelling its numbers considerably, and Toussaint's army marched into Port au Prince, although he himself remained at his base. The capital of St Dominigue saw for the first time these fearsome bandits, as they marched proudly through the city, their heads held high. To the incredulous relief of the nervous inhabitants the discipline of the troops was as stern as it had been on the field: there was no looting, the behaviour of these ragged men, barebacked and barefooted, was rigorously correct, women were unmolested, whites were shown no violence. Their officers' behaviour was impeccable. It was the white General Dessources whom Toussaint had once routed at Mirebelais, who burned the plantations behind him as he withdrew, and the mulatto La Pointe, whom Toussaint had once called a coward, and who had issued the order to take no prisoners, who now set fire to L'Archaye as he evacuated it.

Toussaint had not only gained the day on the battlefield; the victory won, he now showed the enemy not only the calibre of himself but of his people.

8   1796-7: The Commissioners

Toussaint had been appointed a brigadier general by Laveaux and now this appointment was confirmed by the French Directory. Laveaux was to write to the Ministry of Marine: 'The mulattoes are in despair at seeing Toussaint L'Ouverture – a Negro – become a brigadier general,' perhaps Rigaud in particular, though some historians say that Toussaint and Rigaud got on well together, and so they did – for a time and on the surface there were fine words from both – but in the mulatto–Negro antagonism of that time a genuine link was an impossibility. Mulattoes were often more anti-black than the whites. Toussaint knew perfectly well that Rigaud allowed no Negro to rise above the rank of captain in his army. Rigaud might well, and indeed did, admire him as a brilliant soldier, as he was one himself, but Toussaint was still black. His rank was not the mulattoes' only grievance, they were equally in despair at Toussaint's hold over Laveaux.

In the south Rigaud was virtually dictator, he held absolute power and was as dedicated to the mulatto cause as Toussaint was to the black. All important offices were held by mulattoes, ignoring both black and white. The mulattoes had, however, a weakness created by lifetimes of petty jealousies and snobberies; not only did they not get on with black and white, they did not like one another. The envy that Rigaud demonstrated permeated the whole structure of their society – even in freedom.

They were so divided that they were prepared to fight for three different armies, the Republican, the British and their own, and change sides in the middle of a battle at any profitable inducement. Their loyalties had been so fragmented all their lives that they had none left. Their inherent treachery was soon discovered by Toussaint, who wrote bitterly to Laveaux: 'There has been a conspiracy and you must know there is a man of colour at the head of it.'

Laveaux should have heeded his words and been less trusting of his commandant and second-in-command to him at Le Cap – Villatte. Laveaux had removed himself to Port de Paix which was more comfortable as Le Cap was still in ruins. When he was there rumours of Villatte's conduct began to leak through to him. Toussaint, a less trusting man, had long been suspicious and had gently prodded Laveaux to make an investigation. Finally convinced that something was indeed very wrong, Laveaux decided to take a closer look at matters and moved into the Governor's house at Le Cap. He was to find corruption on a grand scale and belligerent disloyalty. When proof was produced Villatte lost all discretion: he had been humiliated, the one thing he could not tolerate, for as a mulatto he had suffered humiliation all his life, and he determined upon revenge. He insulted Laveaux and even threatened him with violence. Laveaux wrote to Toussaint to ask for help. Toussaint replied: 'What! Have they the audacity to threaten you with force. Do they imagine they can do as they please . . . This very day I am sending a delegation with a letter.'

Villatte contacted Rigaud and Pinchinat in the south, and Pinchinat went up on some trivial pretext to confer. All realized that to gain control of the Colony it was necessary to curb Toussaint's influence on Laveaux. His army was essential to them but his policies were not, and they sensed his power. Therefore it had to be Laveaux who was removed in order to keep Toussaint in check, and in Laveaux' place, to gain their ends, there had to be a mulatto Governor.

Toussaint was perfectly aware of these manoeuverings. He had almost daily reports of the situation from a subordinate of Villatte, Colonel Pierre Michel who was a Negro.

On 20 March 1796 there was a military parade at the Place d'Armes in Le Cap. Laveaux returned from it and changed out of his stifling uniform into a dressing-gown and slippers. He had an appointment with an officer of the engineers with whom he was discussing fortifications when Villatte came unannounced into his work cabinet. Six men followed him and then, as he wrote to Toussaint, 'more than a hundred rushed into the room – all were mulattoes, not a Negro, not a white man. I thought they wished me to arbitrate some quarrel and rising calmly from my chair I asked them "Citizens, what is your pleasure?" whereupon without warning they fell upon me. I fought them off and managed to free myself. They seized the engineer and I cried for help. My aide Robert came running but he was unable to reach my side. They attacked me with their fists and sticks. I was in my slippers and lost them during the struggle. I was dragged into the street, bareheaded, barefooted, by the arms, by the hair. They threw me into prison where medical assistance was denied me.' Laveaux was an elderly man and it was a humiliating shock for him. He had suspected that they were plotting against him for he had written to the Minister of Marine that 'Villatte is quite persuaded that he is going to be Governor', but he had not expected mob violence at the hands of men, many of whom he knew and some of whom he trusted.

He was left alone for two days and then visited by representatives of the

Municipality who pretended to be amazed and in despair at his arrest, but they too were involved in the plot and it was declared officially that Laveaux had 'lost the confidence of the people' and they named Villatte as Governor.

Michel immediately sent a dispatch to Toussaint who was in Gonaîves, assembled all the men he knew to be loyal and called out the cultivators to 'defend their friend Laveaux'.

Toussaint digested the news and sent a letter to the Municipality at Le Cap and to underline the letter ordered Dessalines, Moïse and Belair to march on the capital with 6000 men where they joined forces with Michel's troops.

The mulattoes' plan was to place Laveaux on board a ship and send him back to France, but no one had quite enough courage to put this into action. Toussaint from Gonaîves issued a withering proclamation: 'In disrespecting the Governor you have disrespected France', and went on to compare the lot of the people under the Republic with that of those under the British who were 'branded on their cheek and chained as galley slaves . . . you on the contrary live peacefully in your homes but now you sow confusion.' The population was indeed confused, at the first break-down of law and order all the elements of insurrection had broken out again. But 10,000 troops standing on their doorstep had a quietening effect and the mulattoes were forced to realize they had failed and Laveaux was released. He rested in Haut-Le Cap for five days recovering his strength and trying to regain his equanimity. Villatte had gone into hiding with a small group of supporters and Toussaint remained in Gonaîves. He did not wish to take on the mulattoes as well as the British and he knew his presence at this juncture would only inflame matters, but he was anxious to see his friend and could wait no longer. On 27 March at the head of his personal guard of cavalry he left Gonaîves and rode to Haut-Le Cap. Laveaux came out to receive him and with great emotion the two men embraced, clasping each other like father and son, except that Toussaint, the 'son', was the elder.

Their personal happiness at seeing each other again and the temporary abeyance of the mulatto uprising did not blind either of them to the fact that the problem still existed and they discussed it far into the night. Toussaint wanted Laveaux to dismiss Villatte immediately, Laveaux saw in this more potential danger from Rigaud and Pinchinat. Toussaint believed that the 'catechism asks to forgive us our sins as we forgive those who have offended against us, but in an army no subordination, no discipline and there is no army – that at least is what I believe.' Laveaux was still in a state of shock, a time when it is difficult to make decisions, and he could not make up his mind. However with Laveaux' permission

Toussaint sent Villatte a message asking him to come to Le Cap. Villatte did not come, probably fearing a trap.

The next day Toussaint and Laveaux rode into Le Cap together at the head of 10,000 men. Toussaint was in full dress uniform. 'He wore a kind of blue jacket with a large red cape falling over the shoulders, red cuffs with eight rows of lace on the arms and a pair of large gold epaulettes thrown back; scarlet waistcoat and pantaloons with half boots; round hat with a red feather, and a national cockade, these with an extremely large sword formed his equipment.' (Rainsford)

For Toussaint the entrance into Le Cap must have brought back many memories: once he had been only a postillion with a coach behind him as he passed through these familiar streets, now he rode with the Governor of St Dominigue at his side and behind him were his black generals, his personal bodyguard of ninety dragoons with their blue hats and cuirasses, his white, black and mulatto officers, his cavalry and 10,000 men marching with proud precision.

No wonder the crowd cheered, this was a demonstration for all to see, a symbol of what their own land could produce, what it meant to be a free Republic. Military music always stirs the heart and there were scenes of emotional enthusiasm.

More was to come: on 1 April 1796 a dais was raised in the Place d'Armes, the flag of the Republic of France flew high and was draped out of the windows of the ruined houses, the populace was wearing its best and there was a buzz of excitement and anticipation. The army was massed at attention and Toussaint's bodyguard was drawn up on each side of the dais, the horses' bridles clinking as they nodded their heads. Toussaint and Laveaux appeared together, the trumpets rang out and the band played. Then Laveaux spoke; he spoke firmly and clearly in his perfect punctilious French to proclaim Toussaint L'Ouverture Lieutenant Governor and announce that in future he would do nothing without consulting him, and in so doing he gave him a power equal to his own.

Laveaux then addressed the people, saying 'there stands this black Spartacus, the Negro who Raynal prophesied would avenge his race.' Toussaint drew his sword, kissed the hilt and, raising it high above his head, shouted 'After God – Laveaux.'

The mulattoes were stunned, they had expected the reinstatement of Villatte and some dispensations for themselves, but there were none; instead this black man had virtually supreme power over them and the north. The blacks were mad with joy and the whites who had expected nothing for themselves were relieved. Many of them had grown to trust Toussaint; by his actions he had shown his fairness and protection of them and they certainly trusted him more than any mulatto.

Laveaux felt reassured, now he had made the decision, that he had not only a friend but a powerful ally at his side, but perhaps he did not suspect that Toussaint might prove too powerful, even for him. He was still concerned about the mulattoes, particularly Rigaud whom he felt had not shown his hand yet; the British were still firmly entrenched and he was a tired man, his apprehensions made him ill and he could not recover easily from the shock he had received at mulatto hands.

He wrote piteously to the Minister of Marine: 'Ah, Citizen, do not delay, send troops, send Commissioners'; he felt himself unable to deal with the situation any longer.

The French in Paris were themselves uneasy at the mulattoes seeking power and at what they considered to be the supremacy of Toussaint. In the meantime they showered him with honours – he was valuable – they appointed him a divisional commander but they also decided it wise to send out Commissioners from the Metropole to size up the situation and keep it under control, since they had become uneasy at Toussaint's power over Laveaux but, at the same time, they did not wish in any way to antagonize him. The Commissioners landed bearing with them an ornamental sword and a brace of pistols of superb workmanship. They also carried an invitation for him to send his two sons to France where they could receive the finest education and would be the responsibility of the Republic.

The Commissioners were headed by Sonthonax, who had been completely vindicated at his trial; Raimond, a mulatto; Roume, an odd choice as he had already shown himself incompetent in one field, but as so often happens in government he was given another post, this time in the Spanish sector of Hispaniola. They were accompanied by 1200 troops, arms and artillery.

Sonthonax was quick to set to work, impetuously he arrested Villatte and had him deported. He then rashly ordered an investigation into Pinchinat's and Rigaud's part in the affair. Being a fanatical Republican and, it must be remembered, the original emancipator of the slaves (with whom he was, naturally, extremely popular), he was very disturbed by the mulatto domination of the south. Whites and blacks were equally badly treated, jailed for no reason and held without trial for the slightest offence. The mulattoes were so confident of their authority that they were openly corrupt and too arrogant to care who knew it. They extorted large sums of money from the whites: when they rented a house from a white landlord they would then refuse to pay the rent and there was nothing the white could do about it, but Sonthonax was so keen to achieve a quick result in the Colony that he ignored all advice from others with more experience of the situation, which indeed was delicately balanced, especially since it was Rigaud's army which was keeping the British at bay.

Toussaint tried to curb Sonthonax' hastiness but he was brushed aside. The Commission chosen to go to Les Cayes consisted of a mulatto, La Borgne, and two white men, General Des Fourneaux and Rey. Rey was a disastrous choice. Rigaud and he were not merely enemies, but their hatred was implacable. Rey had once attempted to have Rigaud assassinated. His reputation was shabby, a man of flagrant indiscretions so far as women were concerned and a heavy gambler which made him suspect with Toussaint. But Sonthonax refused to listen; carried away by reforming zeal he was determined to set his house in order.

The Commissioners arrived in Les Cayes and Rey although on official duty continued to live his usual life. Rigaud was engaged to a very beautiful girl Marie Villeneuve, whom Rey deliberately and to spite Rigaud seduced. He asked Rigaud to his house for a discussion, and then said to him slyly and conspiratorially, as man to man, 'Rigaud, I am going to introduce you to the most beautiful girl in Les Cayes, but you must promise you will tell no one.' He then led the way into his bedroom, tiptoeing towards the bed. Rigaud, intrigued, followed him. Rey smiled at him over his shoulder and drew the curtains; Marie Villeneuve lay there, naked and sleeping after love. Rigaud sprang at Rey in an attempt to choke him, forcing him towards the balcony; hearing the commotion and the awakened Marie's screams the servants rushed in and separated them. It was not a propitious start for an enquiry into corruption.

Rigaud in any case was nettled at having to be investigated at all and Pinchinat, well aware of his guilt in the Villatte affair, spread the rumour that the Commission had come to reinstate slavery. A riot broke out and before Rigaud could control it 200 whites were massacred. Sonthonax withdrew his men – there was little else he could do.

Toussaint refrained from saying 'I told you so' but he was angry with both Sonthonax and Rigaud and the men involved and he felt that if he himself had had the handling of the affair he would have managed it a good deal better, but he was learning diplomacy fast; he was pleasant and consolatory to Sonthonax, but at the same time he staunchly defended Rigaud for, as he had told Sonthonax many times, Rigaud was too valuable to alienate. But this incident confirmed Toussaint's mistrust of Sonthonax' ability to rule the country. Toussaint felt as so many men living in colonies before and since have felt that the outsider who hurtles in 'dressed in a little brief authority' makes blunders which a man who belongs to that country would never make.

At this time the French Assembly introduced a new directive. St Dominigue was to send representatives to the new French Chamber of

Deputies and to the Senate. Toussaint had decided whom he wished to go and one of them was Sonthonax, but the other, less understandably, was Laveaux. He wrote Laveaux a letter, written in the usual affectionate manner:

My general, my father, my good friend,
I, seeing as I do with grief how since you arrived in this unhappy land you have sacrified your life, your wife and your children, and unpleasant occurrences which I do not wish to have the grief of witnessing; I should like to see you elected to the office of Deputy. For then you will have the satisfaction of seeing your fatherland and that which you will find more dear to you, your wife and your children. And you will be sheltered from the factions that spring up all the time in St Dominigue. At the same time my brothers will have the assurance of our cause being defended most zealously. Yes, my General, my father, my benefactor, France has many men of excellence but where is the man who like you can be relied upon to be a true friend to the blacks? No, we will never see your equal.

Toussaint knew of Laveaux' ill-health and weariness, there is no doubt that this is the letter of a man thinking of a friend – who had indeed given a large part of his life in a foreign and often hostile land – but there remains a sliver of suspicion in the mind, and certainly there must have been moments when Laveaux wondered if his friend was being wholly straightforward, particularly when he heard that Toussaint had also nominated Sonthonax for the Chamber. It seemed rather too coincidental that both Frenchmen holding power in the island should be manoeuvred to leave at the same time. Toussaint had not troubled to tell Sonthonax that he had put up his name. Laveaux weighed the matter: if he did suspect any ulterior motive on Toussaint's part he overlooked it at the relief of being able to see his family once more, for he had returned only once to France during all these years and his children were growing up without him having ever known them. He could continue to be useful to St Dominigue and to his friend. He accepted Toussaint's suggestion with gratitude.

The Electoral Assembly met; to ensure that the voting went Toussaint's way he used rather surprising strong-arm methods. He had said to Laveaux that he would use 'Confidential agents, to impress upon the electors how necessary it is for the welfare of the blacks that you should be chosen to represent them. You will be!' The agents were his nephew Moïse and Colonel Pierre Michel, together with a detachment of soldiers who were armed. Michel spoke on the platform, playing with his pistol as he did so. The electors voted for Laveaux and Sonthonax.

On 19 October 1796 Laveaux sailed for France, Toussaint and he having
said a sad farewell. They continued to write to each other, an intimate
correspondence concerning their own lives, their thoughts and the affairs
of St Dominigue, but they were never to see each other again.

Sonthonax did not take up his appointment, but remained.

Sonthonax did not trust the mulattoes and was often rather peevish about
them: 'their demands appear to know no bounds and they seem to require
every kind of office; yet they do not cease to complain if they are called
either Negroes or whites.' Perhaps this reflected a moment of domestic
irritation for he married his mistress, a mulattress – a Madame Villevaleix,
a rich widow with several children. But on the whole he was popular with
the mulattoes and always endeavoured to do his best for them.

Since his first visit he had become obsessed and his hatred of the whites
grew fanatical. He knew from early experiences on the island of their
treatment of the slaves he had freed and he saw them returning to their
homes, saw that they still dominated the countryside and he hated them
with an unbalanced venom that they knew and returned – it was *he* who
was responsible for the freeing of the slaves, *he* who had forced the colonists to flee or had had them deported, who was confiscating their land and
giving it to the State and arming the cultivators with muskets. 'With this
I give you your liberty, whoever tries to take it from you intends to
return you to slavery.' In fact it was Toussaint who took the muskets
away. Sonthonax said, 'Nobody has the right to make you work if you
do not want to.' Toussaint never ceased telling them, 'Work is a necessity,
it is a virtue.' *He* was the villain, not Toussaint, Toussaint had encouraged
them to return to their estates and had encouraged the émigrés to come
back from abroad. Sonthonax was now refusing to let them in. They felt
that when Sonthonax handed out muskets to their cultivators he was
encouraging murder, which indeed he was. All his affection, all his effort
was directed towards the black masses, not towards the black leaders who
he thought used their status in order to accrue both money and women.
At least he was true to his Republican principles, but he was impractical
and unrealistic; in his eyes the blacks could do no wrong and he saw
himself as their redeemer, not Toussaint, who lived for nothing else but to
be considered their hero, and he would stop at nothing to gain the love
and respect of the black people.

Toussaint was black, he knew his people were people with the same
frailties and virtues as any other race. He disagreed wholeheartedly with
Sonthonax' sentimental idealism. He certainly knew his people's limitations, and especially that they were not ready for the wholesale distribution

of muskets. But he continued to be suave and pleasantly ambivalent towards Sonthonax and to prevent his more foolhardy ideas coming to fruition.

In December 1796 Toussaint visited Le Cap and had a meeting with Sonthonax who made the incredible proposal that they should massacre all the whites and form an independent state based on the great principles of the French Republic. Toussaint could hardly take him seriously and laughing quietly he said, 'Well, Commissioner, when I have declared my independence of France and have massacred all the whites what do you propose I should do with *you*?' He dismissed the proposal and when Sonthonax brought the matter up again, he cut him short. He had no intention of massacring the whites, not merely out of humanity but out of good sense; he was also not particularly anxious to discuss independence or he might disclose the seed that was forming in his own mind.

Toussaint was wearied by this nonsense and was only too glad to get away and be once more on the battlefield as a soldier. In the spring of 1797 he made a sudden attack upon several British outposts, taking them with ease and capturing valuable cannon, arms and prisoners. A grateful Sonthonax appointed him Commander in Chief in a ceremony in the Place d'Armes. After the ceremony and the speeches were over Sonthonax asked to speak to him privately and again proposed that this was the moment to achieve their ends and that all the whites should be banished. Toussaint replied: 'That is to say, Commissioner, that you wish to destroy me . . . you suggest yesterday that the whites should be massacred and today that they should be banished. I am leaving.'

He turned on his heel. Sonthonax, nearly hysterical and with tears streaming down his face, cried out, 'It is finished, I thought we could agree – Oh, promise me you will tell no one what has passed.'

Toussaint ignored him and left the room. However, he wrote a long report to the Directory of all Sonthonax' unbalanced plans. His policy towards the whites never altered throughout his life. It was a curious situation, a black man and a revolutionary defending the whites against one of their own race.

In France the Directory was becoming as alarmed as Toussaint by Sonthonax' behaviour and the pro-white planter group within the Chamber was lobbying fiercely for his recall. He was accused of killing whites, which he had not actually done yet, and of taking state money – which he had also not done, not being that kind of a man. It was felt by many in the Chamber that he should be recalled. Hearing of this, Sonthonax was more determined than ever to pursue his dream of an independent black state with himself in sole control and no competition from any other white man, and what was more urgent, he now realized, no competition from Toussaint.

He was determined to make his dream come true in spite of Toussaint, so he spread rumours among his administrators and stirred up suspicion against Toussaint wherever he could. He tried to insinuate himself with Toussaint's generals, telling them that Toussaint was too overbearing. Finally and with great skill, he created unrest in Toussaint's army. He increased the pay of the men of the garrison at Le Cap while letting it be known within Toussaint's camp that, whereas he considered his soldiers, Toussaint did not. He withheld supplies and implied this was due to Toussaint's mismanagement. He sent an officer to incite Toussaint's officers to mutiny. This scheme was successful but Toussaint arrested sixty-seven officers and shot two, and the mutiny was over.

Toussaint now knew that Sonthonax must go and soon. On 16 August 1797 he marched on Le Cap with a large force, camped near by and then rode into the town accompanied by a few officers. He went straight to the Governor's house and asked to see Commissioner Raimond. He informed him that Sonthonax must leave, he did not wish to offer him violence, and in order to avoid any scene it would be better if Raimond told him that it was time he took up his position in the Chamber, which the Assembly had voted upon a year before. Raimond was speechless and stared at Toussaint unbelievingly. Toussaint was cold but firm, Raimond was frightened because, although Toussaint's manner was quiet, as many reported, he could be very menacing. Raimond agreed to give the message to Sonthonax.

The next day Toussaint gave Raimond his reasons, telling him that Sonthonax intended to massacre the whites and that he had every reason to believe he had been the cause of the mutiny among his men, and that Sonthonax was trying to use the blacks to massacre the whites, which would lead to civil war. The Commissioner replied that the removal of Sonthonax might lead to civil war anyway. Toussaint remained unmoved. Raimond then went in to Sonthonax and told him of Toussaint's accusations. Sonthonax said he wished to speak to Toussaint alone. Toussaint (in his report) stated that he repeated the accusations against Sonthonax to his face. Sonthonax, as usual, became nearly hysterical: 'How can you treat me like this? I am the founder of liberty.' He should have thought back to the day when he proclaimed emancipation and Toussaint wished even then to seize the credit for himself. Sonthonax had not fought unarmed on the battle field for liberty, he had only proclaimed it. Toussaint still remained implacable. He must go. Sonthonax, thinking of his future when he arrived in what might be a far from welcoming Paris, agreed to go if he could take with him a letter signed by Toussaint and his commanders expressing their gratitude and confidence in him. He asked for three days to collect his belongings. Toussaint agreed but added dryly it would probably be better if he wrote his own letter in praise of himself.

The letter was delivered; it was excessively laudatory, but Toussaint and his staff signed it and returned it to Sonthonax. Still he did not leave, although the three days were long past. Sonthonax who never seemed to tire of intrigue was once more trying to muster help, by antagonizing the officers of his garrison against Toussaint. Toussaint was bored with the game, it was over anyway, and he had won. On 27 August at the un-welcome hour of four o'clock in the morning he sent his white Chief of Staff (which under the circumstances was not tactful) to order Sonthonax to be woken, and to inform him that the frigate *L'Indien* awaited him and that if he was not aboard by sunrise Toussaint himself would put him aboard by force. Sonthonax pleaded for a few more hours to collect himself and his family and the request was granted.

At eight o'clock he and his wife and stepchildren left the Governor's house; everything was formal and circumspect; Sonthonax was leaving in order to fill an honoured post which the island had voted him to do. The rumour that he was leaving had spread like wildfire, respectful troops had been ordered to line the streets, sorrowful black faces peered into the carriage windows to catch a last glimpse of the man who had first told them of their freedom. No one cheered, solomnly they lifted their hats and the women bowed their heads and bobbed. Accompanying Sonthonax was the black General Leveille, who had disagreed with Sonthonax being given his congé, and many other white officers. On the quay Toussaint was waiting. He handed Sonthonax a letter, saluted him, bowed respectfully to his family and then they were rowed away to the waiting frigate. Toussaint stood to attention as the guns fired a salute and did not leave until the Commissioner was on board.

He had gone, and Toussaint's decision had been right if ruthless. Sonthonax' hysteria, blind idealism and capacity for intrigue could only have produced another holocaust, if he had been allowed to remain. He may have possessed many virtues, his sympathy for the black race in their struggle was certainly one, but Toussaint knew that any man who suggests wholesale racial massacre as a means to any end is irrational. He could not shoot him down like a mad dog, or imprison him to protect the populace; it was fortunate that he could send him back to his own country, where he could continue to plead the cause of the Negro without endangering anyone else.

Sonthonax denied all charges, saying that 'It is he whose political career has been one long revolt against France. Toussaint has fooled two kings, he may well end fooling the Republic.' It seems he was astute, even if he lacked judgement. He was also a practised and unrepentant liar, living in a world of fantasy in which he could conjure up plots and counterplots and eventually deceive even himself. He only lied when it was unnecessary, which is always foolish. Toussaint only lied when it was vital to do so.

Toussaint knew that Sonthonax would spread distrust about him in the French Chamber which indeed he did, always protesting that any idea of independence had always been Toussaint's and never his. How was he, Toussaint, going to restore the confidence of the French government in him and in his administration? Although the Republic had offered to educate his sons he had not so far taken up the offer. He now made the decision to send them to France to prove his sincerity and his trust. It had always been his dearest wish that they should be educated, as he had never been, and he longed for the day when all his people would be educated; but at least he could start with his own sons. He told them what an opportunity it would be, while their mother wept; she did not care whether they were educated or not – she only wanted her family around her. The boys were excited as their father painted for them a picture of what they might achieve with education, of how they would return to the island as polished as the émigrés and the young white men whom they had so often watched enviously riding through the streets of Le Cap.

Toussaint wrote a long emotional letter to the Directory, not only concerning St Dominigue but the fact that he knew in his heart that he was handing over his sons as hostages. This letter must have been pondered over and altered many times as was his usual custom. He refers to Vaublanc and his inflammatory speeches in the Chamber and then says 'but insidious speeches should not sway wise rulers' and adds 'treacherous agents have come among us . . . but they will not succeed. I swear it by all that liberty holds most sacred . . . My affection for France, my knowledge of the blacks make it my duty not to leave you in ignorance of the crimes of which they are thinking of or the oaths which we renew to bury ourselves under the ruins of our country now revived by liberty rather than to suffer slavery again . . . you will discover that they are counting on my lending myself to their perfidious views for fear of my children. It is not surprising that these men who are willing to sacrifice their country to their own interests are unable to conceive how many sacrifices for a true love of country a father, better than they, is willing to make . . . I unhesitatingly base the happiness of my children on that of my country, which they, and they alone, are prepared to destroy.

'I shall never put my personal happiness before that of St Dominigue, but I know I have nothing to fear. It is into the care of the French government that I have entrusted my children.'

He ends his letter by crying out against Vaublanc and his colleagues

who had advocated the return of slavery. 'Do they believe that men who
have enjoyed the blessing of liberty will calmly see it snatched away? They
bore their chains only so long as they did not comprehend any other life
more happy than that of slavery. But today when they are free, if they had
a thousand lives they would sacrifice them all rather than be forced into
slavery once more . . . But France surely will not betray her principles, she
will not withdraw from us the greatest benefit which she has given us,
she will protect us against our enemies . . . *But if the re-establishment of
slavery in St Dominigue came to pass then I declare to you it would be to attempt
the impossible, we have known how to face dangers to obtain our liberty, and we
shall know how to face death to maintain it.*

'This, Citizen Directors, is the spirit of the people of St Dominigue,
these are the principles which they wish to demonstrate by my words
to you.

'My own feelings you know. It is sufficient to renew, my hand in
yours, the oath that I have made, before gratitude is killed in my heart,
before I cease to be faithful to France and to my duty, before the symbol
of liberty is profaned . . . before they take away the sword and the arms
which France honoured me with for the defence of its rights and for the
triumph of liberty and equality.'

Did Toussaint really believe in the honesty of those who were to care
for his children? He had good reason not to. He did not know when he
wrote this letter that the Vaublanc faction had already been ousted. If he
had, perhaps he would have hesitated before sending them over as virtual
hostages.

When Placide and Isaac set sail a large crowd gathered to see them off,
for they were popular on the island, the leader's children, black boys who
were so honoured to go to France to be educated. Suzanne was grief-
stricken, Toussaint quiet, as they watched the ship growing smaller in the
distance until it seemed to merge into the blue of the sea.

Toussaint's agitation about Vaublanc, and his fear of the threat of
slavery from the Directory, had led him to make an overt demonstration
of his (seeming) goodwill, a goodwill which in fact he himself no longer
felt. It is curious that a man so devoted to his children should have taken
this step and made them pawns to the strategies of power and politics.
Perhaps he would have hesitated if he had realized that a man far more
dangerous than Vaublanc, a man far more threatening to himself, to his
children and to St Dominigue was about to take the centre of the stage of
the world.

9 1798: Negotiations with France, Britain and America

In France the Directory had listened carefully to Sonthonax' account of Toussaint's virtual dismissal of him, and although they themselves had already recalled him, they were uneasy at what they heard: Toussaint appeared to be climbing rapidly to a position of disturbing power, and his impassioned letters upon slavery carried within them a not too veiled threat. They came to the decision that they should curb him before it was too late. They appointed Comte (now, under the Republic, Citizen) Hédouville to be their Special Agent in St Dominigue. He was a man of wide experience, a negotiator and mediator of some renown, known popularly as the 'Peacemaker of the Vendée' (a province of France as refractory as St Dominigue) where he had been most successful in soothing disturbances; but the Vendée with its ancient churches, its peasants in their sabots and its gentle agriculture was not St Dominigue. Hédouville was, like Laveaux, an aristocrat of the old school turned Republican, and a man of keen intellect and painstakingly conscientious but, unlike Laveaux, he did not possess an instinctive liking for or under-standing of the black race and from the outset he felt himself to be their natural superior.

Before he left Paris, Hédouville consulted Laveaux, who of course spoke in praise of Toussaint, and he consulted Sonthonax, who did not. Being a thorough man he decided to see Roume, who had remained in San Domingo, before sailing on to St Dominigue.

On 25 March 1798, whilst Toussaint was negotiating with Maitland and preparing for his triumphant march through the conquered territory, Hédouville landed on Hispaniola. He talked to Roume who described Toussaint as 'a philosopher, a legislator, a general and a good citizen'. Hédouville had now heard the good and the bad of Toussaint. General Kerverseau, the army officer in charge of the former Spanish territory, had told him that Toussaint was 'a man of great good sense' and (perhaps mistakenly) that 'his loyalty to France could never be in doubt, whose firmness equals his prudence, who enjoys the confidence of all colours . . . with him you can achieve anything, without him nothing'.

Feeling himself well prepared, Hédouville sailed for Le Cap. Now it was time to find out the truth for himself, but unfortunately he was already biased, for he had not listened well enough to Laveaux and Kerverseau and Roume, and too well to Sonthonax. He was eager to come face to face at last with the man about whom he had conjectured for so many weeks.

In his first letter to Toussaint he wrote, ever the diplomat, 'I should have met you long before this to assure you of my admiration and interest in your brilliant career, which I have found unusually inspiring.' Toussaint, who was now familiar with gentlemen sent out from the 'Metropole' was unimpressed: 'If you think that I am able to assist you in any way with your important enquiry into my comparatively unimportant affairs, then I am always at your service. You flatter my ability but it is nothing more than an overpowering desire to do my very best, and if perchance I have sometimes succeeded, then this is the least that I can do for my comrades. If the interests of the Republic will be furthered by our meeting, then this can be arranged.' It was not exactly an encouraging letter. However, Hédouville replied effusively: 'I am waiting with bated breath the moment when we shall finally meet here and you will have my undivided attention. I will postpone all my work until you and I have together agreed on the problems of affairs.' At the same time he wrote equally eagerly, or nearly so, to Rigaud.

In the first week of April, just before Hédouville's arrival, Toussaint left his base with his bodyguard of dragoons, commanded by Moriset, a mulatto, to join his men. His dragoons wore superb cuirasses, and a contemporary says 'in precision and equipment they were comparable to Napoleon's Cents Gardes'. Toussaint rode ahead of them on his favourite grey stallion, Bel Argent, in the full dress uniform of a French general.

Together with his staff he made a triumphal march through the conquered towns; everywhere he went he was thronged by cheering crowds, the populace running after him down the streets to catch the last possible glimpse of him. The mayors and leading citizens made fulsome speeches and solemn addresses to him. Toussaint, with his dry and rather cynical sense of humour, must have been wryly amused, but the people showed their genuine gratitude for his humanity and protection of them.

Then came the great day, in the afternoon of 14 April 1798, when Toussaint entered Port au Prince, the capital of St Dominigue, for the first time.

The entire population came out to meet him, white and mulatto alike treating him as a conquering hero; the cathedral bells tumbled out joyously and cries of 'Vive Toussaint', 'Vive le Général', 'Vive le

Libérateur' rang through the streets. The very same men and women who had been grateful for the protection of the troops of His Majesty the King of England now welcomed Toussaint with fervour. But the blacks were cheering their own, the small graceful man who now rode towards them was their symbol of freedom, made flesh, and they worshipped him as a god.

A formal procession had been assembled for his welcome, led by two acolytes, one bearing the Cross and one a gilt-fringed silken banner, followed by choristers swinging censers of smoking incense, then the priests from the whole district wearing their heavily-embroidered soutanes. The mayor, Bernard Borgella, was followed by all the leading citizens, the émigrés from the ancient families of France. Behind them in their carriages, or riding side-saddle on their thoroughbreds, were the most noble and the richest white women who were escorted by a guard of honour on horseback formed from the young male aristocracy of the province. A grand triumphal arch of green branches and flowers had been raised to receive him, and young white girls lined the route that led to the arch carrying baskets of blossom with which they showered him. Toussaint dismounted, threw the bridle of his horse to his groom and walked over to them, thanking them politely and kindly; he had been fond of his master's daughters and perhaps the innocence and prettiness of these girls reminded him of his former 'family'. He then walked to the head of the procession and genuflected before the Cross.

The mayor made a speech of welcome, and four of the highest-ranking planters came forward bearing a golden altar canopy and, kneeling before him, asked him to step onto a dais. Toussaint suddenly became rigid with anger, he knew that these men, now kneeling at his feet, would a month ago have joyfully heard that one of their former protector's bullets had gone through his heart. He stepped back from the fawning group and, feeling that he was being mocked, said, 'A canopy and incense belong to God alone.' Despite the protestations of the mayor that this was the usual reception given to a visiting Governor, he walked quickly away, the procession following him towards Government House where his dragoons were drawn up on each side of the entrance. He ran up the steps and disappeared inside, leaving the charade behind him. Toussaint was not a blunt man, his manners and gentility were often remarked upon, but he loathed fulsome hypocrisy, and the open irritation he showed over obvious flattery often sparked off a sudden and uncharacteristic rage.

That night the whole of Port au Prince was en fête. Flambeaux burned in the streets, and from every window came the glow of candles, the sound of music floating out through the jalousies of the great houses, and in Government House, 150 of Port au Prince's citizens sat down to a banquet with Toussaint and his staff, followed by a grand ball at which the dancers twirled and bowed and sipped their wine till dawn.

In the narrow back streets by the harbour where the air smelt of swamp, and little black pigs scuttled away in the mud, the people danced too, they danced for joy, the smoky flambeaux shining briefly on one glistening, joyous face after another as they leapt high in the air to the sound of the drums and the squeaking fiddle. Feasts of goat, sheep and chicken had been prepared in great iron pots, and had been stirred for hours by the old women, the scent of burning sugar, spice and pepper mingling with the smells of rum and sweat, and here too they danced till dawn, when the church bells rang out for early Mass.

Next morning a solemn Te Deum was held at the Cathedral and, after Mass, Toussaint was presented with a gold medallion bearing his effigy and the words 'Après Dieu – c'est Lui'. After God – he! His mind must have gone back to the time when, standing beside Laveaux, he had said those very words – but he had meant them.

Mayor Borgella then gave an address praising Toussaint for his wisdom and humanity. Toussaint's reply was typical of him, and typical of many of his speeches, in that it reiterated the crux of his policy towards the country, a policy which he had held ever since the early days of the revolution: the necessity for agriculture. He preached this necessity on every likely and unlikely occasion. 'Work together for the prosperity of St Dominigue by the restoration of agriculture . . . the appearance of the countryside through which I passed on my way here has filled me with sadness. This condition alone should have made you see that in joining Britain you were deluding yourselves. You thought you would gain, but you have only lost . . . men who have the liberty to enjoy freedom without licence and to reap the reward of their toil will care for their land far better than it has been cared for before.' He called upon them to aid Hédouville in his task, and he praised him as a distinguished man. In this he showed a generous and open gesture towards Hédouville.

The celebrations and the speeches were over, and Toussaint now went back to work, something he was always eager to do. He conferred with Mayor Borgella, a white man who was both a rich merchant and a landowner. Toussaint discovered him to be sensible and sincere, and he placed his trust in him and abided by his judgement, something he was not quick to do for any man, indeed he was usually slow to delegate even the smallest task. Together they worked for hours reorganizing and planning the future of the district and choosing the most able administrators. The last business was the most tiresome. Those who had any likelihood of being chosen for the administration scrambled over one another to ingratiate themselves with Toussaint. One white man came to Toussaint and applied for the post of Custodian of Government supplies. Toussaint turned down his application ('either because he did not know him, or knew him too well' – Malenfant). The man's wife had recently given birth to a boy and, nothing daunted by Toussaint's refusal, he decided to use his wife to further his purposes. He sent her to ask Toussaint if he would be godfather to the child. Toussaint quickly saw through such a transparent ruse and it angered him, unusually and disproportionately, perhaps because his pride was pricked that they thought him too gullible and imperceptive to see through their scheme.

He turned on the woman and said coldly, 'Why, Madame, do you wish me to be godfather to your son, tell me the truth, is it not your only aim to obtain the post for your husband from me? I do not believe you to be sincere when you make this request.'

'But how can you think so, General? No, my husband loves you, all the whites are attached to you.'

'Madame, I know the whites, if I had their skin it would be another matter, but I am black and I know how in their hearts they detest us. Have you reflected seriously on what you are asking of me? If I accept, might it not be that when your son reaches the age of reason he might reproach you for giving him a Negro as a godfather?'

'But General . . .'

'Madame, God alone is immortal. I am a general, that is true, but I am black. When I die who knows if my brothers will not perish again under the white man's whips. The work of men does not endure . . . You wish your husband to get a post. So be it. I will give him his post. Let him be honest and remember that God sees all. As for becoming your son's godfather I cannot grant your request. The whites might blame you and perhaps one day your own son might too.' (Malenfant)

Hédouville was writing constantly and flatteringly to Toussaint inviting him to visit him. 'Nothing can equal the impatience with which I await your honourable presence.' Toussaint, his work in Port au Prince now completed, assured Hédouville he would take the next opportunity to visit him, which he did, but it was a visit of courtesies only, a long and tiresome journey for nothing. The moment Toussaint left Port au Prince Maitland made a surprise attack in the south against Rigaud, whose army, unprepared, was in danger. He sent a desperate plea to Toussaint, who hastily went south and sent in reinforcements.

In May 1798 the two men met for the first time. Both were small men but there the resemblance ended. Toussaint's grizzled hair had receded and he was now nearly bald. Rigaud wore his straight-haired wig. Compared to Toussaint's deep black skin, Rigaud was almost fair. Rigaud had the rather superficial manners of the French upper classes and during his education in France had lost his creole lisp. In all things he wished to appear French, to be his father, rather than his mother. There was no doubt as to what Toussaint was, he was black.

They were allies, perhaps both hoped for more than that, Toussaint had even referred to Rigaud as 'my good friend'. But the rifts were too deep. Toussaint remembered the treachery of the regiments who had deserted him at the height of battle, he remembered St Marc, he remembered Rigaud's treatment of the 'Swiss', he remembered Villatte and the pitiless men who had taken out their cudgels and beaten his friend Laveaux, he remembered the lies and the trickery and the self-seeking. He had said 'there is a conspiracy and you may be sure there is a coloured man at the head of it'. He knew that the cause that the mulattoes were fighting for was, in reality, one of self-interest; the majority of them cared nothing for the slaves and were as keen to reinstate slavery as any white. Above all he knew that he could never trust them because of their divided past, their divided bodies and divided hearts. But he needed them as he needed Rigaud, they were as much a part of his land as he himself; and somehow they had to come to terms together for the mulattoes were necessary for his plans for his country. At this stage, whatever his private feelings of mistrust may have been, he still made a public effort to heal the rifts that existed between the mulattoes, the whites and the blacks. One day during a public address he lifted two carafes of wine, one white and one red. 'These are different, as you can see,' he told the people; he then poured one into the other, and asked them to notice how when mixed the colours blended and became one.

Toussaint had, soon after Hédouville's arrival, placed his agents within Hédouville's household and what he heard from them he did not like: that he was thought little of, that the republicanism of Hédouville was in reality only a cloak that hid ingrained prejudice and racial antagonism. Perhaps the jibes and jokes at the dinner table, with himself as the target, were only the lighthearted banter of the rather silly young men who were a part of Hédouville's staff, but they passed unchecked by Hédouville and were symptomatic of the way the 'Special Agent' was thinking. Toussaint was a serious man, his jokes were infrequent, and he lacked the form of sophistication that delights in reducing the important things in life to triviality.

Rigaud and Toussaint set off together in the carriage for Le Cap and it is legendary, if apocryphal, that Toussaint during the two-day drive confided in Rigaud his plans for independence – or at least for autonomy within the framework of the French Republic – and asked him to collaborate. Rigaud did not commit himself, and perhaps it was at that moment that Toussaint realized not only had he made a mistake in taking Rigaud into his confidence, but his hopes for collaboration were dim, that there could never be equality between the mulattoes and the blacks. It was to prove so, and it has proved so ever since in the sad country that St Dominigue became – Haiti.

Rigaud was the first to be received by Hédouville, who found him charming, his social niceties familiar, and the Agent overwhelmed him with attention and intimate confidences. Rigaud was flattered, he was being treated as a Frenchman and more than that he saw the chance to ingratiate himself with Hédouville at Toussaint's expense, so he did not hesitate to tell Hédouville of the conversation in the carriage. Toussaint, according to the later evidence of two of the servants at the Governor's palace, had been shown, perhaps deliberately, into the room next to the work cabinet to await his interview. The walls being of wood and open at the top as in all old tropical houses he overheard all of Rigaud's and Hédouville's conversation. It came as no surprise to him but simply confirmed his suspicions of both men. It was disillusioning, but it cleared his mind.

When admitted to Hédouville, he was his usual polite self, while Hédouville was markedly cool with him. He had his spies too and it may well have come back to him that Toussaint had remarked in Port au Prince, on hearing that the Directory had been guided by experience when they had chosen to send Hédouville, 'Guided by experience, eh? Well, that is something that the chosen Hédouville does *not* have.' He certainly was not showing much evidence of it now.

Confronted by a Negro in the undress uniform of a French general but with a yellow madras bandana round his head, Hédouville, like so many before him, underestimated Toussaint's astute intelligence, his power and his strength of character. He too had made up his mind, during the two months that he had been in the Colony, that Toussaint must be removed. The scenes of triumph in Port au Prince confirmed this opinion. Toussaint was far too powerful, so his policy was to rely upon Rigaud and split the two camps as quickly as possible, playing colour against colour. In order to probe Toussaint's reactions he made derogatory remarks about Rigaud, even suggesting to Toussaint that perhaps the time was ripe to arrest Rigaud, following up Sonthonax' orders which had never been carried out. Toussaint was astounded by such perfidy, in view of the conversation he had overheard, and exclaimed: 'Arrest Rigaud! I'd as soon arrest myself. You must know that he is one of the most eager defenders of our cause.' His own faith in Rigaud may have been shaken, but he was not going to admit it to this white intruder. Mistrust was now mutual and complete.

The men on Hédouville's staff demonstrated their inexperience by sniggering at Toussaint behind his back and subtly trying to bait him for their own amusement. None of this escaped Toussaint's sharp all-seeing eyes, and if they had been his own officers they would have been well aware of this; he also sensed that they were taking their directive from their chief. Admiral Farbre, who was in command of the warships which had brought Hédouville to Le Cap, said in conversation with Toussaint that he would be honoured to take Toussaint aboard his ship to France. Toussaint interrupted him before he could say more, adding coldly 'your ship is not big enough for a man like me.' Rushing to his Admiral's rescue and thereby making matters worse, a young officer from the ship suggested how good it would be if Toussaint were to end his days in France, how honoured and welcomed he would be. Toussaint seemed merely amused at such continuing lack of finesse; he replied ironically, pointing to a small shrub which was growing near to where he stood, 'Yes, I will go when this has grown large enough to build a ship to take me.'

So again nothing had been achieved by the meeting and Toussaint proceeded on his own way simply giving lip service to any wishes of Hédouville's.

He next turned his attention to the British, deciding he was bored playing games with Maitland, and it was time they went. He wrote to Maitland and told him, categorically, that he must complete the evacuation of all troops from Jeremie and Môle St Nicholas, otherwise he himself would attack the remaining British forces with 20,000 men, and would show no mercy. Maitland decided that discretion was the better part of valour. He had also been advised from London that a possible trade agreement with St Dominigue might be one way of recouping at least some of Britain's gigantic losses, so he wrote to Toussaint suggesting a meeting. On 31 August 1798 they met near Môle St Nicholas. Toussaint was accompanied by 15,000 troops, to make his position doubly clear. He was welcomed by Maitland and his officers like a king, was received with full military honours and reviewed the British troops from a velvet-covered dais. Then Maitland conducted him to a marquee decked with Union Jacks, which he had had erected in the Place d'Armes, and where an elaborate banquet had been prepared. After the meal ended Toussaint was presented – in the name of the King of England 'as a token of esteem for the humanity with which you have treated the British prisoners' – with the magnificent silver service upon which the banquet had been served. He was also presented with two highly ornamented bronze cannon.

This was all very gracious but it had its underlying motive, a softening-up process in order to make the terms of the agreement more acceptable to Toussaint. However, the banquet had not dimmed Toussaint's wits, he seldom ate or drank much anyway and almost nothing upon important occasions. He demurred at the initial proposals which included a clause that the British agree to acknowledge Toussaint as king of Haiti; as a good Republican he did not give a damn whether the British acknowledged him as king or not. In any case he was not, never had been, and never would be a man who sought grandiose titles, he had been quite content to be Médecin Général and would even have been happy to have remained a colonel, as he told Laveaux; nor did he seek power for its own sake, from beginning to end his only aim was to aid and serve his people, and if that meant he could help them best by being their guide and ruler, then he was prepared to do that, but the titles that went with the position meant nothing to him. He would never have made himself emperor as did Napoleon or Toussaint's own general, Henri Christophe. Maitland had once more underestimated him – as so many whites had, and would continue to do – believing that the title of king would please his Negro vanity; but it was never possible to judge Toussaint by the standards applicable to other men.

The British also offered to protect him against French attacks, though he doubted their power to do that. However, he was interested in their offer of a commercial treaty and in their offer to assist him in a similar commercial treaty with America. He saw the opportunity to export his goods and to import arms if it ever should come to a confrontation with France.

Toussaint knew that in French eyes and the eyes of the five men of the Directory he had absolutely no justification in treating with Britain. Britain and France were at war, but his first loyalty was the protection and the prosperity of his own people, and he got on rather better with the British and with Maitland than he did with the Commissioners who came from France, and if he could make a sensible and profitable deal with the British then he was quite prepared to do so without any pangs of conscience.

Maitland returned to England to place the proposals before the government there. Toussaint informed Hédouville that he had been negotiating successfully with Maitland, but failed to inform him of the secret clauses. Maitland then wrote to Toussaint from London, apologizing for being so long in writing because he had been 'sorely tested with bad weather and unfriendly winds on our voyage'. He had heard from Toussaint, who was displeased that the arrangements that had been made for the evacuation of Môle had been altered, and Maitland assured him that 'nothing will be done which is contrary to those measures agreed between us in the secret convention' [it is curious that Maitland himself refers to it in those terms on paper] 'which cannot fail to give gratification to all those like yourself, M. Le Général, whose singular desire is the protection of humanity controlled in an orderly fashion by a stable government. To convince you of my desire and to be assured that the foregoing is put speedily into effect on the Island of St Dominigue, now under your protection, to promote all the advantages of contentment of peace and commerce, I have received orders from His Majesty's Ministers to visit your island again. But before starting my journey I must tell you that I am to stop a few days in America.' The American visit was to cement the proposed treaty with Toussaint and St Dominigue.

He ends his letter by emphasizing his 'respect for your good self and your esteemed character'. Maitland was later to say that he did not consider Toussaint 'very intelligent', but perhaps that was in the light of later events. Toussaint was certainly able to strike a hard bargain with the English general. Maitland was of course under British orders to encourage Toussaint in order to harass and undermine the French morale. Toussaint may well have been aware of this but his needs were immediate.

In the meantime Toussaint had himself been in touch with the President of the United States.

LIBERTY   EQUALITY
at Cap-Français 6 November 1798 the seventh year of the
French Republic, one and indivisible.
Toussaint Louverture
Général en chef de l'Armée de Saint Dominique
à Monsieur Adams
Président du Congrès des États-Unis d'Amérique

Monsieur le Président,
It has been a great surprise to me and, in a way, most distressing to notice that the ships of your nation have abandoned the ports of St Dominique. By so doing, they have foregone all those trade relations with us, and are thus no longer bringing here the supplies and food-stuffs produced in your Continent in exchange for our rich produce.

I cannot understand, nor is it my business to enquire into the motives, that have prompted the people of the United States to cool towards the French colonies, and if I may, I would hereby wish to suggest once and for all certain guide-lines by which proper methods we might re-establish the navigation to and from our ports and thus, once again to see the American ensign flying within them.

It is in your interest, just as it is in ours, to expand trade, but you must be entirely convinced of this if you are to make an important contribution.

If it is the intentions of Congress, or of your own self, to change any existing arrangements which were formerly set up in this regard and which I have ignored, do not hesitate to inform me; if, to recommence it we must respect our mutual neutrality, and to maintain the great harmony which has always existed between the French Republic and the United States of America, or if to revive it again we must draw up Treaties between our two Republics, you must be assured, Monsieur, that the Americans will find in the ports of the Republic of St Dominique nothing but safety and protection, where the flag of the United States will be respected as that of the powerful friend and ally of France which we know it to be, that strict orders will be given to our ships while at sea to assist, by all possible means in their power, the swift return passage of your vessels to their home ports, and we shall recompense them promptly and correctly for the cargoes that they bring here.

If this promise that I give, Monsieur, to protect the trade of your nation should prompt you to allow your ships to return to the ports of the French Republic in this colony, I shall have been most happy to have contributed thus, and will feel proud to have revived between the Continent and the Republic of St Dominique mutual trade arrangements, which are vital to the interests of the two Republics, which should never have ceased in the first place. Receive assurance of my attentive consideration of your reply . . .

Toussaint Louverture

Toussaint received a reply to his letter on 4 March 1799 from Timothy Pickering, Secretary of State of the United States, in which he was informed that trade with France and its colonies had necessarily come to a halt, because there had been numerous occasions when the French government had seized and destroyed vessels that were trading in a bona fide capacity between the United States and its allies. Thus the United States had passed an act of Congress in its last session, to suspend all trade between France and its dependencies. However in this enactment there had been inserted a clause which stated that, if the hindrance of American ships on the high seas should be reported to have ceased (which was in line with the assurance given by Toussaint in his letter), then it was to be the decision of the President to re-open trade with the island of St Dominigue if the President was convinced of their sincerity in this matter. To this end, the President had appointed a Consul General to represent American interests in St Dominigue, a Dr Edward Stevens of Philadelphia, and as soon as the President was convinced of the safety of American ships in trade, then the restrictions would be abolished completely.

Perhaps the President's and the Secretary of State's decision to play along with Toussaint may have been influenced by other than commercial interests.

On 23 May 1798 Edward Stevens, who had by then been installed as Consul General of the United States to St Dominigue, wrote a letter to General Maitland which makes curious reading: 'While I was at the Cap I was informed by an important black person who was in the confidence of General Hédouville, that the Agent of St Dominique had received positive marching orders from the Directory to invade the Southern States of North America, using the island of Jamaica as a stepping-stone. General Toussaint L'Ouverture had been consulted on the best method of attack, but he was opposed to this, having made a trade agreement with you, and he set about opposing any military expedition against Jamaica in the first place. Finding Toussaint L'Ouverture inflexible, Hédouville turned to Rigaud to organize this enterprise, however Hédouville's sudden departure and absence had put an end to all those preparations for the invasion which had been set in motion. L'Ouverture had taken his irrevocable decision and Rigaud was too frightened to disobey him.'

In this, Toussaint showed more wisdom than Napoleon or Hitler in their Russian campaigns. He knew he had sufficient men, as Stevens, writing to Timothy Pickering, said 'His army amounts to 55,000 men, of which 30,000 are of the line and disciplined. The remainder are militia.' History might have been very different if he had taken the step. Certainly he could have taken Jamaica with ease, and even under Washington the American army consisted of only around 20,000 men, few of whom were regulars or highly trained. The slaves in the Southern States would certainly have risen and rallied to a black army in their midst. But Toussaint's ambitions were not territorial, the welfare of his own people came first. Perhaps he also suspected that it might be a clever ruse by Hédouville to remove him and his army from the scene – but as Hédouville had also tried to involve Rigaud this does not seem likely.

The secret convention, however, nearly foundered before it had even been launched. Unfortunately on 12 December 1798 the *London Gazette* published a report of the treaty – a report which was most likely to go back immediately to the Directory and of course to Hédouville. It was a highly flattering version of the treaty and of Toussaint's role in it. It was also a brilliant example of how the British in war are expert at turning defeat into moral victory. One hundred thousand men are lost in the West Indies for 'the independence of this very important island' to be 'recognized and guaranteed' – one might think that those men had died

fighting for this end and not against it. 'In the cause of humanity a black
government has been organized under the leadership of a black man' and
'the history of the actual war does not present any particularly important
event' – no, indeed, only between 40,000 and 50,000 tragedies and millions
of pounds – 'except that it is more interesting in humanitarian consideration
than in any permanent advantage to Great Britain when one considers
the treaty made by General Maitland with the black General Toussaint
L'Ouverture on the occasion of the evacuation of St. Dominique. By this
treaty the independence of that very important island has in fact been
recognized and will be guaranteed against all the efforts that the French
may make to overthrow it. Not merely without the expense of fortifications or armies but with the benefit of having the exclusive commerce . . .
Toussaint is a Negro and in the jargon of the battlefield has been called a
brigand, but it must be recorded that his behaviour for a Negro is quite
contrary to that associated with his race, and furthermore he has proved
that his character as a man is quite different from that which is usually
associated with the colour of his skin.

'An important point must be made, that in the cause of humanity this
black government constituted and operating in the West Indies under a
black leader, be he Chief or King, taking into account that the black race,
so shamefully stained by their creator, which has received nothing in the
past but accustomed degradation, is now recognized like a sister and
treated with the most perfect respect and equality. All men of virtue will
rejoice at the sight of the standard of the black people, which now flies
proudly high.'

In spite of this, Colonel Harcourt, Maitland's envoy, instead of being
met by a pleasant if determined partner in a treaty, was met by a very
angry man. Toussaint immediately showed his displeasure at the publicity
given to the treaty before it had even been signed. He was obviously
unimpressed by the histrionic and condescending flattery and picked
out the kernel of the matter which was what displeased him. Harcourt
prevaricated; he realized only too well that the good relations established
between Toussaint and Maitland were in jeopardy. He asked Toussaint
to overlook what had happened, and added that in his opinion Toussaint
had made a good bargain with the British and should jump at the chance
to settle matters.

Probably realizing this was true, if not palatable, Toussaint agreed to
accept that (1) Great Britain would not attack St Dominigue on any
pretext whatsoever. (2) Toussaint would not attack Jamaica. (3) Maitland
agreed that Britain would not interfere with the internal affairs of St
Dominigue – while Toussaint was in control of the island (this was
scribbled in in pencil as an obvious afterthought). (4) That during the

duration of the war between the British and the French Toussaint would not interfere in any way with Jamica's interests. (5) In consequence of these mutual agreements it was agreed that Britain was allowed to send ships to assigned ports in St Dominigue for the purposes of trade and that they would receive no interference.

It had been a complicated negotiation, even Roume had attempted to interfere, suggesting that Toussaint at the final meeting with Maitland should arrest him. Maitland was informed of this by a friend, but he trusted Toussaint and went ahead with the meeting, and when Toussaint was rather late Maitland became understandably apprehensive, but Toussaint arrived in a hurry and handed him two letters: 'There, General, read these before we talk, one is a letter just received from Roume and one is my reply. I would not come to you until I had written my answer to him that you may see I am not capable of such baseness.' He had written: 'What, have I not passed my word to the British General? How then can you suppose that I would cover myself with dishonour by breaking it. His reliance upon my good faith leads him to put himself in my power and I should be forever infamous were I to act on your advice. I am faithfully devoted to the Republic but I will not serve it at the expense of my conscience and my honour.'

The treaty document was then signed by Toussaint and Maitland, and it was over. The last Englishman embarked and left the island. How many tens of thousands lay beneath its soil will never really be known. Toussaint's successful conclusion to the war with the British received no praise or thanks from Hédouville whose relations with Toussaint were declining fast.

One of the major problems of the negotiations with Maitland had been the fate of the black armies which had fought under the British. Maitland's first suggestion had been to ship them to Jamaica where they could be sold off as slaves (an idea that would certainly have proved profitable for someone). Toussaint was of course adamant, they were to remain and to be given amnesty. Maitland was forced to submit, he could hardly do otherwise, but he insisted that the émigrés who commanded them should also be given amnesty. Toussaint agreed. All were free to serve under Toussaint if they wished. Many of the white officers he left in the command which they had held under the British.

On hearing this Hédouville was incensed with rage, for not only had he been discarded by Toussaint during the negotiations but now he felt he had found a concrete example of treachery of which he could make good capital with the Directory. He accused Toussaint of breaking the laws of the Republic and wrote him letters of such unpleasantness as to be insulting.

Hédouville was a conceited, self-important man. During his stay in St Dominigue his ego had taken a mauling. He was himself convinced that he was, in every way, superior to Toussaint by colour, birth, intellect, achievement and certainly by the power granted to him by the Directory, and yet somehow he had been made to feel inferior. Toussaint's stature seemed unassailable. He knew that it was he who should have conducted the peace negotiations and yet he was politely ignored and treated as a puppet by both Toussaint and the British. He would have done anything at this point to even the score and restore his self-esteem. Toussaint continued to ignore him and invited back the émigrés from abroad, by which he was simply continuing his policy – the equality of all and the balance of power; if he needed the mulattoes then he needed the whites with their superior education, their knowledge of cultivation and their culture but, even more, he needed this knowledge to spread and be absorbed by all his people. Had he not learned from his masters? He also needed them to counterbalance the mulattoes' dominance. It would take years for his own people to take their place in the administration of the country; so he used the whites in places of trust, and he needed more of them to produce his exports, as his own people could not do this without their help and experience.

A paradoxical situation had arisen whereby Toussaint, a black ex-slave, defended the whites against Hédouville, a French aristocrat. He was rash enough to tell Hédouville that he did not consider many of the whites guilty – merely unfortunate. Hédouville continued to find fault with Toussaint's every decision, and Toussaint heard through his agents in Le Cap of the insulting way in which Hédouville spoke of him, of how he was sneered at by those who surrounded the Special Agent, of the jibes at the expense of 'the old black monkey'. He heard how they had boasted that with 'four soldiers they could arrest the monkey with the handkerchief'.

Hédouville had attempted in Maitland's absence to make a separate treaty with General Dalton and Colonel Spencer but as Maitland was their superior officer, they refused to have anything further to do with such a scheme and both they and Maitland apologized to Toussaint, which provided one more mortification for Hédouville.

Not only was Hédouville contentious about the émigrés, he also made trouble with the cultivators. In an attempt to get them back to regular disciplined work he tried to introduce a system of indentured labour, a three-year contract binding them to a proprietor. Toussaint strongly objected, regarding this plan as partial slavery, as indeed did the cultivators. It seemed as if the 'Pacifier of the Vendée' was remarkably inept in his dealings with the people of St Dominigue.

The unpleasantness and back-biting became too much for Toussaint, so he decided to bring matters to a head, or to end them with Hédouville. He wrote to him: 'Your ceaseless reminders that it is within your power to dismiss me make me think that you very much want to do so.' Hédouville heard that Toussaint had pardoned some émigrés who had celebrated Mass with him. Hédouville attacked him for his open religious faith which was against Republican law. He had gone too far, no one could attack Toussaint upon the subject of his religion, and he tendered his resignation as Commander in Chief to Hédouville. He received no reply. He wrote to him once more. 'If I have asked your permission to resign, it is because having served my country honourably, having wrested it from the hands of its powerful enemies, having put out the fires of civil war to which it was for so long subjected, having for too long neglected my beloved family so that I am now a stranger to them, having sacrificed my own interests, my time and my years so that liberty may triumph, I wish now in my old age to save the honour of my name from insult for the sake of my children . . . If you do not grant my request I shall make it to the Directory itself . . . Mankind is inclined to envy the glory of others, men are jealous of the good that they have not themselves achieved, a man often makes enemies by the simple fact that he has given great service. The Revolution in France provided many examples of this dreadful truth. Many great men have paid the penalty in exile, or on the scaffold for the service they have given to their country and it would be imprudent of me to leave myself open any longer to the arrows of slander and malevolence.' He added that his only desire now was to retire quietly into the bosom of his family, that he was for the moment utterly disillusioned, his spirit was tired: 'I know too much now about the heart of men not to realize that it is only with my family I can find happiness.'

Hédouville did not reply. Instead he immediately set about disbanding the black army and abolishing the post of Commander in Chief. The army was to be divided into three smaller parts, each responsible to and under the direction of the Special Agent. His plan was approved by the Directory.

Toussaint himself had been disbanding his troops, urging them as he did so to go back to the land, but his motives were very different from those of Hédouville. Toussaint, whose eye saw all, noted that Hédouville was disbanding the blacks but that mulatto troops were being retained, and all the forts in the coastal towns were being turned over to whites or mulattoes. The implication was obvious; his men perceived this too and there was an uneasy mood of unrest and tension in the black army.

Hédouville's first target was the Fifth Regiment under Moïse,

Toussaint's nephew. When Hédouville announced to Moïse that it was to be disbanded they quarrelled sharply and openly. Moïse was a handsome, dashing young man, but was also wilful to the point of arrogance, and unlike Toussaint he mistrusted and hated the white man. Hédouville was more determined than ever to dispose of him.

Moïse had two brothers in his regiment, Adrien and Charles Zamor. Charles Zamor quarrelled with a fellow officer which led to a duel; although Moïse attempted to end the matter the animosity continued and the town took sides.

Hédouville saw an opportunity to use this for his own ends; one day when Moïse was away on duty, he dismissed Moïse from his command and replaced him by an elderly black advocate called Manginat. Moïse was popular not only with his troops but with the people and on returning Moïse confronted Manginat. White troops opened fire and Charles Zamor was killed and Moïse himself forced to flee. But, he had not served under Toussaint for nothing; he appealed to the source, the people, telling them that Hédouville was against them and would return them to slavery. Hédouville called on Rigaud to come to his aid from the south, thus deliberately inciting civil war; but he had not reckoned on Toussaint who, like a war-horse scenting battle, lost all his doubts and depression and went into swift and immediate action. He scribbled an order to Dessalines commanding him to march on Le Cap and arrest Hédouville, then, like Moïse, he roused the people. He had only to speak and tens of thousands stopped their work, seized whatever arms they could, and marched.

Hédouville felt the stirrings of panic; as a last attempt he sent Vincent who was Toussaint's old and trusted colleague to parley with Toussaint, but it was far too late, old friend or not, Toussaint arrested Vincent and then himself marched on Le Cap.

Outside the town he rode into the midst of the cultivators who surrounded it, telling them to keep calm, that he, Toussaint, would save them, they had nothing to fear, he would protect them, and it was a cleverly played and successful piece of strategy. At the sight of thousands of relentless black faces, their numbers growing and stretching far into the distance, their machetes or old muskets in their hands, Hédouville did not wait for Toussaint's arrival but fled aboard the warship that had once been offered to take Toussaint away. Toussaint sent a message to Hédouville inviting him to return and telling him that he had nothing to fear at his hands. This gesture was the final humiliation for Hédouville. He set sail for France.

Before he left, however, he made a last throw in his attempt to foment a civil war. It was his policy and it was to become the policy of the

Directory. He wrote to Rigaud: 'I am forced to leave the Colony by the overbearing ambition and treachery of General Toussaint L'Ouverture, he has sold out to the English, to the émigrés and to the Americans, and he does not hesitate to violate the most solemn oaths without giving it a thought. I urge you to assume the authority of Commander in Chief of the south which was formerly in command of the Commander in Chief.'

Toussaint entered Fort Liberté and was greeted with emotional excitement, the crowds surrounded him and Bel Argent, reaching out to try and touch him, and calling out to him 'Papa Toussaint', 'Papa Toussaint'.

The next day he made a public speech in which he reinstated Moïse. The unfortunate Manginat was forced to stand in front of him, under arrest, and had to listen to a speech of blistering sarcasm: 'At the very moment when I had driven the British from the Colony and was about to enjoy the fruits of my labour after so much effort, Hédouville finds a Manginat. Yes, a Manginat. Are you Manginat? Well you are certainly a clever schemer, are you not? Hédouville choose a Negro to destroy brave General Moïse . . . I reinstate Moïse in his former functions . . . Hédouville says that I am against liberty, that I want to surrender to the English . . . who ought to value liberty more, Toussaint L'Ouverture, slave of Breda, or General Hédouville, Marquis and Chevalier de St Louis? If I had wished to surrender to the English, would I have chased them away? You must understand that Toussaint L'Ouverture is now on his own and at the mention of his name everybody must tremble.' This was the first time Toussaint had ever spoken like this, he rarely showed arrogance and it was the first time he had made it open and clear that he considered himself their leader and no one else.

That evening he talked to Moïse of his intentions for the future; he was unusually elated and confident. He told him: 'Hédouville has spread the rumour that he is going to France to raise an army. He thinks he can frighten me but I have been making war for a long time and if I have to continue I am prepared . . . My soldiers will always be ready to defend their liberty. I don't want to fight France, until now I have saved this country for her, but if she attacks me, I shall defend myself.'

When Hédouville returned to France he wrote a report to the Directory in which he stated in cold blood: 'it will perhaps occur to you that it is important to create seeds of division between them, to embitter the hate which exists between the mulattoes and the blacks, and to oppose Rigaud to Toussaint.'

That he succeeded in his intention to create a war of colour was the worst tragedy that had so far struck St Dominigue. A tragedy that has continued, on and off, for a century and more, not black opposed to white, but black opposed to mulatto. It was not the fault of Toussaint or of

Rigaud, who was to say: 'All my life I have been obedient to blacks from my cradle on . . . isn't my mother who brought me into the world a Negro?' But both sides were to forget their mothers and the bloodiest war of all was launched upon St Dominigue, engineered by Hédouville and the cynical men who sat moving their pawns in the Metropole.

10 Civil War: Negro Against Mulatto

Toussaint continued to set his house in order; he asked Roume and General Kerserveau (in order to make some kind of conciliatory gesture towards the Directory) to come over from San Domingo. He asked Roume to act as Commissioner. He was aware of Roume's admiration for him: 'The merit of Toussaint is so excelling that I have difficulty in understanding why some people do not find qualities in him to praise, but only to criticize and malign.' Toussaint also sent General Vincent to France bearing protestations of loyalty towards the Directory, which in the circumstances must have appeared hollow.

So far, so good; but Rigaud, still under the influence of the departed Hédouville, was open in his disapproval of Toussaint's treatment of the Agent.

To smooth matters over Roume held a meeting between Toussaint, Rigaud and Beauvais, the mulatto who was in command of Jacmel, and La Plume, a Negro who was commander of Léogane. Nothing was achieved by this meeting, and then a very unfortunate incident took place in the town which was under Rigaud's jurisdiction. Twenty-nine Negroes and one white man had been imprisoned and crammed into a small window-less shed. When the jailers finally opened the door they found a pile of suffocated corpses. It was given out that they had died from the fumes of a recent coat of whitewash, but not surprisingly this was believed by no one and feeling ran high among the blacks, particularly as no mulatto had been a victim. Toussaint wrote bitterly to Rigaud: 'It is always the blacks who suffer in these deliberately provoked disorders.' The enmity was growing. Rigaud had expelled some blacks from his province; he wrote to Toussaint: 'How is it that these cannibals are enrolled on the side of the West and North when I have deported them from the South?' On another occasion he referred to Toussaint's troops as 'cannibals'. It is just possible that he was not merely attempting to be insulting, but that the deported men were indeed cannibals. Cannibalism has been witnessed and verified in association with Vodun, 'the goat without horns' as the victim was called; but it seems – since he repeated the phrase – that he was just being deliberately provoking. Rigaud felt he could afford to be insolent, for he was still confident that Hédouville would return with an army and that together they would dispose of Toussaint.

Toussaint had now come to the conclusion that conflict was inevitable. He publicly denounced Rigaud, accusing him of ruthless ambition and saying that he would murder his own mother and father for advancement. He further said that Rigaud refused to take orders from him because he, Toussaint, was black. The conflict of race was growing. Rigaud defended himself: 'Indeed if I had come to the stage when I would not obey a black, if I had the stupid pride to think I was above such obedience, how could I expect obedience from the whites . . . Is it not a black who was my schoolmaster at Les Cayes. Doesn't that make it clear that I have been accustomed to obeying blacks all my life?' He added, with obvious intended sincerity: 'from the beginning of the revolution I have braved all for the cause of liberty. I have not once betrayed my principles and never shall. I believe too deeply in the Rights of Man to think there is one colour in nature which is superior to another.' And yet no black man in his army could rise above the rank of captain – so often his actions and reactions were the reverse of what he felt he *should* believe, while his own weaknesses, his own complexes about his colour, betrayed the better side of his nature. In Toussaint's army there were thousands of mulattoes and in Rigaud's thousands of blacks, but the whites were with Toussaint.

The accusations and counter-accusations continued, culminating in Rigaud denouncing Toussaint for his secret part in the British peace negotiations and publishing Hédouville's letter on his treachery. Finally Rigaud proclaimed that he no longer acknowledged Toussaint as his Commander-in-Chief.

The pot was coming to the boil, as mulattoes left Toussaint's army, and whites travelled from the south to seek Toussaint's protection. On 21 February news came that Rigaud was deliberately massacring blacks. Toussaint was in Port au Prince which was in an uproar. He rode through the town, shouting to the citizens to follow him to the church. There he climbed a rostrum to speak, he was visibly moved and trembling, in his hand he held a sheaf of papers which he waved on high at the crowd. 'Here,' he declared, 'I have the proof of a vast organized conspiracy against my authority and I hereby formally accuse the mulattoes as the perpetrators . . . Everyone is aware of what you want. You want to rule the Colony. You want to exterminate the whites and enslave the blacks. Consider well before you take that fatal step.' He brought up the old contentious subject of the 'Swiss' again, knowing that it would further arouse the people. 'As for Rigaud he is lost . . . the armies of liberty will crush him, the rebel and the traitor.'

Rigaud struck first, attacking Petit Goâve which was commanded by

La Plume. Rigaud had 4000 men, La Plume 700, and Rigaud won an easy victory, after which his first act was to have eighteen white men massacred. 'All the whites in Port au Prince rose in a mass, and desired permission to march against him, but Toussaint objected to it, observing that they had already suffered misfortunes enough by the Revolution, and that he had men enough to finish the contest and protect them without subjecting them again to the horrors of war.'

Toussaint's army was at the outset less well equipped than that of Rigaud who had been bringing in a steady stream of ammunition from St Thomas, Jamaica and the United States. The British and the Americans were quite prepared to trade with both sides.

On hearing of this Toussaint wrote to the President of the United States.

'Commander in Chief of the Army of St Dominigue to Mr John Adams, President of the U.S.A.

Mr President,

Mr Ed Stevens has shown me the letter which you have written relative to the measures which you have taken in your proclamation, and I view with great pleasure that you have avoided taking sides with the factions now exposed to the fury of civil war.

Rigaud, who commanded the Southern Territory of St Dominigue, under my orders, to satisfy his insatiable ambitions, had raised the standard of Revolution against his lawful chief, and against the National Authority, igniting the firebrands of discord, he has plunged this lawabiding territory into civil war. He started the hostilities without warning at Grand and Petit Goâve, he has assassinated many whites, and this is but the beginning of his heinous crimes. His criminal and atrocious misdoings have left no alternative to the Government Agent but to brand him as a lawless rebel, and to muster an army to punish his outrages. In consequence, the army of the Southern Department of St Dominigue has been mustered. However, the machiavellianism of this rebel has ensured that he is well advanced in the preparation of his infamous projects, by infiltrating his poisonous ideals into the West and North of this country.'

Toussaint continued with an explanation that anything that the President can provide will be greatly appreciated to help to get rid of 'the odious Rebel Rigaud'.

Adams was slow in his decision to trade, but eventually he did, in direct opposition to his predecessor George Washington who had thought it was 'lamentable to see such a spirit of revolt amongst the blacks'.

Toussaint needed aid and he was having internal trouble in his territories; mulattoes there were rising and coming out openly for Rigaud, but less understandably the maroons were also rising against Toussaint. His efforts to put them to work as cultivators had not proved popular.

Toussaint could hesitate no longer, he launched a vigorous major attack, Dessalines attacking the mulattoes in Port au Prince and the maroons in the hills. Christophe was to attack Le Cap and dispose of the mulattoes there. Toussaint himself surprised St Marc and put down the mulatto rebellion in the port. Many faced the firing squad. He had acted with his usual swiftness but with unusual ruthlessness.

He rode south to confront Rigaud, but on the way he was ambushed by a mulatto party, and his white doctor who was riding at his side was killed by a bullet intended for him, and Toussaint's hat was swept off his head by another bullet. He remained calm, simply dismounting and getting into a carriage; after a while, however, he remounted his horse and, staying some distance away, sent the carriage ahead. As it rounded a bend there was a burst of gunfire; Toussaint rode quickly up to it, but the assailants had fled, leaving the coachman dead.

It was important for Toussaint to know Beauvais' commitment; they had a mutual admiration for each other and Toussaint felt there was a good chance of the commander of Jacmel declaring for his side. Beauvais' conscience was troubled: he found it impossible to decide what was the right action to take. Instead of making a decision he quietly opted out. Leaving Jacmel at night with a few companions, he boarded a ship and sailed for France. Toussaint laid siege to Jacmel which was one of the most beautiful and elegant towns of St Dominigue but a mulatto stronghold, where the entire population was mulatto. To this day it retains the romantic elegance that made it dear to the mulatto heart, a small corner of the France of their fathers set in the beautiful and wild scenery of the land of their mothers. Situated round a natural bay, a semicircle of hills protected it. It was a difficult town to take, but Toussaint was patient and, like a cat by a mouse hole, he waited.

From this siege there emerged a hero, a mulatto officer called Pétion, a young man of great intelligence, wisdom and courage who was later to become one of the early leaders of Haiti.

Inside Jacmel the people, flies caught in the web of war, slowly starved. Toussaint was in command of an army on one side of the town, Christophe on the other. Toussaint suggested to President John Adams that the sea should be policed by American ships in order to stop supplies, but there was too much profit to be made for the Americans to concede that gesture, they continued to supply both sides, as did the British. It is not an admirable but certainly a familiar role played by great commercial nations.

Toussaint proceeded to put the town under a relentless bombardment. Saint-Remy wrote: 'Soon to the miseries that overcame the troops, there were added the disease and deaths that were brought about by famine, in fact for some time the soldiers had been rationed to four ounces of bread a day.' The inhabitants had eaten first the horses, then the dogs, the cats and the rats; they ate the small birds, the lizards, the grass in the squares, the leaves off the trees and then there was nothing left. 'A soldier whose body was shattered by a cannon-ball was immediately set upon by two women who quenched their thirst with his blood and by reason of their great hunger tore at his flesh whilst it was still palpitating. Notwithstanding these fearful scenes the garrison, obeying Pétion to the letter, continued to demonstrate great bravery and steadfastness without complaint or murmur.' (Saint-Remy) The weak had died early, the little children went soon. Pétion could stand the brave suffering no longer: he sent the old men, the women hardly able to walk and the children out of the two town gates. He trusted in Toussaint showing his usual humanity, which he did, so that those who passed more dead than alive through his lines were cared for, fed and looked after tenderly by their besiegers until they were strong enough to walk over the hills to safety. For those who passed through the gate on the other side of the town opposite Christophe's forces, there was a different end to the siege of Jacmel: Christophe's men watched as they stumbled forward and then Christophe gave the order, his soldiers raised their muskets and every old man, every woman and every child was shot down. Their men watched helplessly from the walls of the besieged town, until all lay still under the pitiless sun. The future king of Haiti had started as he was to continue. For his own sake, Toussaint should have paid more heed. In fact, this was almost the only occasion when Toussaint did not punish an officer for an unnecessary act of cruelty. He remained silent. In this terrible struggle it was now total war for both sides.

Pétion had to make a decision, since surrender would have meant death anyway. One night when the moon was covered, he and his men attempted to escape from their trap, but Toussaint was too wise and experienced not to surprise such a move. Almost all the garrison were wiped out, although Pétion himself escaped.

The siege had lasted five months and cost the lives of 2000 men, but it is not recorded how many civilians died.

Throughout the south the mulattoes fought with the ferocity of animals. Their whole way of life, their pride, their class, their colour, their very existence was in jeopardy, threatened by these hordes of 'cannibals' who had swept down upon them and showed them no mercy. St Dominigue was a tortured land torn into bloody pieces by the unreasoning hatred, the passions aroused by race and colour. Rigaud shot his own men if he suspected them of weakness in the struggle. In the close confrontation of the battles of those times men cut each other's throats with knives, they tried to strangle each other, they fought with their teeth and with their nails; the hand-to-hand fighting was the most vicious ever known. It had become and was to be known as 'the war of knives'. On Toussaint's side Dessalines and Christophe were ruthless to prisoners, and Rigaud's men attacked the civilian population as if their bloodlust could never be satisfied.

Rigaud himself appears to have been insensible to what he had started. In the midst of taking a town he would seize some pretty, scared girl and take her to bed, or drink and dally with his women camp followers. The scenes of horror and violence merely seemed to increase his appetites. Nobody has ever denied that Rigaud was a brave and brilliant soldier, but now, just when he should have proved those qualities, he demonstrated the baser side of his complex character. It seems that it was only after Jacmel had fallen that he realized that his cause might be doomed, and the South and all he and it stood for be lost to him. He became desperate, his proclamations read like the screams of a man in agony. He called Toussaint 'a monster thirsting for human blood, a wretch who knew no gratitude, a traitor to the Republic, the ravager of St Dominigue, the executioner of Jacmel, the persecutor of the Agents of France and the tool of the English'.

Dessalines finally forced Rigaud's strongly-held position at Mirogoâne and defeated both Rigaud and Pétion and as he drove them before him to their final point of retreat, Les Cayes, Rigaud burnt all behind him, so that the people themselves and even his own mulattoes rose up against him as the devastation brought famine along with it, and Toussaint's victory became assured.

While the battle had been raging in the south, Roume in Le Cap, perhaps under the orders of the Directory, had attempted to raise a revolt in Jamaica. He sent two secret agents over to the island, but they were discovered by the British. It was an indiscreet and ill-timed venture. His men were taken and hanged, and the British in retaliation seized one of Toussaint's convoys bearing heavy cannon and destined for use in the siege of Jacmel. Toussaint was infuriated, this was the time when he needed the British arms most; he sent for Roume who refused to come, so Toussaint rode north at his usual speed showing his fury plainly. Toussaint was a patient man, but this act made up his mind; the Agent must go, now that his hare-brained fruitless scheme had considerably lengthened the siege of Jacmel. He could not afford unreliable men around him and he did not forgive him.

Toussaint returned to the south, secure that Rigaud was virtually

beaten. Now was the time to appeal to the people. He issued a proclamation endeavouring to unite the country and to heal the wounds: 'I am
merciful, I am humane, I stretch out my arms to you, the arms of a father.
Come all of you, come! I will receive you all, you from the south as well
as those from the north and from the west, who have been enticed by
Rigaud to leave your wives and families to join him. If Rigaud who is
responsible for all this tumult were to come to me openly and acknowledge his fault, I would receive even him. But if he remains stubborn it
should not prevent you, the fathers and the mothers of families, from
coming to me. I will welcome you all with open arms. As when the
prodigal son repented he was welcomed by his father.'

He ordered all clergy to conduct a grand Mass and to give thanks to
Jesus Christ for victory and to ask for blessing upon those of both sides
who had died: 'I ask all the soldiers who attend Mass to say from the
bottom of their hearts "Thanks be to God for his blessings to us, and may
he continue to care for our souls and to show us his mercy".' The stricken
island longed for peace and he was offering it with his usual humanity.
The people remembered his acts of forgiveness in the past and they wanted
to believe him; the alternative, if there was one, was worse.

Toussaint Supreme:
The Country at Peace

In Paris a youngish man with smooth black hair, a round fat face and compelling black eyes had come to power, a bourgeois of ruthless determination who moved the men he commanded around as if they were chequers on a board. His name was Napoleon Bonaparte and he had risen through military prowess to become the First Consul of the French Republic. The Directory was no longer sending its commandments to the island of St Dominigue; one man was now in control not only of France, but of half of Europe and France's possessions beyond the seas – the First Consul.

The bourgeoisie in general fear the black man, theirs is the attitude of the 'petits blancs'. They fear he might usurp their position in society whereas the aristocrat does not. Toussaint and Laveaux had made this discovery and found their relationship mutually satisfying and rewarding. Napoleon, a Corsican peasant, a 'petit blanc', did not possess a heart generous enough to be a liberal man. He could never forget material possessions. He inquired of his advisers whether the best financial results obtained in the colonies were from slavery or emancipation – at that time clearly the reply was slavery. 'Then,' he said, 'the sooner we return to that system the better.'

No one can deny that Napoleon Bonaparte was an exceptional man, he possessed the energy of genius, a quality which he shared with Toussaint. Another quality demonstrated by both was the personal consideration of the smallest detail; Napoleon read all the reports, every possible piece of documentation on St Dominigue and he absorbed the fact that while he had been fighting in Egypt some unknown black slave had defeated a considerable British force in the Colony and before that had routed the Spanish. This ex-slave had even been given the rank of full General of the French army.

Toussaint had sent General Vincent to Napoleon as his spokesman and Rigaud had also sent a delegation. Rigaud was ignored by Napoleon, but the First Consul needed time to weigh up Toussaint. He made the decision to return General Vincent to the island as a part of the new consular commission, and confirmed Toussaint's position as Commander in Chief,

Roume to continue as 'Special Agent'.

Toussaint had informants in Paris, and he had evidence of Napoleon's policy towards slavery: there were still slaves in Martinique and the rumour flew fast that in Guadeloupe it was intended to restore the old system.

In the meantime there was Rigaud to contend with. Toussaint sent the returned General Vincent to parley with him. Vincent was met by a man who had become completely irrational: Rigaud wore sidearms and waved a pistol, he threatened to kill himself – holding the pistol to his head, but not pulling the trigger; he sobbed, he screamed vituperation against Toussaint and then sat chewing at his handkerchief in the corner of the room, his eyes wild and unseeing; he produced a small dagger from his sleeve and played with it, drawing it backwards and forwards across his throat. Vincent talked to him kindly and said that he had visited his son at school in Paris, and briefly Rigaud seemed to comprehend his surroundings, then once more became outside himself. It was clearly impossible to make peace terms with him, he was not capable of reasoning. He had made preparations to set fire to Les Cayes by daubing the buildings with tar but then could not come to the decision to implement his instructions. Finally, still wearing his straight wig but not his uniform he said a sad farewell to his officers and set sail for France. His lack of reason had not prevented him from sending his family ahead, or from loading three ships with every valuable he and his relations possessed. On landing he hastened to Paris to seek an interview with Napoleon. In his usual emotional manner he railed at fate and particularly at Toussaint. Napoleon found failure a bore but he heard Rigaud out without comment and then said, 'General, I have only one fault to find with you, you were not victorious.'

Toussaint entered Les Cayes which was, like Jacmel, a mulatto stronghold; the population were nervous and ingratiating and he was stern, but he stood by his word, no one was to be made an example of. Verbally he showed his scorn to those of Rigaud's supporters who attempted to toady to him, saying to one man whose sycophantic flattery as usual infuriated him, 'Get out of my sight'. The mulattoes' pride would not allow them to serve under Toussaint, many of them left the country sailing for Cuba, Jamaica, Trinidad or the United States.

He intended impartial justice to all, but made perhaps the most important single mistake in a life of humanity. He appointed Dessalines as commander of the region and then himself left. Exactly what commands he gave to Dessalines are not known, but he must by now have realized the brutality of Dessalines' nature. Dessalines, who later became the first leader of a new country, Haiti, did not hesitate when in power to massacre

every single white man, woman and child on the island and to leave their
bodies piled in public places until they rotted away. He did not hesitate
now to kill every mulatto officer he could drag out of hiding and every
official of any prominence. His troops bayoneted fifty officers who were
first bound to stakes on a spot still known as Croix-des-Martyrs. Mulatto
historians say he killed 10,000 people, obviously an exaggerated figure, but
the fact remains that Dessalines acted in direct contravention of Toussaint's
promises and his orders. When he heard of this Toussaint covered his face
with his hands; he remained at his desk silent and unmoving but when he
looked up his face was stained with tears and he said unsteadily, 'I only
asked him to prune the tree, not to pull it out by the roots.' But he had
shown a small sign of the weakness that once he would never have shown,
in allowing his generals to become too powerful. He wrote admonishing
Dessalines but he, who once had had Jeannot shot for his treatment of the
whites, did not have Dessalines put before the firing squad for his treatment
of the mulattoes. Dessalines remains the culprit, but Toussaint's instructions to 'prune' were totally misunderstood.

Toussaint then turned his attention to Roume and San Domingo,
although Roume was only incidental to the Spanish issue. From the time
Toussaint à Breda had mounted his horse and ridden to the rebel camp at
Galliflet there had only been one dedicated aim for him to pursue, whatever the sacrifice: the end of slavery, 'freedom for all' as he had said, be
they black, white or red,' and yet only a few miles away, across the
mountains, slavery still existed. The ships from Africa still brought their
cargo, the slave-market and the whip still existed, and in the city of San
Domingo the slave traders from Cuba and Puerto Rico still looked over
human beings and selected them as if they were wares. Toussaint was
determined to take over the Spanish side to create a unified, free
Hispaniola.

He asked Roume's formal permission to invade, but Roume would not
grant it, possessing no instructions from Bonaparte to do so. He was
determined to stand firm, but so was Toussaint. He sent Moïse to see
Roume, and Moïse politely suggested that Roume and his family might
prefer the seclusion of their estate at Dondon; outside he had carriages
waiting and without even giving them time to pack their belongings they
were ushered out and driven away. Toussaint had made Roume's submission doubly secure by his old trick of rousing the people who were
marching on the capital, mustering once more against the enslavement of
their brothers. Toussaint wrote boldly to Napoleon that having decided to
take San Domingo he had found himself 'obliged to invite Citizen
Roume to give up his duties and retire to Dondon until further
orders' and he added 'when you have need of him, I will send

him to you'.

Few men, if any, had dared in recent years to address the First Consul in such a cavalier manner. It was noted and not appreciated. When General Vincent had landed on the island as the First Consul's Commissioner he carried with him an edict from Napoleon which had mentioned that there were 'special laws' to be enforced in St Dominigue at a later date. Toussaint went ahead with all that he felt sworn to achieve before any 'special laws' came into force. Perhaps he no longer cared, he did not know Napoleon; since he came to power he had become accustomed to dealing with men whose calibre had always been lower than his own, he did not realize that one day he might come face to face with a man who was more ruthless than he.

The Spanish under Toussaint's old sparring partner Don Garcia were not at all happy about being taken over. Moïse crossed the border with 10,000 men and Toussaint made a flanking advance. Against such hardened and formidable troops the Spanish crumbled. Spanish colonists all lived a life of ease, submission seemed to be a part of their nature and Toussaint was a kind adversary, so Don Garcia was quite prepared to argue no further and, when informed that they could worship as they wished, the priests, who held a large degree of control over the Spanish section, were content. Paul Louverture, Toussaint's brother, was instated – in Napoleonic manner – as Governor. The slaves were emancipated and Toussaint made a stirring speech as always encouraging and admonishing the idle ex-slave; 'I have never considered that liberty meant licence and that when they are free they have a right to live in idleness . . . in fact they should, and it is my wish, that they work harder in the new estate than they did before'.

The slaves hardly noticed their emancipation, their life had been as idle as their masters', they were scarcely aware of Toussaint, and San Domingo returned once more to its long siestas and bullfights.

Toussaint had put Roume and his family aboard a ship and now the whole of Hispaniola was his to rule. He could have become self-indulgent like so many leaders who have achieved their aim, but he did not; tireless as ever, he never considered himself or anyone who surrounded him. Industry was a necessity to him, the reason for his existence, and he could not understand why this was not so with his people. He issued proclamation after proclamation in stirring patriotic words endeavouring to make his people understand the necessity for work. He bribed the whites to come back and run the estates by promises and investment, and having succeeded in this he found that his people were not prepared to return to a life of agriculture. The black man dislikes long hours of monotonous work, unlike the Italian or Spanish peasant who will work all day in a tempera-

ture far exceeding that of the West Indies. The black man feels the heat of
the sun and it is a myth that the sun does not burn or exhaust a man whose
skin is black; in fact, it appears that the Negro feels and suffers more from
the heat than the Latin.

Toussaint was faced with a problem which was almost insuperable:
his people were free and, being free, did not wish to work. If they had
their garden, with their pig and chickens, a few yams, cassava and peas
which they could tend before the sun came up and then rest for the remainder of the day, they were content. Any extra produce they could sell
in the Sunday market represented a bonus with which to buy clothes and
trinkets. On the rocks, by the shore, or in their hollowed-out canoes
made from the 'silk cotton' tree, they could fish or even scoop up the
small 'jacks' as the shoals made a suicidal dash to flounder upon the sand.
They did not *need* to labour. They were warm, they had enough to eat
and they slept under the thatched palm leaves; when they awoke, the sun
made everything surrounding them grow and glisten, and a dropped seed
would instantly germinate.

Toussaint, faced with this dilemma, published an edict that anyone who
was not employed was liable to arrest. It seemed that the only alternative
to financial ruin or to reinstating slavery was to continue to run the
country as if it were an army. His generals took over sections of the island
and, treating the cultivators as if they were soldiers, forced them back to
work. This policy was open to abuse, and Dessalines re-introduced the
whip until reprimanded. Somehow, by superhuman effort, by riding
through the island himself and speaking to the men on the plantations and
inspiring them with his own passion to make his dream reality he managed
to re-establish the sugar industry.

After twelve years of civil war the population was considerably
diminished. There had been 30,000 whites, now there were only 10,000.
The blacks had suffered proportionately: out of 500,000 probably around
a third had perished. No one had the heart to fight any longer, all longed
for quiet and a time of convalescence, and for someone to give them
the incentives that would bring first hope and then progress.

Toussaint reorganized the courts of law, justice was to be for all;
taxation was minimized as an incentive to the proprietors, and the civil
service, where endless idle clerks sleep at their desks, was pruned to a
minimum. Severe laws were imposed against corruption, smuggling and
general dishonesty. He was particularly severe with anyone prominent in
society who failed to set a good example. To those who possessed the
natural advantages of intelligence and possessions he was unrelenting, to
the simple and the have-nots he showed endless patience, and like a father
with a slow child he encouraged. He wrote to the old Jacobin, Abbé

Gregoire, seeking advice on schools; Gregoire sent priests to the island who inaugurated high schools throughout the country. Toussaint felt that the influence of the Roman Catholic church was in its own way a form of self-discipline which his countrymen needed.

Unlike many men of action he loved beauty, not only the natural beauty of the countryside which surrounded him, but beautiful objects, not for their worth but for the pleasure they gave him. He loved jewellery, as anyone who has seen the watch which he possessed which is now in the National Museum in Haiti will realize. He encouraged art and brought artists into the island as teachers; the Haitian school of primitive painters is now famous. Toussaint and Christophe, the black products of the new thought of Rousseau and Voltaire, were the first men to encourage their nation to draw something other than the designs of the 'veves', the Vodun patterns of Africa.

He rebuilt the widely scattered towns. This he supervised personally. He had stables of thoroughbred horses stationed at various vantage points throughout the island. At night in the cool, with the moon lighting his way over mountains and through rivers he rode, startling the inhabitants of Les Cayes, Jeremie, Léogane by a dawn arrival, when he would immediately set to work, drawing up plans ,interviewing alarmed and sleepy officials, inspecting the troops at the garrison and demanding detailed reports from all who were in positions of responsibility.

He ate little and was nervous of poison – a heritage from his days of slavery. On his routes across the island he had trusted 'tanties', old women whom he knew who cooked for him the peas, the fish broth, the callaloo and pumpkin soup that were sufficient to sustain him for many hours. Sometimes when tired he would tether his horse by a river, strip and dive into a rock pool, rubbing his body with the silky silt, then take a branch of a sweet-smelling shrub, a 'ruction bush' to thrash his shoulders and back till he felt refreshed and renewed, then on again once more.

Le Cap was the town he most wished to restore to its former elegance. He loved elegance, of manners, of speech, of surroundings. Once when visiting a French officer's home the stylishness of which particularly pleased him he said to those who were standing beside him: 'You see that, my sons will live like that.' He was not a vain man, but now in a period of peace he took great care of the appearance that he presented, he wore his round hat with plumes, his blue uniform and buckskin trousers, but also he wore a 'flesh-coloured cloak' which swept the ground. His personal jewellery was beautiful and tasteful.

The company that he kept was mixed. As a Republican he was determined upon a classless society, but as intimates, curiously enough, he seemed to find the whites most sympathetic. His close associates were a Frenchman, Citizen Pascal who had married a beautiful mulatto, Abbé Molinière, also French, and an Italian, a priest called Marinit; but there is no evidence that these men were really close friends. Some men do not need friendship as a support. Laveaux was the only man who seems to have stirred in him some kind of craving for love.

Marcus Rainsford, a British officer who posed as an American, visited Le Cap at this time and witnessed for the first time 'a real system of equality'. He noted with obvious surprise that: 'The enjoyments of life were to be found in a high degree in the capital of St Dominigue. The men were in general sensible and polite, often dignified and impressive; the women frequently elegant and engaging.'

There, in Le Cap, Toussaint created from past memories the world of those who had once been his masters but a world now that belonged to, and could be enjoyed by, all. There were coffee houses of the English style and a hotel was constructed, the 'Hotel de la République' – 'an edifice' Rainsford says 'of elegant appearance'. He adds: 'Toussaint not infrequently dined here himself, but he did not sit at the head of the table, from the idea (as was asserted) that the hours of reflection and relaxation should not be damped by the affected forms of the old regimen, and that no man should assume a real superiority in any other place than the field. He was in the evenings at the billiard table, where the writer conversed and played with him several times'; and Rainsford adds that if he did not always experience 'the refinement of European intercourse, he saw no room for insincerity' and that Toussaint was 'free from the affectation of sentiment'. 'A conscious ease and a certain "gaieté du coeur" presided over every repast.'

Apart from painting Toussaint encouraged another art, the theatre. The old theatre was splendidly rebuilt and the traditional works were played in the manner and style beloved by the Comédie Française of today, except that the actors and actresses were black. They surprised Rainsford by their accomplishment, but if he had known black people intimately before he would not have been so surprised, the talent of the Negro for mimicry is unsurpassed.

Rainsford noted that many of the rich blacks hesitated over Toussaint's instruction to rebuild the town, 'as if in rebuilding their former residences they should create new masters'. But not all felt that threat: 'The interior of their houses was in many instances furnished with a luxe beyond that of the most voluptuous European, while no want of transatlantic elegance appeared, nor, among a general fondness for show, was the chasteness of true taste always neglected. The service of their domestics, among whom were, for what cause was not ascertained, some mulattoes was performed with more celerity than in many instances in Europe.'

Toussaint built for himself a house – a palace, rather – of the greatest luxury, which appears to have been one of his few self-indulgences; it had marble floors, French furniture created by master cabinet-makers, silk hangings, carved and painted ceilings and a garden copied from the pattern of those he remembered that were created by the white 'mistresses' of his youth. On his work desk he always had a vase of fresh and sweetly-scented flowers.

He employed five secretaries who were on duty night and day, because he slept so little. At three or four in the morning he would be walking up and down, dictating to one then another, striving to put his thoughts on record, to communicate with and inspire his people, or those in France who, he knew, would eventually control his country's destiny. He was one of those exceptional men who never wastes one moment of their time, perhaps because he knew that time for him was running out. The only rest and relaxation that he took was when he returned to his plantations, which he had, like all the black leaders, acquired. Toussaint's favourite plantation was Ennery. He wrote 'my wife, like myself, wished me to acquire the "habitation" of Ennery for the sake of my children.' He wanted his children to relive the typical plantation life that he had known, and it should be remembered that Toussaint had been a slave of privilege. He owned four plantations when he came to his final power: Dekao, Ennery, Beaumont and Sansay. Le Moniteur, the Haitian newspaper, wrote in 1799 that 'the "habitation", the estate of the General, is of all the most pleasing and the most picturesque which is to be seen in the Colony. Nine leagues from Gonaîves and three from the Spanish border, it exists in perfect and agreeable solitude. The main house and the huts of the cultivators are situated on a high plateau, below which plantations of coffee surround the river which flows from the Spanish side and which in its course encircles the house twice on the terraces below. At one glance one can see the whole estate spread before one. The landscape is bordered by high mountains which make the valley and the view most charming. Everything in the house and on the estate is kept in the most perfect order.' In the ruins of this great house a monument was erected to Toussaint.

It was there that his wife Suzanne lived and there in the fresh and quiet uplands he shed the skin of the General, the leader of a nation. He wore old working clothes and a tattered straw hat; he sat in the shade with his 'bon martis' talking of nothing and everything; or sat as the sun set and the moon came slowly up turning all into silver, holding fat, comfortable Suzanne's hand and stroking her soft familiar skin. It is recorded that when together they held hands like children or very young and inexperienced lovers, that they hardly spoke but smiled at each other with sleepy contentment.

When administering the city of Le Cap, he not only had almost the entire responsibility of ruling the country but he was regarded by the people as a Solomon; matrimonial problems, delinquent children, neighbours' quarrels were all brought before him, and somehow he found time for all. He also found time for those who now lived abroad; whites, many of them widows and short of money, wrote asking him to help with their business affairs. It makes extraordinary reading going through those letters from scattered former French aristocrats to whom Toussaint the ex-slave replied so punctiliously: 'For more than three years I have asked the Citizen Descheux, your mother, to return to her property, my advice unhappily has not prevailed over that of her brother.' And 'I shall neglect no means to put the Citizen Fortier in a position to look after your interests' and wearily 'if your mother has left with her brother it is not my responsibility to persuade her to return.' He was indeed the father of his people of every colour. These people included Josephine de la Pagerie, now Josephine Bonaparte. She had been born in Martinique but her former mother-in-law Madame de Beaurmhais, still owned property in St Dominigue. Napoleon, the First Consul, had married a Creole girl whose black and lustrous eyes and vitality intrigued him and whose voluptuous body totally enslaved him. His love-letters to her, written from the battlefield, when he thought that perhaps that body might be possessed by another, are some of the most openly vulnerable letters ever written by a man to a woman. He wrote of the bandana with a curl escaping which she tied round her head 'a la créole' as she slept, the only garment on her naked body. He wrote in frustrated misery how he did not understand her ways, could never know whether she was true or false, how he did not know, when she laughed, if she laughed at him. It is hard for men to understand women and it was very hard for a European 'petit blanc' to comprehend the style, the largesse of the life lived by the 'grand blancs' whose islands were their castle. Napoleon resented those islands, he resented the life that Josephine still yearned for, resented the memories, the intimacies, perhaps even the blood she shared with those dark, unfathomable people, who occasionally visited his home and to whom she chattered, using unfamiliar creole words and gestures which she used only with them, creating another shuttered screen between him and herself.

When Napoleon came to power Josephine, who like most Creoles was painstakingly acquisitive, wrote to Toussaint inquiring about her mother-in-law's property at Léogane. Toussaint wrote back, and they frequently corresponded in a cordial yet businesslike manner. Under her instructions, he put the property in order and the revenue from the estate was forwarded to Josephine. At some point during this correspondence he mentioned that his sons were in Paris and asked Josephine if she would be kind enough to entertain them, to keep an eye upon their progress and send him news of them. Josephine invited the two boys, Isaac and Placide, to Malmaison for luncheon one day in June. There, among her roses, she walked with them and flirted a little; like her, they were Creoles and they were young and handsome, they already understood the language of eye and touch although they were only children becoming men. They shared with her the heritage of sun and sea and island life, all were at ease with one another, the play upon words, the 'picong' came equally easily to her lips, to the black boy and to the mulatto. In their presence she was back again in a green and humid valley, where the lawns stretched down to the river and where every morning the slave bell rang, where once she had stirred in her four-poster bed and turned again to sleep while the soft deep voices below murmured on their way to work. She was homesick, island-sick, and so were they. Her creole lisp was theirs, her childhood and youth had been spent with faces which were black; her wet-nurse was her first memory, her earliest companions the children of the household slaves whom she had chased through the cigarbox rooms of the great house, who picked her up and caressed her if she tripped, and who stroked her silky hair which felt so strange to them. They had been so proud of her beauty as she grew, but they had also scolded and reprimanded her, even more than her own mother, if she in any way fell below the high standards they felt to be necessary for a 'grand blanc'. She was theirs, their pride and their joy, Mademoiselle Josephine, their young and beautiful mistress. All this was remembered once again as she plucked purple roses with crinkled petals and gave first one to Placide and then to Isaac. She was back once more where the arches of bamboo curved over the river and the wild tannia dipped the tips of its great leaves into the water, where once she had cooled her little white feet, where childhood companions, younger versions of Isaac and Placide, had sat beside her as above them the golden orioles flashed their yellow wings. Now in Malmaison there were only sparrows, and the sun however brightly it shone was always dimmed, and her present life was not one continuous admiration but nowadays only one of commands and criticism. She invited the boys often; Napoleon did not criticize her for that, it was part of his plan.

For Toussaint, Josephine's attention to his children was both comforting and flattering, but it is doubtful if he was deceived. Meanwhile there was no time to be lost: the roads, the irrigation, the ports, the export trade, the education, the arts and justice, the administration of all St Dominigue took every moment of his time. The roads of St Dominigue were of special interest to him. The island was virtually a military camp and so communications within that camp were of primary concern. Toussaint opened up the roads of St Dominigue and San Domingo so that it was possible, for the first time, to travel the length and breadth of Hispaniola.

In his concern for efficiency he did not neglect the humanities. Children, the future of his nation, and particularly the humblest, were his prime concern, and not only their education but also their health. On the largest of the old estates the slave hospital had always existed, its efficiency balanced upon the care, or lack of it, of the manager or proprietor's wife, whose concern for the well being of a slave child was at the best Christian, and at the worst financial, but Toussaint really cared. One of the first measures of his administration was to prevent the enforced work of pregnant female cultivators, and during his term of office the black population increased and infant mortality noticeably dropped.

Toussaint was everywhere. No inefficient administrator was safe, they might be sure that if they idled their chief would suddenly appear in their office to check up on the books; the financial position of every town and every estate was known to him, as well as the prize pupil in every school, the officer who refused to marry his mistress, or the priest who misbehaved with his housekeeper. All were equally known. La Croix said: 'No one knew what he intended, whether it was his intention to stay or to leave, from where he came or where he was going. He would announce that he was to be in Le Cap when he was at Port au Prince; when everyone thought him to be in Port au Prince he would be found in Les Cayes, at Môle St Nicholas or at St Marc. He would start a journey in a carriage, but then after a few miles he would mount his horse, order the vehicle to proceed with its guards while he would suddenly appear where he was least expected only accompanied by a few officers.'

He held two levees at the Governor's Palace, known as the 'petit cercle' and the 'grand cercle'. The 'petit cercle' consisted of his intimates, and included people of influence within the Colony; the rich, the talented and the amusing were guests and so were women of exceptional beauty, but for the first time in the West Indies their colour was ignored. For the first time strangers from other islands, captains of trading ships, mulattoes, Negroes and planters grew to know each other. Toussaint had made a tentative experiment of this kind of social gathering at Mirebelais, where for the first time all the colours and the classes of the island mixed; but now he had made his 'cercle' international. It was shocking only to visitors from the Metropole or from British or Dutch colonial islands; to the people of St Dominigue it was a relief, but a relief which was not allowed to last.

His 'grand cercle', again in the Government Palace, was for the people. He entered, attended by trumpeters, his officers following behind, rather in the manner of democratic royalty of today; he would stop at certain preselected points, exchange a word with some worthy man or unfortunate widow. He would then leave the assembly which anyone could attend. Sometimes, after his formal appearance, he would return and walk among the crowd and, as he had done in his earliest days as Médecin Général, stop and talk to them. He knew that the source of knowledge was the people and the only way to obtain that knowledge was to return to the source. He found the time to do all this; for a very private person, which he was, social life was most exhausting and yet he knew it to be necessary for the good of his country and so he performed it in order to achieve more knowledge of those over whom he ruled.

Americans formed a part of this society, traders and sea captains having married mulatto girls. Early trade from Boston to Jamaica and St Dominigue created some of the greatest fortunes of 'old money' in the United States today. Rum-running was a profitable venture long before prohibition, and St Dominigue was so close to America that import was made easy.

The freedom of the individual was limited, it must be admitted. Perhaps the structure of the society could best be compared with the life in Cuba today. Work for every class was enforced, the military were all-powerful. The children too were encouraged to work, not only in school but in agriculture. The profits of merchants were closely watched and the estates, though still managed by whites, were run upon a cooperative basis. No one was penalized in any way for their colour, the equilibrium between the races remained steady, it was only under Toussaint that this happy and rational balance was achieved. It could have been expected that with a black victory the persecution of so many years might have been reversed but it did not happen. General Vincent said of him to Napoleon, 'Races melt beneath his hand.' The Christian Church remained powerful and Toussaint launched a concentrated attack upon Vodun and against general lawlessness.

So, life in St Dominigue at long last became calm and stable, far more stable than for many years before the revolution had engulfed it. The people of all colours now dared to hope, allowed themselves to believe in a future. The days of work returned, and after work the nights of sleep that no longer contained fear. Gentle family pleasures became familiar once more, the music played as night swiftly fell, the 'after crop' dances, the early morning picnics in the still dew-laden air. There was time once more for small indulgences, time to cultivate their gardens, to walk to market beside donkeys loaded with flowers, shiny fruit and provisions, time to gossip without the apprehensive glance over the shoulder, time to test their cockerel's prowess and shout their wagers from throats rinsed with rum. The churches were filled each Sunday and now after Mass it was not only the 'grands blancs' who paraded their finery, they were joined by the mulattoes and the blacks and it was noticed that the blacks outdid all the rest in magnificence and style.

In view of this stability, and the surge of economic growth in the Colony, it might have been thought that the 'Metropole' would have been content to let matters rest and leave the man who had achieved this progress in such an incredibly short time to continue his work. But to Napoleon, Toussaint was suspect and for many reasons, both rational and irrational. Toussaint was black, in itself an irritant, because Napoleon could not tolerate the black, or even the mulatto; when still young he took pleasure in taunting fellow officers who were mulattoes. Toussaint was an efficient, even brilliant administrator whose success owed nothing to Napoleon's influence or directives. His military prowess was undeniable and had become a near-legend not only in France, but in Britain and the United States. He was a disturbingly shrewd statesman and had managed with the coolest effrontery to elicit the aid of John Adams, the President of the United States, with whom he had negotiated a trade pact, disregarding France's preferential trading priorities, which understandably weighed heavily against him in Napoleon's eyes. There were other, less important but equally irritating reasons which did not allow Napoleon's mind to rest, which pricked on his disaffection for Toussaint – Josephine and her heritage, the émigrés in France and Napoleon's own overweening pride and vanity. It seemed to him that this black man was attempting to emulate him, Napoleon. But above all it was Napoleon's own ambition, not these petty reasons, which was moving the First Consul to action. Beyond St Dominigue lay the distant and tempting prospect of Louisiana. St Dominigue was essential to France's colonial structure, and Louisiana might with the help of St Dominigue become a part of that structure. The new world lay within grasping distance from St Dominigue, and Napoleon was not sure that he was prepared to share that prize with Toussaint, an ex-slave and an African.

The trade pacts between Toussaint and the Americans which so infuriated the French were, ironically, found most unsatisfactory by Toussaint. One day he said, throwing down a pile of bills in a fury, that 'the Americans are more Jewish than the Jewish'. Yet they were necessary to him, they were the only people who would give him arms and he knew that he was going to need more arms than he had ever needed before. He added, 'I have however succeeded in making them accept 300,000 francs in bills of exchange from the Treasury, payable in two months after the presentation. If they are not paid I am a failure here.'

Toussaint knew that his time was running out; at the moment he was the master, but how soon would those 'special laws' mentioned by Napoleon be enforced? He ruled, but as far as Paris was concerned, he had no real right to do so. He was driven by something outside himself, some instinct, some genius which never let him rest, which exhausted those who surrounded him, particularly his generals, who, having achieved their position, now looked for a life of ease. He said to General Vincent, his white adviser from France, 'It is impossible for me to stop, something from above urges me on, and I cannot resist.'

He could not, he said, give in, that now he was 'above the earth in a land where eagles fly'. Did he mean that he was another Napoleon? Napoleon's emblem, he should have remembered, looked sideways. He had attained the impossible and of course there was no way back, but he was at the very top of the most fragile branch of the tree and every day his position became more precarious and, unlike an eagle, he could not fly.

In the climate of recovery and peace Toussaint made a decision. He burned his boats. He created a new constitution which included self-government of the island. It was not a very revolutionary constitution. He himself was to be Governor for life. Catholicism was to be the religion of the new state. Slavery was to be abolished for ever. After Toussaint's death elections appointing a new Governor and ministers were to be held every five years. Of the ten men who drew up this constitution six were white and three mulatto, and they all agreed that the colour of a man's skin was to be no bar to him socially or constitutionally, in public service or in private life; and yet, oddly enough, Toussaint insisted in social circles that while a coloured or black woman was to be called Citizen a white woman was always to be addressed as 'Madame'.

The new constitution, although so mild, caused general consternation. The whites gave lip service to it – what else could they do? – but they were horrified, they were French, they felt that their last link with security was being destroyed. The mulattoes and freed blacks found nothing in it encouraging for them, and Toussaint's own generals were openly rebellious and dismayed. Moïse called Toussaint an 'old fool' and said, 'Who does he think he is, King of Haiti?' They did not possess his ideals; now owning large tracts of land, their revolutionary ideals were tailored to fit their pockets and the return of slavery might well have been welcomed by them.

One of the sadder results of the forming of this independent constitution was the rift it caused between General Vincent and Toussaint. He had once suffered arrest at Toussaint's hands but this he had accepted and still remained a genuine and honest friend. Toussaint asked Vincent to carry the official document to Paris and to present it to the First Consul. Vincent felt the new and independently constructed constitution to be an ill-advised and provocative move and, being faithful and fearless, he told Toussaint so frankly. Toussaint unexpectedly lost his temper with

Vincent, who stood quite helpless, an elderly white man before his old
black friend. They both realized that there was no meeting point of
contact; whatever their friendship, the barrier of race and the different
attitudes of centuries rose between them. To prevent a return to slavery
was all that existed in Toussaint's mind, and he was not prepared to accept
the expedience of a white man who had never been and never would be a
slave. Toussaint, usually so civil, shouted at Vincent and rushed from the
room, then mounted his horse and rode away. Sadly, Vincent agreed to
carry the constitution to Napoleon. He wrote to Toussaint a regretful
letter from Florida on his journey to Europe, warning him that this
decisive step towards independence was folly. Toussaint did not reply.

In all the chief towns the constitution was read out, the troops paraded,
the church bells were rung, there were public dinners and dances, salutes
of guns and fireworks, and Te Deums were sung in every church.
Toussaint was crowned with bay leaves, but for the first time the rejoicing
had a hollow note. The populace noticed the increasing numbers of ships
from the United States carrying arms, artillery and supplies. They heard
the rumours that men were to be brought from Africa to serve in the
army. (Toussaint had 'ordered' 20,000 men, whom of course he would
have freed, but still . . .) The French sailors who sailed in told the people of
the might and power of Napoleon; they did not want another war, all
they craved for was peace, a time to draw breath and to enjoy the new
prosperity, the good fortune that had suddenly fallen upon their land.

Once again an exodus began; the émigrés, perhaps understandably in
the circumstances, were insecure rather than fickle and once more they
packed their mules, piled high their carriages with their valuables and
made for the packets that would convey them back to France. Toussaint
was wounded by this; he had welcomed them back, protected them from
their own white Commissioners, received them as intimates and favoured
them even above his own and yet many of them were now, after all
that he had tried to achieve, not prepared to stand by him. To one man
whom he had known, a member of his 'petit cercle', he said, 'Why do you
wish to leave? You whom I trust and esteem.' The man replied, 'Because
I am white,' and added that many like himself would welcome forces
from France. It must have been a bitter blow to Toussaint. He pointed
out that the arrival of French forces in St Dominigue would be ruinous
for all, not only for himself. He then looked at the man he had believed,
mistakenly, he could trust and said, 'If you feel you must go I will not
detain you' and then added: 'Take with you a letter to the First Consul
which I will give you . . . tell him what I have achieved here, tell him of
the prosperity of agriculture and of trade. It is by that I wish to be remembered and judged . . . Our liberty belongs to us, not to France,

we shall defend it or perish.'

In Paris Napoleon Bonaparte read the new constitution of the island of St Dominigue. He wrote a letter to Toussaint which he never sent, a letter hinting at a partnership in some new military exercise against Jamaica, in order to blunt the thrust of British sea power in the Caribbean, against the United States in order to obtain global power? Something, and we shall never know what, changed his mind.

Much later, in St Helena, he was to admit that he made a mistake in attacking St Dominigue: 'I should have been content to rule the island through the intermediary of Toussaint.' Josephine said that she had advised Napoleon to keep Toussaint at the head of affairs in the Colony and that any interference would make the people fear a renewal of slavery. She knew her people. She added 'I was never able to convince him'.

The expected reaction, the letter from Napoleon, did not arrive. Toussaint spent more and more of his time inspecting and strengthening the coastal defences of the island. Both Christophe and Moïse were becoming openly rebellious towards him. It was the familiar reaction of the young stag who prepares to attack at any sign of hesitation on the part of the old, acknowledged leader. Moïse became openly indiscreet, he was in control of the northern territory, he had aroused the people before on Toussaint's behalf against Hédouville, now he aroused them against Toussaint and against the whites. He told them everything they wished to hear: 'Why should they work on the white man's land? Why did not Toussaint allow them simply to work their own gardens and enjoy the leisurely life that should be the heritage of freedom?' The details of the produce grown in each area controlled by different generals had to be returned to Toussaint's central control and checked by him. In Moïse's area the quantity dropped, noticeably. Toussaint reprimanded Moïse who was blatantly rebellious; calling out the cultivators, he and his troops invaded the plantations, dragged out the white owners and killed them, they looted and rampaged through the northern territory and towns, breaking into shops and warehouses and murdering anyone who stood in their way, and Moïse was at their head. Christophe may have had his own feelings about Toussaint but he certainly did not want Moïse stealing a march on him and taking over as the new revolutionary leader; so he attacked Moïse. Dessalines felt the same and he also chased the new rebel army, but it was Toussaint who fell upon Moïse without mercy. Three or four hundred whites had been slaughtered but by the time Toussaint had meted out justice well over 1000 blacks perished. He lined up the more obvious ringleaders and prisoners before a firing squad. Every tenth man was ordered to step forward and was shot. Toussaint watched on horseback; it was necessary for him to be there so that not only was justice done, but was seen to be done. Moïse was court-martialled and Toussaint person-ally insisted on the death penalty. Moïse had been his favourite, like another son, an intimate of his household and his most trusted officer, from the time of the Spanish wars on, but there was no hesitation on Toussaint's part. Moïse faced the firing squad bravely. The north was troubled and demoralized and for the first time the people felt unsure of 'Papa Toussaint'. This was not what they had expected. To some it seemed as if he too was endeavouring to return them to slavery. They were still not convinced that any kind of organized labour was not in itself slavery, even though money was received for that labour. Poor Toussaint, even to him his task must have seemed so colossal as to be insoluble, above all he wanted freedom, but he also wanted progress; his plan for his people was to look forward, not to revert to men sitting under the big shade trees and women scratching away at some small garden, but education, the enjoy-ment of life with every faculty; now he found even his generals turning towards the easy way, looting from those who had gained possessions by their own efforts, rather than being prepared by labour to acquire them themselves. It was on the day of Moïse's execution that, heart sick, Toussaint heard that a large force destined for St Dominigue had left the shores of France.

12 1802: The French Campaign

With his usual efficiency Napoleon wrote out a detailed plan of campaign for the take-over and intimidation of the island of St Dominigue, but at first he did not implement it, he had many other problems on his hands, and in particular the British. To a man who envisaged the complete control of the world, including Russia, India and even the United States, St Dominigue was one small island to be gobbled up and digested when he wished.

When General Vincent presented Toussaint's constitution to Napoleon he brought it to a man already prejudiced, even obsessed. It infuriated Napoleon who flew into one of the rages that his circle of officers dreaded. He displayed the manners of the peasant, which he was, towards Vincent, cursing him, and Toussaint: 'this gilded African,' he shouted, 'I will not rest until I have torn the epaulettes off every nigger in the colonies.' Vincent was embarrassed but helpless; Napoleon turned his back on him and summarily dismissed him.

Thinking of Toussaint's reliance upon him, Vincent wrote a plea to Napoleon on Toussaint's behalf; he knew the quality of Toussaint and he tried his best to convey this knowledge to Napoleon: 'At the head of vast resources is this man, who is the most active, the most indefatigable that one could ever imagine. It is true to say that he is everywhere, especially where danger threatens and where his cold and sensible judgement inform him his presence is necessary. His sober habits, his faculty, unique to him alone, of never needing rest, his ability after the most tiring journey of being able to attend to his administration, of replying to a hundred letters in a day and even exhausting his secretaries. Added to which he has the ability to charm and beguile all, which sometimes he carries to the point of deceit. In effect, he is a man so much superior to all who surround him that respect for him and submission to him reach to the point of fanaticism with many of his followers. His power in St Dominigue is boundless. He is absolute master of that island and his will is law; although some prominent men, but very few blacks, know his aims, they are powerless.'

Sitting at his desk in Paris, far away from Toussaint and from St Dominigue which he had grown to love, Vincent added a final plea to

Napoleon: 'Sire, leave it alone! It is an island of content within your dominion. God destined this man to govern. Races melt beneath his hand. For you he has saved this island from the British. He refused the enticements of George III and saved it for France.'

Napoleon's views were vehemently expressed; he wrote: 'Toussaint L'Ouverture with his wayward authority has proclaimed and taken action (at the same time he has the gall to inform France what he proposes) which not only offends the authority but the very dignity of the Constitution itself has been outraged (and why, good God) of all things to proclaim the Independence and raise the flag of Rebellion. Toussaint L'Ouverture has chosen a course of action which is quite impossible and that which the Metropole considers most intolerable. At this time they don't even wish to discuss the matter further, these black leaders, these ungrateful and rebellious Africans. With them it seems impossible to establish a straightforward system which respects the interests of "La France" as well as those of a newly born country, no further discussions – eh!'

Napoleon was so angered by Vincent's sincere and honest pleas that he banished Toussaint's advocate and a good servant of France to Elba – an ironical choice. When Napoleon himself arrived there, Vincent was present to greet him.

The secret plans for the invasion of St Dominigue, written in Napoleon's hand, were put into force. It was the largest expeditionary force that Napoleon or indeed the French had ever sent overseas. Perhaps Napoleon's forward thinking was that once he had the men there it was only a stepping-stone or two to the New World. Eighty-six ships of the line and transports carried over 30,000 men. They sailed from Brest, Toulon, Le Havre. The war with England was temporarily over and the British, true to their trading tradition, were quite willing to offer supplies from Jamaica. Holland, too, from her dependencies in the Caribbean agreed to back the assault, the thought of the profit to be accrued from supplying arms being the swiftest way to still any nation's conscience. While the original 30,000 men were upon the sea another 20,000 were to be mustered and sent as reinforcements.

Admiral Villaret Joyeuse was in command of the fleet, and the Commander in Chief of the army was Charles Victor Emmanuel LeClerc who was married to Napoleon's beautiful and wilfully immoral young sister Pauline. He was only twenty-nine years old but he had fought brilliant campaigns for Napoleon, particularly in Italy. He was a slight young man who did not at all resemble a soldier, in fact in his appearance he was rather precious; he had red-gold hair which he wore in profuse and carefully dressed curls, a pouting, rather petulant mouth and the large and slightly protruding eyes which were considered an asset at that time. A contemporary – Armoud – wrote of him: 'He is like a presumptuous child, sated with premature fortune and honours.'

Pauline was incurably frivolous, she appears to have looked upon the whole expedition as a spree, a new titillation which might remove the boredom from a life which consisted of nothing but pleasure. That neither of these young people had any conception of what they were going to face is underlined by the fact that accompanying them on the warship was their four-year-old son Dermide Louis Napoleon, and of course his nurse, under-nurse and nursery staff. Dermide remained unscathed in St Dominigue, but died in Italy while still a child after Pauline had married Prince Borghese.

Pauline had a new wardrobe created suitable for a warm climate (and therefore revealing); she auditioned a small company of actors and dancers for her evening entertainment and engaged a full string orchestra. The transports were loaded with furniture, bales of silk, decorators and seamstresses. Crate upon crate of china and glass was carefully packed. What fun it was all going to be, once they had disposed of those wretched black generals, on this beautiful island that her sister-in-law had described to her.

As the whole world remembers and Canova has recorded, Pauline was an exceptionally pretty young woman. She was described by a contemporary as having 'a voluptuous mouth, and is rendered interesting by an air of languor which spreads itself over her whole form'. Poor Pauline, when she boarded the ship so gaily she had no premonition that her handsome young husband and, it is said, many of her lovers, would never leave St Dominigue. That, swollen with weeping and beside herself with grief, she would shear her head of its flaxen curls and place them in her husband's coffin.

Aboard the ships that sailed were thirteen generals and twenty-seven brigadier generals. There were also mulattoes, Rigaud, Villatte, Pétion and several others; but Napoleon did not trust them and LeClerc was given instructions that they were to be watched and if they caused any trouble they were to be immediately deported to Madagascar.

Amongst all these important Frenchmen and natives of St Dominigue there were two youths, Toussaint's sons Isaac and Placide; they had been removed from the Collège de la Marche, the Lycée Colonial, by Napoleon because they had a part in his scheme. They were accompanied by their tutor, the Abbé Coisnou. It is said, but has not been proved, that Toussaint knew that his children might be used as pawns by Napoleon, so he endeavoured to get them over to London and via Jamaica to St Dominigue, but they were so well guarded that the plan proved impossible. The chief of police was held personally responsible by Napoleon for their secure transportation aboard ship.

Before leaving, Abbé Coisnou escorted the children to the Tuileries where they were presented to Napoleon, who treated them graciously and asked them to convey his compliments to their father. He gave them a letter which he had written to Toussaint, the letter being placed in a beautiful enamelled box. The boys were overawed and very impressed. General LeClerc was present and they were introduced to him by Napoleon who said, 'This is my brother-in-law who will be in command of the army.' They were told that France did not intend to make war upon their island, and that Napoleon admired their father whom he considered 'a great man'. It was a display of total hypocrisy but Isaac was still only sixteen years old and he was very impressed. Placide was now twenty-one, not a boy of great intelligence according to his school reports, but keen to follow his father as a soldier. They were further flattered by a dinner given in their honour at which LeClerc himself was present. Napoleon gave them gifts and then they set sail, two young men who by now were completely won over by Napoleon's treatment of them and by his graciousness, and they were quite prepared to do anything for the great General, such was the state of their hero-worship.

His instructions to LeClerc would have altered their opinion of him. LeClerc carried with him thousands of proclamations appealing to the people of St Dominigue, which were intended to woo them into a surrender without, it was hoped, having to use much force. The proclamation read:–

Whatever your origin or your colour, you are all French; you are all equal and all free before God and before the Republic.

France, like St Dominigue, has been a prey to factions born by internecine squabbles and foreign wars. But all has changed; all nations have embraced the French, and have sworn to them peace and amity; the French people have embraced each other, and have sworn to be friends and brothers. Come also, embrace the French and rejoice again to see your European friends and brothers.

The government sends you the Captain General LeClerc, he has brought sufficient forces for protecting you against your enemies and the enemies of the Republic. If it be said to you their forces are destined to ravish you from your liberty, answer: the Republic will not suffer it to be taken from us.

Rally round the Captain General, he brings you abundance and peace. Whosoever shall dare to separate himself from the Captain General will be a traitor to his country, and the indignation of the country will devour him as the fire devours your dried canes.

Done at Paris   The First Consul

Napoleon Bonaparte

The inference is clear, there were no enemies of the people in St Dominigue. The enemies of the Republic were only Toussaint and his generals.

Napoleon promised them freedom, but he always intended to reimpose slavery. He also intended to abolish all education for Negroes. White Creoles only were to be educated and only in France. All white women who had prostituted themselves with Negroes were to be deported immediately to France. Public meetings were to be prohibited and all propaganda concerning the equality of the Negro was to be banned by law. As soon as Toussaint surrendered he and his followers were to be shipped to France. If he did not surrender he was to be captured by whatever means possible and shot within twenty-four hours. No black general and no black officer over the rank of captain was to be allowed to remain in St Dominigue.

There can have been few orders of such a cynical nature ever written: 'In the interviews with Moïse, Dessalines and Toussaint's other generals treat them well. All Toussaint's principal agents, the whites and the men of colour must in the first period be treated kindly according to their ranks, and in the last period send them all to France.

'All the blacks who are in a high position must during the first period be treated well and flattered but in general one must remove their popularity and their power . . . All whites who have fought with Toussaint will be deported to the Guyanas . . . All mulattoes and blacks who are of a bad disposition whatever their rank will be deported to the Mediterranean to the island of Corsica.'

Trading between France and the island was to be restored and all trade taken away from the Americans for, as LeClerc was to note, 'These men are not French, they only know the United States. It is the United States that has brought here the guns, the cannons, the powder and all the army weapons. They have encouraged in Toussaint the idea of fighting back . . . because they hope to maintain exclusive trade.'

But Napoleon was not too concerned about this: he thought it possible that the Americans might attempt to interfere if it came to a struggle but he was confident of dealing with both them and Toussaint with his enormous forces.

On 29 January 1802, two squadrons of the French fleet hove into sight off Le Cap. This was only a third of the main fleet as they had become separated at sea. Forewarned of their movements, Toussaint and his staff watched them as they sailed in and unfurled their sails, so that the crosses of their masts stood up black against the last blaze of the sun turning the sea to lavender. Toussaint, always a separate man, sat apart astride his horse. All were silent, only the horses moving and pawing the sea turf, but they knew aboard those ships there were anything up to 12,000 trained fighting-men and the most efficient artillery that France could muster. Toussaint knew this was only the first wave of many. He remained silent and then, in the cool rush of air that follows sunset, he said, quietly and without emotion: 'We are doomed. All France has come to invade us.' He leaned forward and patted Bel Argent's neck as if to find comfort in familiarity, then suddenly without another word he wheeled him round and spurred him away.

It was a fault of Toussaint that he did not communicate with his officers – or seldom – and that he only gave them orders. Now in the greatest crisis they had faced they needed reassurance but, either he did not know how to give it or he was not prepared to reveal his plans. A lifetime had taught him to trust no one; he needed time to collect himself and to think.

The first action of LeClerc was to send an order to Christophe who was in command of the garrison of Le Cap to receive him, his generals and officers and to quarter 5000 men. Toussaint, when appealed to by Christophe, gave categorical orders for him not to do so. LeClerc then landed an envoy bearing a flag of truce and men who posted Napoleon's proclamation throughout the town. Even the Mayor, César Télémaque, an old black man and faithful to Toussaint's cause, was persuaded to read it out to the people. Naïve and easily deceived, they were eager to accept the proclamation at face value. They were weary of war and they too had climbed the cliffs and seen the formidable fleet. The population was, as usual, divided. The whites were only too happy to welcome the French. Toussaint was right when he said at this point, 'Do not trust the whites, they will betray us.' The mulattoes were maintaining their neutrality waiting to see which side might be the better ally; the 'petits blancs' welcomed anyone who was not a black general; and no one consulted the cultivators who, with their previous experiences of white masters, might have been shrewdest of all.

Christophe steeled himself as he sensed the mood of the people and to the envoy he sent a reply, 'You will not enter the city of Le Cap unless it is burnt to the ground and on that smouldering rubble we will fight you again.'

LeClerc was biding his time in the roads and squabbling pettishly with his generals upon military policy, while the tension upon both sides was making all nervous. Christophe under Toussaint's orders made his final preparations for the fate of Le Cap. He summoned the garrison to whom he appealed, and he assessed their loyalty – all agreed to follow him to death.

On 2 February 1802, Rochambeau, the French general, attacked Fort Liberté and salvoes of his powerful guns split it apart. It was now war. Christophe ordered the population of Le Cap to evacuate the town immediately and to fly to the hills. The people were both terrified and desolated; they knew only too well what these orders meant: fire. All their new-found peace and plenty, their newly-built houses, the great warehouses full of goods, all were to go up in smoke, and who knew if anything would ever be recovered. They protested, they wept, citizens of influence went down on their knees before the Hôtel de Ville in front of Christophe, but he was adamant.

Forced on by the soldiery they left, the rich with their carriages loaded with boxes piled high with tumbled clothes hastily snatched from their presses, thrusting their way through the ragged bands of the poor who carried their children and a nodding chicken under their arm and bundles upon their heads, while mules, their side panniers bulging, were whipped on past those who rolled barrels or lugged the most valuable items from their stores. So rich, poor, black, white, mulatto made their way up the mountain of Haut-Le Cap. Up the steep, winding stony path, those who fell were trampled upon by the more ruthless and fearful. When the carriages lost a wheel and capsized, frantic women tried to grab what belongings they could, and horses bearing whole families stumbled to their knees. No one helped the others in their misery, since terror brings out in the human race only very few Good Samaritans. When they had reached safety on the mountainside, tens of thousands of people stopped, watching their city and the quiet blue sea, and waited for all they had striven for, all their security, to disappear under searing tongues of flame.

They saw a small sloop sail in towards the shore at dusk and they heard a cannon fire. In Le Cap the signal was given and instantly every soldier came out of the garrison carrying flambeaux. They were led by Christophe on a charger; he was possessed, frenetic with rage. All the public buildings, the newly-appointed Government Palace, the theatre, the ballroom, the customs offices were set on fire, while Christophe galloped amongst his men urging them on. Their faces and bodies ran with sweat, were streaked with ashes, their eyes glowed red reflecting the flames, the common soldiers' bare feet were burned by smouldering cinders and they choked on the acrid smoke, and yet, like battle, it brought a form of joy and some of them laughed as the buildings crumbled behind them. The inhabitants who had defied orders and refused to leave were burned behind their barred doors. Christophe took a savage pleasure in burning his own house, in setting flame to everything that his position and money had brought him ever since he had been a slave and a waiter in a dockside restaurant. He stood and watched the flames lick up the silken hangings of his over-luxurious mansion, and then he left it, spurring the men on once more. All the trappings of eighteenth-century civilization vanished in a few hours and were never to return to Le Cap in quite the same way again.

On the cold mountainside the priests urged the people to kneel and pray, and comforted the hysterical and weeping, when suddenly the arsenal of the garrison exploded with such tremendous force that everyone knew there was no hope. The force of the explosion blasted with such fury against the rocks of the mountain above their heads that they split and great boulders tumbled down upon the packed and helpless multitude, killing many who still wept and prayed.

Soldiers in the town, too, were killed, but Christophe and Toussaint had achieved their purpose: when the French landed they would find nothing to shelter them or feed them except charred and reddened earth; this was all that remained of what had once been the fairest city of the Antilles. The French fleet saw the holocaust and were infuriated, and bewildered too: what sort of men were these they had come to face, what passion stirred them that they would destroy their miniature Paris in order to be independent? Their own revolution had dimmed in their minds and memories.

On shore the weary population were mustered together by the soldiery and forced to follow Christophe into the interior; they trailed behind the soldiers, only allowed a minimum of belongings, now following once more the fortunes of war. The people were disenchanted at every level. They were not soldiers or idealists, and the first stirrings against Toussaint began to spread.

Toussaint was strangely remote, detached in a period of vacillation and depression. He knew the sufferings of his people and felt their growing disillusionment but he had not yet decided how to conduct his attack against the French forces. His front stretched for the whole length of the island; it was too broad, a situation he had never liked, so he hesitated. He had gone to the Spanish part of the island with Dessalines to organize resistance there and communication was reduced almost to nothing between him and the generals.

LeClerc and his officers landed and were both dismayed and angry at the scene of desolation which confronted them, and no one more than LeClerc's wife Pauline, who had expected to find a Government Palace to move into where she could hold balls and receptions and dazzle the creole populace. LeClerc placated her as a husband must, and she moved into an old fort-like building which hung over the sea about half a mile away from the town. Its ruins today look unpromising and it must have taken many hours of work by her staff to make it acceptable to her. The glare from the sea and the lowness of the position made the air stiflingly enervating, it is no wonder that she had 'an interesting air of languor'.

LeClerc issued a proclamation of his own, a subtle bribe in which he said: 'Attach yourselves sincerely to the French government. It will not burn your towns or your dwelling places.'

In his history of Haiti Spencer St John stated that it had been Napoleon's intention to solve the problem with as little destruction as possible, but that 'General LeClerc did all he could to cause an armed resistance, as a peaceful solution would have given him no military glory'; this is probably correct, he was a young man, opinionated and rather vainglorious. St John continues: 'therefore instead of sending Toussaint his children and the letter he bore from Bonaparte, he tried to surprise Cap Hatien.'

The island had heard a rumour that the children were on board and he mentioned them in his proclamation: 'The French government intends to reward General Toussaint . . . the young people do not have to be the victims of the anger of the older generation. I will send them to him tomorrow.' This appears to be a clear admission of culpability. He did not send them to him 'tomorrow' because Toussaint was not there to receive them; he was attempting to rally his forces throughout the island. In fact, LeClerc did not send them to Toussaint for two months.

The French under General Boudet then attacked Port au Prince from the sea. Dessalines who commanded the capital and the province was not there – he was with Toussaint in the Spanish sector – or it might have been a very different story. Toussaint's white Chief of Staff, General Agé, was temporarily in command in Dessalines' absence. General Boudet landed and under a flag of truce requested surrender – as he had 3500 troops accompanying him it was rather a forced request. There was a parley and Lamartinière, one of Dessalines' brigadiers, refused to surrender, declaring that he would destroy the town and everything in it including himself rather than give way. He rose from the large table that all who were present were sitting around and, turning to a fellow officer Lacombe, demanded the keys of the magazine, Lacombe, a white man, refused to hand them over. Lamartinière drew his pistol and shot him dead then snatched the keys from his pouch, which shows the spirit of those still loyal to Toussaint; but General Agé intervened, so that the French were allowed to advance to the fort whose doors were opened to them by mulatto officers. It appears that blood or colour prevailed, whatever the cause or the ideal at stake. Lamartinière and a band of faithful men waited on the ramparts till the French were inside the fort, then they opened fire, shooting down hundreds, Pamphile La Croix being among those wound-

ed. Then Lamartinière and his men leapt down and retreated towards the
hills. The French had achieved a comparatively easy victory. Lamartinière
had attempted to set fire to the town as he and his soldiers passed through
it but sudden rains damped down the fires. Port au Prince is surrounded
by low swamp and quagmires and consequently by mosquitoes; some of
the French soldiers complained of pain and fever and some died; although
the real rains had not yet started, it was a warning which no one heeded,
and in any case disease was the enemy which the French could not
conquer.

Toussaint in San Domingo heard of the firing of Le Cap. Changing
horses, he galloped through the night over the pass that led down to the
northern plain, riding at such a pace, with such skill and certainty that his
posse of officers was left far behind him. 'The Centaur of the Savannahs'
caught up with Christophe's force of blackened and exhausted soldiers and
civilians in the dawn. He approached them at a gallop and Christophe
knew whom he confronted. Toussaint was grim.

He wrote in his memoirs that he had 'not intended the burning of Le
Cap'; perhaps at that time he had not, it was Christophe who had acted
precipitately in the passion of the moment, but it had undoubtedly been
agreed between Toussaint, Christophe and Dessalines that theirs was to be
a scorched-earth policy.

In the dawn light, both on horseback, Christophe and Toussaint conferred, coldly and briefly. Perhaps they had lost confidence in each other;
they had been as one when they were victorious, but defeat brings doubts.
Toussaint was making his way as swiftly as he could towards Gonaîves
and the fortress there, and he ordered Christophe to Grand Rivière. It was
a sad meeting, there is little to say when luck starts to run out, and when
it runs out, it runs fast. A few hours later, after Toussaint had left
Christophe, his horse was shot from under him by French snipers whom he
had not expected to have advanced so far. He was shaken, but he mounted
another horse and rode on to Gonaîves.

Toussaint had now formulated his policy of war, it was not as com-
prehensive as he would have wished, but he was not a great general of
defence, only of attack; but now he was no longer the scourge who swept
down upon armies and obliterated them, so he had to take the only course
open to him. The French, backed by naval power, were attacking on all
fronts. He knew his only hope was to withdraw his forces, burning
everything as he went, and then to retreat to the interior, forming a
strong nucleus that could then attack the French later when their lines
would be more attenuated. He knew also that his army could at any
time be reinforced by the cultivators. If the French wanted to wage war he
would too, and in a way more horrifying than they had ever imagined.

He wrote to all his generals of his new plans: 'There is no reason to despair, Citizen General – if you can, endeavour by force or guile to set the city on fire. As it is built of wood, a few trusted subjects should be enough to achieve this work. Do you not possess men who are faithful enough in your service to perform this?' And then he added – and this was the whole strategy of his war plan: 'Remember, that while we wait for the rains, which will deliver us from our enemies, fire and destruction are our only hope. Remember, too, that the land which we have watered with our own sweat should never be allowed to give our enemies sustenance and life. Destroy the roads. Throw the corpses of your men and your horses into the wells. Command that everything be burned and destroyed, so that those who have come to enslave us again may never forget the image of the hell which they so well deserve.'

This was a new, embittered Toussaint, not fighting for his own life, which he had never valued, but for his bewildered and now falsely beguiled people.

Half his generals never received his letters of instruction; they were intercepted by infiltrating French, the bearers of them were shot and the messages sent back to LeClerc and Boudet. Toussaint in desperation sent double messages, placatory ones for French ears and secret instructions for his generals: 'burn, retreat, but never surrender.' The French tortured the messengers or searched their bodies. They then handed on the messages suggesting surrender to bewildered generals, who were unbelieving, but were forced by their own eyes and Toussaint's words to believe that after all they must give in. Toussaint's own brother Paul received the flowery note that he should surrender to Kerserveau and show loyalty to the French as all was lost. He saw no other course but to capitulate. The secret instructions he never received, they were forwarded to the Ministry of Marine and read by Napoleon instead.

The bishops and priests who had formerly orchestrated Te Deums for Toussaint now rang the bells for the French. It had always been an island of divided loyalties, but those very same priests who had marched with the rebel army and had swung incense in Toussaint's honour now blessed the French as they entered the towns. 'Don't trust the whites' was becoming fact. The same men who had knelt at Toussaint's feet hastened to declare their loyalty to France and the First Consul. Toussaint, who had protected white men even above his own people, said: 'They will betray us if they can. Because of this you may act as you wish. Whatever you do will be well done.' But he was to learn the saddest truth of all, that there were few of his own he could trust either.

He wrote these instructions but, by his own nature, could not act upon them. It was admitted by the French that his treatment of white prisoners was always humanitarian, whereas the French did not hesitate to shoot down the wounded or those who surrendered. On one day they shot 600 black soldiers,but then, the French did not regard them as men but, still, in spite of 'equality' and 'fraternity', as animals.

LeClerc was disquieted by the burning of Le Cap, but equally disquieted by the outbursts of violence which his soldiers encountered from the people. The whites and the mulattoes were only a fraction of the people and he learned from his agents of the mounting hatred in the countryside; he could not envisage defeat – at this point it seemed an impossibility – but he was beginning to realize the iron that had eaten its way into the souls of these new people whom he was encountering for the first time. He decided it was now time to make use of Toussaint's sons, a weapon he had not before thought necessary. He summoned them, accompanied by the Abbé Coisnou, and ordered them to wear the military uniforms which had been one of Napoleon's gifts to them. He told them that he was going to convey them to see their father and, of course, their mother. He sent a messenger, under truce, to Toussaint carrying these intentions. The boys were nervous and bewildered in LeClerc's presence; they had seen Le Cap in flames, and had heard the terrifying explosion; they had believed that upon arriving they would see their father and mother immediately, but it was now two months since they had landed and the French who surrounded them gave them no word of assurance, or made any move to bring such a meeting closer. They had been courageous enough to write a letter to LeClerc asking him when they would see their father but had received no reply. They no longer trusted his quick smile and the blue eyes that revealed nothing. Abbé Coisnou attempted to reassure them and LeClerc told them that they were to be entrusted with the great honour of taking the cloisonnée box containing the First Consul's letter to their father. LeClerc assured them that he had 'the highest hopes of coming to an understanding with your esteemed father'.

Late at night they left, escorted by the Abbé and a small party of outriders; they passed through the French lines and slept in a tent which was a novel experience to Isaac, if not to Placide, and one he enjoyed. They slept as young men do and then awoke to ride on towards Ennery.

It was good to smell familiar air again, in the town the blend of swamp and wood-smoke, and in the hills the sweeter smell of crushed ferns and grass and the sudden drenching smell of blossom.

Word travels fast in the Antilles. Small groups of people waited at the junctions of the roads to see Toussaint's boys, the young black masters. When they neared the plantation gates a crowd had gathered; at last it was the homecoming of which they had dreamed as they sat in their school-

room in the hard grey light of a French winter. Now, as their own people
with their comforting black faces ran towards them and cheered them,
they believed, in spite of what they had overheard the French officers
saying, that their father was indeed a great man. At the top of the bowleg-
ged stone steps their mother and their young brother and cousins were
waiting. They dismounted and ran up towards their mother who could
not stop her tears; she kissed their cheeks, the palms of their hands,
stroked their hair and caressed the backs of their necks. She was much
older than they had remembered: an old black woman now, and enorm-
ously fat compared with the ladies of Paris, she did not wear scent but
smelt of sweet coconut oil; as she held them close they remembered that
familiar nostalgic smell and the warmth and comfort of childhood, and
they too wept.

Toussaint had not yet arrived but had sent word that he was on the way;
in the meantime Abbé Coisnou was diplomatically persuasive with
Madame L'Ouverture, imploring her to use her influence upon her husband to abandon his attempt to hold the colony 'for the sake of her sons'.

The boys heard the clatter of horses' hooves, and their father's quick
steps running towards them, and then once again they saw the love in his
eyes and felt the strength of his wiry arms enclosing them. For a long time
he held them both close and then he turned to the Abbé.

Coisnou in his account of the meeting says with a calculated cynicism
only possible in a man who believes his own conscience to be clear: 'I saw
them shed tears and wishing to take advantage of a period which I conceived favourable I stopped him at a moment when he stretched out his
arms to me.'

'Can this be Toussaint L'Ouverture,' he said, 'who is offering me his
hand?' Toussaint replied, perhaps seeing through the insincerity, 'Well,
who else?' Nevertheless, always well-mannered, he thanked Coisnou for
the educating and care of his sons and for guiding them safely to him
through the lines. Isaac then handed his father the box with Napoleon's
letter. He made suitably polite comments upon the beauty of the box,
read a few lines of Napoleon's letter and put it down then, realizing that
the Abbé obviously considered a letter from the First Consul an honour
and of supreme importance, he said, 'I will read this later when I have
time to give it my full attention.'

The letter could not have deceived Toussaint – it would hardly have
deceived his children;

Citizen General,
   Peace with England, and all the powers of Europe has established the
Republic as powerful and great and has also decided the government to

occupy the colony of St Dominigue. We are sending there General
LeClerc our brother-in-law as the Captain General, and as first Governor of the colony. He is accompanied by enough troops to respect the
sovereignty of the French people. In these circumstances we hope that
you will prove to us, and the whole of France, the sincerity of your
feelings constantly expressed in different letters you have written to us.
We think highly of you, and have pleasure in acknowledging the great
service you have rendered to the French people . . . Aided by your
talents and the force of circumstances that have made you a leader, you
have brought to an end the civil war . . . made religion honourable and
the belief in God who leads us all. The constitution that you have
drawn up incorporates many good things . . . The circumstances in
which you found yourself, surrounded as you were on all sides by the
enemy from whom the Metropole could not rescue you nor supply you,
made that cons'itution legitimate . . . But today in the circumstances that
so luckily attend you, I am cērtain that you will be the first to surrender
to the sovereignty of the nation which counts you as one of its most
illustrious citizens, by the services which you have shown to it and by
the talents and strength of character that nature gave you. Contrary
conduct will be incompatible with the view that we hold of you. It will
not only forfeit your numerous rights in the recognition and goodwill
of the Republic, but it will create an avalanche which will engulf you,
to the misfortune of all brave blacks whose courage we admire and who
will, sadly, have to be punished.

We have made this known to your children and as evidence of the
sentiments we encourage, we return them to you.

Assist us with your influence and your efforts. Citizen General, what
more do you desire? The liberty of the blacks? You know that in all the
countries we have been, we give it to the people who do as we wish . . .
After all the service you have given are you not forgetting the honours
and the future that might await you?

The iron hand in the velvet glove becomes more apparent as the letter
continues. It is a poor letter, written in rather bad French, repetitive and
confused in meaning, a letter very inferior to Toussaint the ex-slave's
many outpourings. Napoleon continued threateningly: 'Tell them that if
their liberty is dear to them they cannot enjoy it without the title of a
citizen of France, and that all acts contrary to the interests of their mother-
land, and against the Captain General will be a crime against the national
sovereignty.

'And you, General, remember that as the first of your colour to have
great power, and to be distinguished by your bravery and military

talents. You are before God, and before us responsible for their conduct.'

It is a symptom of Napoleon's feelings and prejudice that in the only letter that he ever wrote to Toussaint he could not forbear to mention his colour. In the circumstances it was not even relevant. The letter meanders on, so that it is not surprising that Toussaint put it aside to read later.

After the emotional reunion with his children and seeing Suzanne still in tears, Toussaint walked round the room while he collected himself; he then looked at Coisnou, quietly and for a long time and then said: 'You appreciate, Monsieur Coisnou, that the words which you have brought me from the First Consul are absolutely in opposition to the behaviour of General LeClerc, his lieutenant, who has descended upon St Dominigue like a thunderbolt and without so much as by your leave is disembarking a large army.' Toussaint paced away from Coisnou and then faced him again, a small but determined man. 'He should remember,' he said 'that I still carry a sword.' He paused again, and then continued: 'For what reason should he wish to declare this most unjust and imprudent war? Is it because I have delivered my country up to the scourge of a foreigner? Because I have planned and worked with all my energy for the attainment and for the respect of my people, because I have established order and justice?' Then suddenly, more angrily, he said: 'Why have my efforts been so considered that my sons have been sent back to me in this miserable way? If, as you all say, General LeClerc is frankly seeking peace, why then does he not halt the march of his troops? He will impose upon St Dominigue a most unwelcome oppression by this unmerited invasion.

'Monsieur Coisnou,' he continued, showing sudden temper, 'I will write to him in this vein and you, sir, and Mr Granville, my youngest son's tutor, are hereby charged to take it to him.'

Coisnou had not expected to be confronted by a man like this, a man of exceptional character. He certainly had not expected this ex-slave to speak to him with such politeness. LeClerc too, when it was too late, was to write to Napoleon 'this is no ordinary man'; but he did not yet comprehend this and he wrote on 9 February 1802 with confidence to Napoleon: 'I have sent Toussaint the children with your letter, saying that if he wishes to declare that the fire at Le Cap was not done under his orders, and that he will bring back his troops, I will accept his surrender.'

Toussaint talked to his sons and to Coisnou, endeavouring to present the situation to them as he saw it. Suzanne made this task more difficult, all she could understand was that if he gave in to all LeClerc's demands then her boys would be with her once more, family life would return and that she would see more of her husband whom she loved. Isaac and Placide, remembering their instructions from Napoleon, pleaded with their father to come back with them to Le Cap and see LeClerc. He looked at them gravely, dressed in their miniature honorary uniforms, and he said: 'I will not attempt to influence you; but, my dear children, you have to make your choice, is it to be France or St Dominigue? Whichever you choose, I shall always continue to love you as I do now.' Poor young men, it was a pitiful moment for them. Isaac, the child of Toussaint's blood, declared, and it cannot have been easy for him, for France. Placide, Toussaint's stepson but his favourite, threw himself into his father's arms and wept. He then said he would follow Toussaint, fight with him and for him and against slavery. Toussaint showed no difference in affection to either boy, but embraced them both. It is ironical that it was his own son who denied him and Placide, the mulatto, the child of another, who followed him. Madame L'Ouverture held Isaac close but she had nothing to fear from Toussaint; he clasped the boy's shoulder and then turned to Coisnou and said, 'Take back my children if it must be so, I will be faithful to my brethren and to my God.'

In the meantime he wrote to LeClerc and told his children to take the letter with them. He wrote in his memoirs that he had refused to subordinate himself to LeClerc and that if he persisted in his invasion he would defend himself. LeClerc said, 'I have received the letter that you wrote to me and which was handed to me by your children, it appears that you have not been rightly informed in the manner in which events have taken place.' He went on to say that it was only after General Christophe's refusal to cooperate that he was 'forced to take a hostile attitude'. He did not, of course, mention that he had already taken Fort Liberté. Toussaint says in his memoirs: 'It was not me who started the hostilities,' and he was right and yet LeClerc went on to tell Toussaint 'there is yet time, surrender to me, I could learn from your ideas, you have a great reputation, you can preserve it intact . . . You have to choose, Citizen General, between the title of Pacifier and that of Devastator of St Dominigue . . . remember that the French government whose army has forced Europe to peace will employ all these means to reconquer this colony and that however numerous your troops you will, in the end, be obliged to surrender.'

LeClerc wrote in this manner to Toussaint but at the same time distributed proclamations to the people which were in a different vein: 'these leaders have stolen the colony . . . their treacherous intentions are unmasked. General Toussaint has sent to me his children with a letter in which he assures me that he desires nothing but the good of the colony . . . I have ordered him to join me, I have given him my word to employ him as my lieutenant general, he has not replied . . . I am taking to the battlefield and I am going to show this rebel the strength of the Government of France. From this moment he will be, in all the eyes of the

French inhabitants in St Dominigue, a monster who prefers the destruction of his country to sacrificing his power.'

It is probable that Toussaint was always, from the moment of invasion,
aware of all Napoleon's instructions to LeClerc. He had efficient agents in
the Metropole and agents amongst LeClerc's own men.

There was no turning back, he could not surrender, the time for
confrontation had come, whatever the outcome. 'I am a soldier,' he said
in a proclamation to his men. 'I fear God, but I fear no man and if I must
die, I will die like a soldier, with my honour untarnished and with no
regrets . . .'

LeClerc was confident, he wrote with certainty to Napoleon, reinforcements were due to arrive at any moment, and he felt that he had
a growing hold upon the people. The only small doubt in his mind was
the fact that unaccountably and for no known cause his soldiers were
falling sick and dying of this wretched fever which was so rapid that a
man could die in hours. 'I have 600 men on my sick list' he wrote to
Napoleon, and then, only a week later, 'I have already 1,200 in hospital,'
adding that he had great need of even more reinforcements. Pauline
wrote reassuringly to her brother that his nephew was well, but she
confessed to Josephine that she was depressed by the atmosphere of
sadness caused by the sudden deaths that occurred on the island.

LeClerc received his reinforcements; under General Grantheme
2500 more men were shipped to the island. With the confidence which
this brought him LeClerc issued a new proclamation: 'I come to restore
prosperity and abundance, everyone must see what an insensible monster
Toussaint is. I promise liberty to the people of the island and I shall
respect their property and their person.

'The General Toussaint and the General Christophe are put outside
the protection of the law, all citizens are ordered to pursue them and to
treat them as enemies of the French Republic.

'From the day on which the French army shall occupy a position all
officers whether civil or military who shall obey other orders than those
of the generals of the army which I command, shall be treated as rebels.

'The cultivators who have been seduced into error and deceived by
the perfidious insinuations of the rebel general, may have taken arms,
shall be regarded as children who have strayed, and shall be sent to their
plantations, provided they do not seek to incite insurrection.' He then
promised amnesty to any soldiers of Toussaint's army who surrendered.

Few of the cultivators heeded him, they rallied to Toussaint. Some of
his officers, however, defected without even attempting to put up a fight.
General Dommage, to whom Toussaint had written 'Don't trust the
whites', surrendered after being captured by his own subordinates and

General La Plume in Les Cayes welcomed the French.

LeClerc wrote to Bonaparte: 'Among countless letters that have fallen into my hands from General Toussaint . . . I send the enclosed addressed to General Dommage in command at Jeremie . . . which contains instructions to raise *en masse* the cultivators and to beware of the whites. Toussaint L'Ouverture gave the order to General La Plume to burn the town of Les Cayes.

'I have letters addressed to Dessalines, Christophe and Maurepas, by the way, which all announce the same dispositions . . . and prove quite clearly that if I had allowed myself to be taken in by the wild protestations of Toussaint I would have been nothing but an idiot.' Evidently neither man had deceived the other.

LeClerc quickly took the coastal towns; he had an army of 25,000 trained men with which to do it. Toussaint was now fighting a battle of retreat.

LeClerc wrote to Napoleon: 'The army of St Dominigue in the course of five days have routed the chief of their enemies, obtained possession of considerable quantity of their baggage and a portion of their artillery. Desertion is frequent in the rebel camp. Clerveaux, La Plume, Maurepas and many other black chiefs, and men of colour have submitted. The plantations of the South are entirely preserved and the whole Spanish part of the island has surrendered.'

Toussaint, fighting a rearguard action, massed his men at Ravin à Couleuvre, a narrow mountain pass through which General Rochambeau was attempting to force his way into the interior. Toussaint was in personal command of around 3000 trained men and Rochambeau had 5000 of Napoleon's picked men; but Toussaint also had the support of 2000 cultivators, men who were untrained but who were fighting for their lives and the future of their families. An awareness of this strength of feeling even filtered through to some French minds. La Croix writes of a black man asking him if he thought that the French intended to restore slavery. He could tell by La Croix's face that this was so. The man said, 'Oh, my daughters, my poor daughters. I cannot bear it.'

General Rochambeau to his extreme chagrin and surprise was beaten back by these men. He re-attacked and was beaten back once more. He had said in his orders to his officers before the battle that they were only fighting slaves who would scatter and flee before them. He discovered his mistake after Toussaint had inflicted heavy losses and taken many prisoners.

The French attempted a pincer movement, encircling Toussaint's forces. Christophe came to Toussaint's aid, beating back the French division commanded by General Hardy. Christophe's men fought with great bravery but he too was forced to retreat.

Toussaint consolidated his position by retreating to the fortress of Crête à Pierrot, which had been built under British supervision during their invasion of the island. The British, who always travelled with their engineers, had a passion for military architecture; there are still many examples of these constructions, some of them remarkably pleasing aesthetically, scattered throughout the West Indies to this day. The fort commanded the approach to the mountains which rise above St Marc. Toussaint, while he established a force there, was playing a waiting game with Rochambeau, taking pleasure in waging the brand of warfare at which he was most expert: the sudden foray, the appearance and disappearance of men as if by magic. And he was in hill country, the land of ravines, gorges and winding passes where his men, so skilfully trained at this type of fighting, could gain a gradual and telling advantage which they could never achieve on the plains.

Toussaint placed Dessalines in charge of his campaign which centred upon the fort and Christophe was in personal command of Crête à Pierrot. Under Dessalines, Toussaint put Lamartinière who had displayed such ruthless decision and courage when the French first landed. He explained to his men that it was essential to hold the position. He spoke to them as 'his children' and Dessalines, Lamartinière and the junior officers were included. All of them were now desperate men, but they were united as never before and, sadly, were never to be again.

LeClerc sent General Debelle into the attack against Crête à Pierrot. Christophe was ready to meet him with, as it appeared to Debelle, a negligible force. Christophe showed little resistance, the French advanced confidently as they had thought 'the slaves' were fleeing before them. What they did not realize was that these 'slaves' who were considered by them to be so foolish had several days before prepared a long and deep trench within firing-range of the fort. The French advanced with speed when suddenly Christophe and his men vanished into the trench and scattered; at the same moment the French, fully exposed, were subjected to salvo after salvo of withering fire from the fort, and in a matter of moments 400 of Napoleon's best soldiers fell dead or seriously wounded.

This was their first experience of a new kind of warfare, to which they were to become bitterly accustomed. General Debelle was wounded and as the remnants of his force retreated they encountered what they were to call the 'infernal guerillas'. In every tree there were snipers so that, as they attempted to drag their wounded with them, they were shot down. As they rushed colliding through the undergrowth in panic, there lurked behind every rock the threat of ambush by men who seemed to be only black shadows, who appeared and then disappeared soundlessly but whose fire was deadly.

LeClerc could not believe that one of his generals, an experienced soldier, could be routed by a band of guerilla slaves. He sent in two more crack divisions to take the fort, under Generals Boudet and Duga but, incredibly, they too fell into the same trap and both generals were wounded as their advancing forces followed Christophe's decoys into the open ditch. At that time LeClerc opposed the fort, a small, isolated building in the middle of nowhere, with 12,000 men. Inside the fort there were only 1200 defenders. Now as the French forces surrounded Crête à Pierrot, they brought in their heavy artillery, but still Toussaint's army held out; besieged now they grew short of food and, more important, water. There was nowhere to bury the dead who were killed by cannon fire, and no one had time to tend the wounded. In the heat of the Antilles a body rots and must be buried on the same day death occurs. The conditions inside a building can be imagined: the living were forced to throw the dead from the ramparts, and the stench was sickening for both defenders and attackers.

Inside the fort they sang and beat their drums to keep up their spirits. They even sang the 'Marseillaise', their voices ringing out deep and clear in the night, drowning the sound of the croaking frogs. The French soldiers heard them and were subdued by the courage of these men as soldiers often are by the bravery of their enemy, and the soldiers of France remembered then that it had not been long since their fathers and their mothers had set fire to the Bastille in the name of freedom.

The situation for the defenders in spite of bravery and defiance was becoming untenable but undeterred they ran up a red flag at each corner of the fortress, declaring to all that there was to be no surrender.

The cultivators were mustering, these were the men in the fortress's one hope of relief; but the mulattoes under Pétion were also rising and coming to the aid of the French, and Toussaint's own generals who had surrendered with their troops were also closing in on the little fort.

Toussaint sent out a rallying cry: 'Courage, mes braves, courage . . . can you forget your slavery, the torture and the cruelty you have suffered for three centuries. Bare your breasts and look again at the mark of the branding-iron upon them. The French do not fight for liberty or for their country but for the ambition and hate of the First Consul. They have not suffered the humiliation of the branding-iron . . . Again take courage, those who do not die by the sword will perish in our climate which will avenge its own. Their bones will lie by our rocks and our mountains, or will be bleached beneath our seas . . . Freedom will spring again for us from their graves.'

LeClerc had said that he intended 'to conduct this war with vigour', but he was having to show more vigour than he wished.

Napoleon had written to him 'this is a military campaign like any other, no negotiation was ever considered.' Certainly it was a military campaign, but it was not evolving at all as anyone in the Metropole had expected, and it was, for LeClerc, so difficult to explain the circumstances of his lack of immediate military success. 'They are worse than Arabs', he said, trying to give Napoleon some idea, after his experiences in Egypt, of the kind of resistance and the ferocity of the men he encountered.

Scouts from the fort infiltrated General Boudet's lines; they knew how to move at night. They claimed to be deserters and then, having gleaned what information they could of the numbers and condition of their enemy, ran suddenly like hares, evading bullets by throwing themselves in the river and escaping to the forces of Dessalines which were mustering on the hills and causing the French harassment from the rear. The cultivators too would suddenly appear in small bands as the French were at ease, old men and women, who appeared friendly and innocent, bearing provisions, welcome fruit and vegetables, and then, suddenly from within the bush there would come a burst of fire and the old men and women who had seemed so frail were instantly as agile as monkeys in the trees and vanished as a few more Frenchmen fell and their blood seeped slowly into the earth of St Dominigue.

LeClerc however still wrote with confidence to the Ministry. 'Immediately after the capture of Crête à Pierrot I made an attack with a detachment of troops on Mirebelais which I occupied' – he does add – 'feebly'. He then continued over confidently: 'General Hardy is going to the north where he will have met and beaten General Toussaint.' In the same letter he says: 'I have suggested to General Boudet that he writes him a letter making openings for his possible surrender. Although he has at this time only 2200 soldiers and about 2000 cultivators in his command, he could still cause us a lot of trouble. Consequently, I must make some effort to rid myself of him. Toussaint is not at all an ordinary man, he has a strong character and a good mind.'

It was now March, the rains might come at the end of April, so the morale of the French grew lower. They began to comprehend, as had happened with the English before them, that they were not fighting ordinary men.

La Croix states in his memoirs that 'it was clear that we no longer inspired the fear of death and this is the greatest misfortune that can befall an army.' He was right because the fear of the return of slavery was a greater terror. There are not many things worth dying for, honour and glory are only words, but freedom has moved the hearts of men for centuries.

The fort at Crête à Pierrot still held but, inside the men had almost no water left, they drank their own urine, sucked on balls of lead, they could not sleep for thirst and they were growing weaker.

Pétion the mulatto led a violent attack on the fort, intending to finish the resistance, a man of St Dominigue against his own people showing more passionate persistence than the French; but the fort still held after three days of constant bombardment and the red flags still flew.

Further north Toussaint was raising the cultivators in numbers, and even threatened Le Cap. In one of the sudden swoops for which he was so famous he took from the French Marmelade, Dondon and San Raphael. One day he saw from a vantage point a brigade of his own men who had deserted under Maurepas massed against him. With characteristic lack of fear he spurred his horse and rode towards them, riding alone until he faced them. 'Soldiers of the North,' he shouted at them, 'will you fire upon your General and your brothers?' The black soldiers lowered their arms and some fell on their knees before him, but a faction of white officers raised their muskets and fired at him, at which his personal bodyguard galloped in to draw fire and so he was saved, but one of them died later in Toussaint's arms. Like a cossack he lifted one of the wounded who had fallen and galloped away with him on his horse.

The officer who died was carrying a letter from Dessalines telling Toussaint that he had come to the regrettable conclusion that with the weight of the French forces it was impossible for him to relieve Crête à Pierrot and that a message must be smuggled through to the fort to give the orders to evacuate. Toussaint did not agree with Dessalines that the situation was hopeless. He made preparations himself to march on the French but before he could set off across country Dessalines had acted on his own initiative. A blind old man and a black woman who seemed hardly able to walk stumbled into the French camp. They did not seem to comprehend anything the French said to them, but by now the French were suspicious of any cultivators, however old and seemingly harmless, and the soldiers beat them with sticks in order to try and make them confess that they were spies. La Croix ordered them, however, to be released as they did indeed appear to be not only ancient but deaf and dumb. It was only when an officer suggested shooting them that they showed they were not deaf or blind or even mute, by running like the wind towards the shadows beneath the walls of the fort; when out of range, they began to dance defiantly, leaping up and down, a war dance dimly remembered, then the gates opened briefly and they entered. They were, of course, brave spies coached by Dessalines and they brought his order with them, to evacuate the position but not to surrender.

Lamartinière rallied his men. Some of the wounded asked for poison rather than falling prisoner to the French; then at nine o'clock, three hours after the sun had set, the 800 survivors of the siege of Crête à Pierrot came out in attacking formation and fell upon La Croix's men. Beaten back, they turned and attacked General Rochambeau's flank and, incredible though it may seem with 12,000 men massed against them, these pitiful survivors broke through, General Rochambeau himself was forced to run for his life and the heroes of Crête à Pierrot passed through the wooded gullies and streams to join Dessalines in the hills.

La Croix was to write later: 'It was a remarkable feat . . . More than 12,000 of us surrounded that fort and yet he escaped us, leaving only his dead and his wounded.' In fact the 12,000 men had been reduced by 2000 during the siege, and on other fronts LeClerc had now lost 6000 men in battle and, more significantly, 8000 were now either in field hospital or were being shipped away because of sickness, a foretaste of what was to come. LeClerc himself was sapped of strength and wrote to Napoleon: 'My position worsens day by day, illness is removing my men thirty to fifty lost a day, 200–250 admitted to hospital.' The practice of loading the sick onto ships and taking them out to sea where the cooler air gave a fraction a chance of recovery was becoming a small, if only a small, solution.

The cultivators, who did not sicken, were growing in strength and continued Toussaint's relentless policy of burning the land, destroying the roads by digging pits, pushing rocks from the cliff-faces of the ravines as the French marched by or pulled their cannon below. Even the seemingly innocent women and children washing their clothes in the river beds would turn and, standing naked, would hurl the rounded river boulders like cannonballs at the soldiers attempting to pass. La Croix said, 'they sprang from the ground at Toussaint L'Ouverture's command, they were everywhere. His name was on all lips. It was only of him that they spoke.'

LeClerc was forced to write to Napoleon with optimism, presenting a good front, for he knew the First Consul, although he was his brother-in-law he was also his exacting master. He wrote that General Hardy 'will now have met and beaten General Toussaint' – his confidence was misplaced, but how else could he write? He mentions Toussaint's strong character and intelligence as a defence against any shortcomings he might be showing as Commander-in-Chief of Napoleon's army. Napoleon was not deceived. The First Consul was 'affected painfully' by the 'loss of so many brave men' and the wounding of no less than four (Debelle, Deveaux, Dugua and Boudet) of his most talented and respected generals.

The 'bandits' were proving themselves to be stronger and stronger, and the rains were beginning. LeClerc wrote, 'my troops are exhausted with fatigue and sickness.' LeClerc was also encountering, as Toussaint had done, the problems of dealing with the loyalties of the mulattoes who had accompanied the army from France to St Dominigue. Pétion had attacked Crête à Pierrot and fought with his usual bravery, but Rigaud seemed expendable to LeClerc, who recognized a troublemaker by instinct and report. He had him and his family arrested and deported to France. The mulattoes then melted away from the French army, and the whites continued to die. LeClerc's position by April was that he had only 11,000 white soldiers (many in poor health) remaining and that he was forced to rely on 9000 Negroes whom he did not trust.

LeClerc had been advised by his staff that it would be a wise move to send a small posse of men, perhaps six, secretly to seize Toussaint at his camp in the hills and so be rid of him. He suggested this plan to General Kerserveau who snorted with derision – saying of LeClerc's advisers 'they are cox-combs everywhere, six! I would not even attempt to take him with 600.'

Like a spider in a web Toussaint watched and waited, and then to the dismay of his own followers and the surprise of LeClerc, Toussaint made a bid for peace.

13   1802: Betrayal and Deportation

This move was a feint, simply a move on the chessboard of the game of war. The rainy season had come early and so the French were dying, just as the British had. Their forces had not proved as formidable as Toussaint had envisaged when he first sighted them from the hillside above Le Cap. In fact for all their successes throughout Europe and the Near East, Napoleon's great army had shown itself to be, in action in Dominigue, amazingly inept and naïve.

Toussaint's one major weakness as a general was that he abhorred any unnecessary loss of life, even that of his enemies. He now felt secure that the French threat had diminished and that victory was in sight, so why continue the bloodshed? It made sense to him because of his natural humanity to prevaricate for a time, to negotiate terms while the rains took their toll, and then, as he had done so successfully with the British, he would deliver the coup de grâce if it should still prove necessary.

Dessalines in the meantime continued to murder every white within sight so that 'the cries of the victims disturbed the night' while the priests tried to save the women and children and Dessalines' wife, herself, rescued those she could. It was just this situation which Toussaint was trying to prevent. He knew Dessalines, he suspected Christophe, he saw the ruthless cruelty of the French and he wanted to stop it all before it was too late. He was sickened by the suffering, by the destruction of the land, by the starving children. He wanted peace but also the guarantee of freedom.

He had not replied during this time to Napoleon's letter and now he used this as a pretext to get in touch with LeClerc. He sent a formal letter, which meant little, to Napoleon by two French officers who had been his prisoners, who took it to LeClerc.

LeClerc wrote to the Ministry of Marine that he suspected Toussaint wished to surrender. The negotiations were tortuous, and neither side, as was natural, trusted the other.

Toussaint's protestations of loyalty towards the Republic were rightly regarded by Napoleon as nonsense. But his letter does include one important truth which, when it was too late, was admitted by both

LeClerc and Napoleon; in it he said 'I have never been guided by ambition but only honour.' Both Napoleon and LeClerc, ambitious men themselves, were unable to comprehend this. Toussaint added that he was willing to take any steps in order to arrest the spread of the evil that had overcome his land.

LeClerc was now a desperate man, his whole reputation in France depended upon his emerging from St Dominigue with this reputation intact. He could not, he knew, make peace with Toussaint, he must conquer; Napoleon did not appreciate losers. So he was determined to succeed another way. He knew, quite rightly, that it was only too easy to split the fidelities of the leading Negro generals; many had joined his ranks and if he could entice Christophe and Dessalines to his side, Toussaint would have no bargaining point in any kind of treaty; abandoned by his generals and their armies, he would be helpless.

LeClerc set about the matter with energy. First he attempted to bribe Toussaint's nephew Belair to abandon his uncle and the cause, adding, of course, that the rewards would be well worth his while. Belair was not, like LeClerc, a venial man (he later died rather than betray his country). He read the letter and then handed it straight back to Toussaint. Through a mulatto emissary, Vilton, LeClerc then sent a communication of a similar nature to Christophe, which he read and then sent on to Toussaint. Christophe did not reply. General Hardy was then persuaded by LeClerc to get in touch with Christophe in person. But there was still loyalty among the generals to Toussaint; Christophe was an intelligent man, as was Belair, and they knew it was only a matter of time before they would crush the French, and they understood and supported Toussaint's policy.

LeClerc made another attempt; he wrote personally to Christophe suggesting that he would be even more greatly rewarded 'if he gave us the opportunity of securing the person of Toussaint L'Ouverture'. Christophe sent this letter also to Toussaint and replied to LeClerc that he 'was not capable of such perfidy . . . he is not only my chief but my friend.'

So Toussaint trusted Christophe as loyal to the cause of freedom and sent him to negotiate with LeClerc. He stated in his memoirs, 'I gave him my permission and he went.'

Toussaint was too trusting: Christophe performed a sudden and complete volte-face; he gave over the army under his command and swore loyalty to LeClerc; he handed over to France, 1200 men, the First, Third and Fifth Brigades, together with 100 cannon which Toussaint had concealed in the hills and 2000 white prisoners. In his treaty he also guaranteed to dismiss the cultivators within the army, who were likely to remain loyal to Toussaint, and he swore not to ill-treat the whites;

and on these terms he was granted the retention of his rank, all privileges and, of course, money. He was a traitor. Toussaint could not at first believe it, it was only when officers and soldiers came to his camp from Christophe's forces that he began to realize the truth. LeClerc wrote smugly to the Ministry of Marine that 'Christophe's submission has set Toussaint in consternation.' Toussaint wrote a mild letter to Christophe asking him to come and explain the position, and Christophe replied that he most certainly would, when he could find the time – but he never did find the time.

Christophe's treachery might be explained by his personal vaulting ambition; he achieved in later years many things for his country, but when he died he was a megalomaniacal tyrant (probably it was not his fault, but was the result of a syphilitic condition). He died by his own hand and his people – many of whom he treated even worse than they had been treated in slavery – rejoiced, taking their revenge upon him by killing his children.

His only explanation at the time for his behaviour was that he was 'tired of living like a bandit'. He obviously regretted the burning of his house in Le Cap. But he made up for this, by building in later years the grandest palace – Sans Souci – in the West Indies, where all the marble floors were cooled (in the Roman manner) with water from a diverted stream running beneath them. It possessed its own theatre and ornamental gardens which were laid out like those at Versailles. The pink stones of its walls are reputed to be stained with the blood of the thousands of Christophe's subjects who built it. Skilled artisans were imported from Europe and cabinet-makers, decorators, and artists from France, Italy and England contributed to its beauty. It is a ruin now, the bats nest in the corners of its great salons, but it is still beautiful.

Toussaint, who had been suffering from one of the periods of apathy and depression that beset him, suddenly threw it off. He announced that he would be prepared to meet LeClerc face to face at Nornets, near Le Cap.

He wrapped his yellow madras bandana round his head and put on his full dress uniform. His son Isaac was told to accompany him. His dragoons in their cuirasses and navy-blue hats rode beside him. He was not mounted on Bel Argent since, as he wrote in his memoirs to Napoleon, 'General Hardy passed through my properties with his armies which he has ravaged, and took all my animals, including a horse called Bel Argent which I valued above all else.' Suzanne and Jean Paul had also been surprised by General Hardy's soldiers and were forced to flee; Suzanne in the ensuing panic lost touch with Jean Paul and his tutor, and Jean Paul, who was a child of only seven, was taken prisoner by Hardy.

As he neared the town the people thronged round him and cheered him, but a group of whites and mulattoes jeered at him, but he was unmoved, he simply shrugged and said to the officer beside him, 'Men are so everywhere, once they were at my feet, these same men who are cursing me, but they will regret me some day.'

This meeting with LeClerc could never have been successful for either, but it was not helped by the fact that as Toussaint rode among the enthusiastic crowd he suddenly reigned in his horse and stopped. He saw Bel Argent being ridden by a Negro officer who had gone over to the French. He narrowed his eyes and showed one of his rare displays of pure rage, which made those accompanying him fearful. One of the men of LeClerc's staff who came to greet him was unfortunately that same General Hardy who had acquired Bel Argent. It was not an auspicious beginning to a meeting requiring delicate diplomacy. Toussaint rode grimly through the ruined streets, hardly acknowledging the crowd; his dragoons too were grim, though the crowds might cheer, for Toussaint and for them it was not a light-hearted occasion. It was noted by all that when Toussaint arrived at the temporary Government House (an old convent) his bodyguard drew their swords. They remained at attention with sabres drawn throughout the entire evening.

LeClerc came out to meet him, arms outstretched, but Toussaint did not step forward to be embraced.

'General,' LeClerc said, 'allow me to show my admiration for the way you have shouldered the responsibility of the government of San Dominigue...'

Toussaint maintained his mood of sternness and asked LeClerc why he had come bearing a sword to St Dominigue which was a peaceful country. LeClerc brushed this aside. 'Your presence here', he said, 'shows your generosity and your goodwill. Between us we will restore this island and make it blossom again.'

Toussaint, quite rightly, did not believe a word of LeClerc's flowery declaration. He attempted rather wearily to get down to the relevant business in hand.

This business concerned Dessalines. In the preliminary negotiations which the emissaries had brought, Dessalines had been the stumbling block; the fact that he had slaughtered so many white civilians as well as prisoners had not endeared him to LeClerc. However, Toussaint assured LeClerc that he could be trusted because, although he admittedly had faults, 'he understood military discipline'. Toussaint made a great misjudgement. Dessalines had for some time been going his own way in the field and off it, even disobeying Toussaint's military orders, for which he should have been warned, but he was not. So LeClerc and Toussaint agreed that Charles Belair, General Vernet and Dessalines were to be retained in the service of the army at St Dominigue, all of which meant, of course, nothing at all. Belair was later shot on LeClerc's personal orders.

The farce continued, LeClerc inviting Toussaint to eat with him and his officers. Toussaint's brother Paul L'Ouverture was present; perhaps Toussaint was unaware of the mix-up of his letters to him, or simply had become completely disenchanted but, as his brother came towards him, he said sharply 'Stop' and then before everyone present he said, 'Your surrender should only have come after mine,' and turned away from him. One of the generals present said, 'Each of us was eager to see so extraordinary a man.'

But the situation was awkward for all; the French officers attempted conversation with Toussaint who either simply looked at them in silence or grunted and made no reply. LeClerc produced an effect when little Jean-Paul suddenly appeared in the room, Toussaint was happy to see his son safe and for a moment relaxed but, remembering the circumstances of his capture, and remembering Bel Argent once more, he glared at General Hardy. An officer was foolish enough to say that he could not help but doubt his loyalty to the First Consul, adding as an aside which was quickly overheard by Toussaint 'one does not get flour out of a coal sack.' Toussaint replied, 'It is possible, General, but out of this sack may come a substance which dissolves bronze.'

Dinner was a sad affair. Toussaint sat on LeClerc's right but, perhaps because he suspected poison, he only picked up a piece of cheese which he nibbled. La Croix said 'he looked ill and did not even eat any soup'; he refused the wine and asked for a glass of water. He hardly spoke, but sat with his head tied up in his madras bandana, occasionally glancing at a man who had particularly offended him by his conduct. LeClerc perhaps with the lack of tact that embarrassment brings asked him, as one soldier to another, where he would have obtained sufficient supplies if the war had continued. Toussaint showed a brief moment of humour, smiled and said, 'Why, Capitaine General, I would have taken them from you!'

He left after that, he and his dragoons rode out of Le Cap, but there were few to see them go. They rode to Marmelade and the hearts of all were heavy. It had been agreed that his ninety dragoons were to be stationed in Le Cap under LeClerc's orders. His troops of crack grenadiers were to be sent to Plaisance.

Two days later at Marmelade Toussaint lined them up in front of him and spoke to them from horseback and thanked them, he spoke individually to the officers and then dismissed them; by then many of the men were weeping. Toussaint was so moved that he remained sitting his horse motionless until the last man was out of sight, and then he turned and cantered slowly towards the hills and the peace of Ennery. For the first time for many years he was completely alone and without escort as he rode quietly along the shaded country paths, and there was no reason any longer for him to hurry.

The people saw him ride past them scarcely acknowledging them, but outside his plantation house at Ennery a large crowd had gathered; one man ran up to him and seized the bridle of his horse, saying imploringly, 'Papa, Papa Toussaint, Papa have you abandoned us?' This stirred Toussaint to life again and he said, 'Non, mes enfants, your brothers are armed and all the officers are at their posts.' He then rode through the gates to Ennery; when he was there he sat on the gallery, gazing over the hills, but his eyes were blinded by his thoughts. The next day at dawn he was up, working before the men had even emerged and wearing an old straw hat and faded clothes, the Toussaint of ten years before. In the evening he sat with the labourers under the silk-cotton tree talking to them as equals. He made energetic plans for the development of his plantations and spent his days as the overseer, not of a nation, but of a property. He seemed content but, of course, he was still waiting.

The first hint of aggression towards him did not take long to manifest itself. LeClerc sent 500 white officers up to the small garrison at Ennery which was near his estate, as an open gesture of menace. He complained to LeClerc but his complaint was ignored.

Perhaps now he recognized the fact that he was to be made the sacrifice, he was to be 'the scapegoat without horns', and knowing this to be so he rested immobile.

It was Dessalines who became the final instrument of the French against him, Dessalines who was only too willing to turn against his brother. Dessalines became LeClerc's lackey; he had been ruthless in murdering whites, something which Toussaint had chastised him for; now he became equally ruthless in murdering blacks, the cultivators, the guerillas, anyone who was for Toussaint, were mown down by Dessalines in his new role as a lieutenant of LeClerc. In the Haiti of today, Dessalines is regarded, even reverenced, as the greatest of all national heroes, but he was, in fact, rather a trumpery character. He used menace to promote himself, which is a successful weapon in war, but he used it in time of peace and he was assassinated by his own men not very long after he had betrayed Toussaint.

LeClerc wrote to Napoleon that Dessalines was not only bearing tales against Toussaint but against Christophe. One of the saddest facts about revolution is that the leaders so often betray each other. The slave rebellions throughout the West Indies would frequently have succeeded but for the fact that the leaders were so contentious with each other. LeClerc wrote to the Ministry of Marine of the 'reports that have reached me from all the generals – even from General Dessalines'.

If only Christophe and Dessalines had supported Toussaint, LeClerc could have been completely vanquished, as the British had been, without the loss of life which subsequently followed.

Toussaint's quiet life at Ennery was disturbed by the news that his troops, including the dragoons, were deserting the French to whom they had been assigned in name and were flocking to him and camping within his plantation. When he rode through his land he found more and more of his people squatting there and asking for his help, guidance and reassurance. LeClerc accused Toussaint of trying to rebuild a new guerilla force. Toussaint most likely found the hundreds of people now living on his land an irritation rather than a comfort and he wrote back to LeClerc, protesting in this vein and stating that he might even be forced to move from Ennery.

LeClerc became nervous as to where he might move. He wrote to Napoleon: 'I informed you in one of my last despatches of the pardon I had been induced to grant to General Toussaint. This ambitious man from the moment of his pardon did not cease to plot in secret, though he surrendered it was because Generals Christophe and Dessalines clearly saw he had deceived them and that they were determined to continue the war no longer . . .' Poor LeClerc was duped. Christophe and Dessalines were as determined to continue the war as Toussaint, to continue it, in fact, until there was not one living Frenchman on the island.

Toussaint wrote a letter which seems harmless but which was later produced as proof of his treachery; he wrote to an agent of his – Fontaine – on 27 May: 'It is said that General LeClerc is in ill health in Tortuga, of this you will inform me, if you see the General be sure to tell him that the cultivators are no longer disposed to obey me . . . I have to ask you whether anyone near the person of the General in Chief can be gained to procure the release of D . . . who would be very useful to me from his influence at La Nouvelle and elsewhere. Acquaint Gengembre that he should quit the Borgne where the cultivators should *not to be set to work.*'

Clearly these are secret and rather incomprehensible instructions, possibly even a form of code. This letter fell into the hands of LeClerc, and gave him yet another reason to mistrust Toussaint. LeClerc made up his mind to dispose of him, using others to accomplish his purpose. He was forced to make a concrete move of some kind and he wrote to Napoleon: 'I have now 3600 men in hospital', adding, 'I need 25,000

Europeans under arms' and pleading for reinforcements. He also said that his decision to arrest Toussaint 'is necessary because I must show some form of strength'. LeClerc is to be pitied rather than despised for inhumanity, his own health was, as he wrote, 'unsteady', but he had a cold mind. When General Hardy who had been a good work-horse for him died he merely wrote him off as a 'mediocre general' whom he would not miss, and added that the only problem was he did not know what to do with his children. It is astonishing that generals travelled with their young children accompanying them on their campaigns, but it is true.

LeClerc used General Brunet as the decoy to ensnare Toussaint. Brunet wrote to him asking if they could meet; 'We have, dear Citizen General, to discuss matters of which I cannot write, but which can be settled within an hour of meeting. If I were not so exhausted by my labours and trivial matters, I would have come to see you, this day; but since I cannot find it possible to leave, will you come and see me?' He added 'If you have recovered from your indisposition', so it appears that Toussaint's health had begun to fail, a fact which may well have influenced his indecisiveness and the weariness of his eventual decisions.

Brunet continued with treacherous falsity, 'You will not find in my house all the comforts I would wish to put at your disposal' – he had, indeed, lost fifteen of his household from yellow fever – 'but you will meet a frank and honest man.' He asks that Madame Toussaint 'whose acquaintance I am anxious to make' should accompany Toussaint and ended by saying that Toussaint will never find a friend sincerer than himself.

Toussaint should not, indeed cannot, have believed this nonsense. Warnings had come to him, Paul L'Ouverture had smuggled through a message to him, his own secret agents must have warned him and yet he went. He wrote later: 'I was instructed that an aide-de-camp of General LeClerc, passing through Ennery, said he carried an order to have me arrested which was addressed to General Brunet. General LeClerc had given me his word of honour and promised the protection of the government, so I refused to believe this.'

He rode to Brunet's headquarters and arrived at about eight o'clock in the evening. Brunet welcomed him effusively and they talked quietly for a few minutes, then Brunet asked to be excused for a moment and went out of the room. Immediately ten officers entered the work cabinet where Toussaint was sitting; they carried drawn swords and some had pistols in their hands. Toussaint believed that they had come to assassinate him and with catlike grace he leapt to his feet, his sabre ready. Ferrari, Brunet's aide-de-camp, lowered his own sword and said, 'General, we have not come to lay violent hands upon you, we have only the order to secure your person.' Toussaint looked at them all and then quite quietly dropped his sword and sheathed it. He said, 'I shall not resist the power you have obtained over me, but my wife is feeble and my children can do no harm, suffer them then to remain at home.' He seemed calm and when they bound him did not even struggle.

Still bound, strangely meek and withdrawn, he was pushed by the French soldiers into a carriage. He asked Ferrari quietly if he could be untrussed: 'You must understand,' he said, 'that I feel this is an unnecessary indignity.' His protest was ignored. It was midnight as they set off; Ferrari sat opposite to him in the dark of the carriage which lumbered over the uneven roads towards Gonaîves with its escort of dragoons. Along the route his people slept; perhaps they stirred as they heard the clop of horses' hooves, the creaking springs and the iron wheels of the carriage, perhaps some who were late to bed noticed the bands of soldiers stationed in the shadows of the trees, or closely guarding the cross roads; and when the small party entered the town and drove down to the harbour, they may sleepily have heard the echoes of muffled orders sounding back from the walls in the quiet of the night before they turned over and slept again. It would not have entered their heads that in the carriage that passed sat Toussaint L'Ouverture, their leader, their inspiration for the future, bound up like a chicken for market, helpless and a prisoner.

On the deck at Gonaîves in the dawn at 'day clean' he was dragged, stiff and weary, from the coach, frog-marched by two soldiers down the slippery green-fringed steps of the quay into a waiting pirogue and rowed across the water, which the early sun turned into patterns of yellow amongst the blue, towards the French warship *Creole*; then he knew that there was to be no return. He offered no resistance as he was forced up the ladder. Once on board the quarter-deck he was greeted with courtesy by the Captain. Fighting men of stature have respect for one another, and he was immediately unbound and offered some loose silver and a change of linen. The Captain, under strict orders, could offer him little else, but as one man to another at least he made an attempt to restore his prisoner's self-respect. Fear and despair make a man sweat and the simple offer of clean clothes and fresh water can be a benison that once again brings hope.

Once Toussaint was aboard the ship immediately set sail northwards for Le Cap. Out in the roads, Toussaint was transferred to a frigate, the *Héros*, where he was taken to a small cabin with a sentry placed at the door.

Toussaint asked for writing paper, but he never wrote anything, but simply sat for hours staring at the blank white page, quill in hand, frustrated by the limitations of his French. He could not, without the aid of a secretary, give expression to the outrage and the passion against injustice which he felt. What he had to say, so that not only his own people but the world would know the truth, must be put down with the style and the eloquence of the leader of a nation; for this his Creole patois was inadequate, and he knew he would be open to ridicule in the assemblies of Paris, the Parliament of London if he spoke in the language of the slave.

He wound his watch, the hours passed slowly, he gazed out of the porthole at the waterfront of Le Cap, so near, but now never further away. He saw his people going about their everyday business, shouting jocular abuse to each other as they hauled the hempen sacks of the produce which he had exhorted them to grow. Behind the town there rose the familiar contours of the hills he had climbed and ridden as a boy, their peaks swathed with shifting grey clouds. As the ship turned with the tide, creaking on the anchor chain, he saw the curving coral coves where once he had swum, throwing himself, flat-bellied, on water so clear that when he opened his eyes he could see his own feet behind him, little bubbles threading between his toes.

He saw as he stared out of the small brass-rimmed porthole the schooners pass on their way to the other islands and to the Americas, their patched sails billowing out as they caught the wind. The sailors on board, glad to breathe the salt air after a week in port with too much rum and too many quickly taken and forgotten women, never noticed the face of an old black man with grizzled hair looking out at them from the side of the ship framed like a miniature in the porthole, an old man with intense, dark eyes except for the sky-blue rim of age surrounding the pupils.

The ship was moored for several days during which time the Captain paid Toussaint several visits which were mutually awkward. Toussaint asked only for news of his family, otherwise he remained silent. At dusk one evening a boat rowed out towards the *Héros*. Toussaint's family were on board. He saw his wife's tranquil face crumpled now but trying to control her fear and apprehension, trying to behave as he would wish her to, braving everything in the hope that soon she might see him again and feel his arms around her. He saw his two sons with their veneer of French sophistication, wearing the high collars and velvet coats of Paris, determined to retain their pride, his nephew Bernard Chancy with the bearing of a soldier, his two nieces Louise Chancy and Victorine Thuzac tearful and bewildered, his valet Mars Plaisir, his wife's maid Justine and his youngest boy Jean-Paul looking around him with bright, interested eyes, still young enough to believe that almost anything is an adventure.

His family boarded the *Héros* but on LeClerc's and Brunet's orders they were not permitted to see Toussaint, and only Mars Plaisir was allowed access to him.

General Séverin who was responsible for the complete body of prisoners presented himself to Toussaint who rose as he entered the cabin, and after the usual stiff formalities Toussaint said quietly and without passion in his soft slurred Creole: 'In overthrowing me you have cut down in Saint Dominigue only the trunk of the tree of liberty, it will spring up again from the roots, for they are many and they are deep.' The words were prophetic, they were not said merely to give himself hope and reassurance, or as a gesture to posterity; Toussaint knew this to be the simple truth.

The news of Toussaint's arrest and seizure emerged slowly, seeping out through the indiscretion of a soldier, or an officer in his cups; then the drums passed the news into the heights of the mountains, the traveller on horseback, the boys on mules, shouted it out as they passed through the villages, and a stunned population came to the realization that this was not just a rumour but was reality. Bewildered, leaderless, they did not know what action to take next or who they could turn to.

LeClerc played upon this confusion believing he had managed a devious piece of strategy with success. As far as he could ascertain the black generals' reaction remained docile, even anxiously compliant. On 11 June he wrote to the Minister of Marine Affairs 'in any case they detest each other and are well aware that I could destroy them, each one with the aid of the others.' Of the troops he was less sure, but he added 'blacks are not brave and now they are scared,' an over-confident refutation of former opinions and statements made by him. He was taking no chances, however, and he wrote to the First Consul: 'After the deportation of Toussaint a few men attempted to make trouble but I have had the ring leaders deported or shot.' He added that he had had one of Toussaint's mistresses arrested 'who came here for the purpose of assassinating me'. LeClerc loaded fifty rebel black leaders onto a frigate with orders to leave them in Corsica. 'I have written to Citizen Miot to employ them in public works. I will make plans for the immediate departure of twenty rogues, loyal to Toussaint, for Cayenne.'

Deliberately and cold-bloodedly he removed members of Toussaint's family who he felt, because of their association with the leader, might have an emotionally disturbing influence upon the populace. He ordered Toussaint's nephew and much-loved friend Charles Belair to be arrested and shot without a trial. LeClerc who was considered to be such an honourable soldier, such a flower of France, also ordered Belair's young wife to be shot beside him. As they faced the firing squad, she tore the bandage from her eyes and, turning to her husband, said 'Come, mon ami, let us die bravely.'

Pauline LeClerc held her nightly soirées in her house on the edge of the sea at Le Cap, the French musicians played the latest airs from Paris and as she danced her gowns were much admired, but her behaviour was considered less admirable; she was such a flagrant flirt that even the most decadent of St Dominigue's old colonial society were amazed and an American visitor was virtuously shocked to find an aide of LeClerc's stroking Madame's feet and legs as she reclined on her chaise during the long hot afternoons. Pauline LeClerc found time to send 'cargoes of Parisian fashions' to Lady Nugent, the Governor of Jamaica's wife who was delighted to be 'altogether looking like a Sultana'. Lady Nugent, who was a sincere follower of Wilberforce, however, had believed that Toussaint 'must be a wonderful man and I really do believe intended for very good purposes'. Dresses of 'spangled silver' however, are very difficult to withstand whatever one's principles and Lady Nugent in return sent a carved and painted wooden horse to Dermide LeClerc for his nursery.

In fact, whilst Pauline danced away the cool night hours, her husband was dying and he was aware of it; he wrote to his wife's brother Napoleon 'a man cannot work hard here without risking his life and it is quite impossible for me to remain here for more than six months . . . my health is so wretched that I would consider myself lucky if I could last for that time!' Of his troops he added 'the mortality continues and makes fearful ravages.' In a few months 14,000 men died of yellow fever, including fifteen general officers, and LeClerc was left with only 5000 effective men.

He had become a desperate man, he knew that yellow fever was not only killing him but four-fifths of his army as well. He suspected that Toussaint had known this only too well and had simply been biding his time before making a well-premeditated attack. In order to justify the arrest of Toussaint and to turn his suspicions into concrete fact, he contrived two very clumsily forged documents which were offered as evidence both in St Dominigue and in Europe. These documents attempted to show proof that Toussaint had been engaged with other black generals and officers to overthrow LeClerc and the administration as soon as yellow fever had weakened the French army sufficiently. Toussaint was later to deny this with passion: 'This is an atrocious and abominable lie, a dastardly action on his part.' The documents were most certainly forged but Toussaint's intentions must have been exactly as LeClerc supposed and feared. How could it have been otherwise, for it would have been impossible for him to have sat by and seen his people delivered back into the slavery which he knew to be Napoleon's intention.

Toussaint on board the *Héros* knew nothing of the reaction of his people, or the fate of his friends, although he must have feared for all, and he was sadly aware of the growing treachery of some of his colleagues and he mistrusted the machinations of LeClerc, but he was helpless and ignorant, simply passing his days floating on the calm water.

On 15 June the *Héros* sailed for Brest across an ocean Toussaint had never sailed before, towards France which once he had called his fatherland, a land he had never seen.

He was still not permitted, for the entire journey, to see his family though Mars Plaisir continued to attend to his needs. Toussaint wrote: 'I was subjected to a crossing of thirty days, during which I suffered not only great fatigue, but also was witness to the most unpleasant annoyances, such as it is impossible to imagine unless one had experienced them.'

When on July 9 the *Héros* moored in quarantine waters south of Brest, Placide was allowed to visit his father and to act as his secretary, and Toussaint was able, at last, to put down on paper some of the anguish which he had felt while cooped up in his cabin. He dictated a letter to the Ministry of Marine, protesting against the illegality of his arrest, but more particularly against the arrest of his wife and family: 'My wife has no responsibility to account for; I alone am responsible.' He also pleaded on behalf of any of his staff whom he feared might have been arrested: 'Anything they might have done was done at my orders, there can be no possible justification for their arrest.'

From Placide he must have heard of the humiliation which his wife and niece were subjected to when they were captured, how they were searched by the French soldiers, although obviously they were concealing nothing, how their jewellery was wrenched from them and how his young and pretty niece's bodice was ripped apart by the soldiers who molested her and jeered at her tears and her shame. He heard how his house was ransacked and his silver and valuables looted. But the humiliation of his family pierced Toussaint more deeply than anything which he had himself endured. He could not comfort them, only send word back by Placide that they must hold their heads high and show the hostile world around them that they were his, that they were Aradas people, the descendants of kings and the kin of a ruler of a nation. He told them to trust in God, but on board the *Héros*, cramped in a small cabin, with an unknown future lying ahead the white God must have seemed very far away and uncaring to a black family from St Dominigue.

When the ship docked, as Toussaint was to write later: 'My children were taken to a destination unknown to me, and my wife to another of which I was also kept ignorant.'

Madame L'Ouverture, together with Isaac, Jean and her niece, was escorted to Bayonne, then kept there as prisoner under surveillance. Because of his age and greater potential danger Placide was placed in the prison of the small fortress of Belle Isle with its unscaleable, towering cliffs. Bernard Chancy was put in prison at the naval headquarters at Toulon. Toussaint was detained in Brest at the fort until arrangements were completed for his transfer. He was allowed to join his family for the first time in weeks for a few moments on the dock at Brest before they were separated again. Still under guard he walked towards them, with the ground heaving under his feet after so many days at sea, but he was composed as he embraced them all, formally kissing them on each cheek and trying to transfer his strength to them. It is recorded that the sailors on board wept as they saw this pathetic public farewell, without even the privilege of privacy allowed for the family's grief. As he turned and left them, he was immediately hustled into a large coach with outriders, only his valet Mars Plaisir being allowed to accompany him. As he passed through the town towards the fort, it is unlikely that he even noticed the tall grey houses, the windows of glass, the chimney pots; all must have appeared to him nothing but a chimera. Grief removes observation except for the smallest details that are close and familiar: the nails of one's hand, a small stain on one's clothing. It removes physical pain too, only making one's body stiff and clumsy and one's eyes heavy and unseeing. Grief is mercifully its own drug.

He was told after a few days in the fort that he was to be transferred from Brest; if he was then informed of his destination it would have meant nothing to him. He was taken from the fort in a large berlin which was followed by a chaise, the coach drawn by four horses with two postillion leaders and an escort of horse artillery. The route was a closely guarded secret; the prefects of all départements and the military commanders of all garrisons were alerted to be on the look-out for any gatherings of horsemen along the way. The precautions taken seem exaggerated, for how many followers had Toussaint in France to come to his aid? How many ex-slaves to lend him their support? Ideologically a few Jacobins and a few abolitionists may have deplored his treatment, but they were not prepared to do anything positive to save him. As the jolting unsprung coach hurried along the route with its detachment of guarding soldiers, avoiding all the major towns, Toussaint must have been wryly aware that in the eyes of the First Consul he had once possessed some importance, even if he did not now.

Through the half-drawn blinds he snatched glimpses of an unknown world, saw gangs of white men and women working in the fields, saw them cutting the alien golden wheat and whiskered barley with their long scythes instead of chopping cane with the familiar machete. As he travelled on he saw in the distance the towers of Orléans cathedral and perhaps he thought of another who, although only a woman, had fought and died for being true to what she believed. He saw the grapes coming to harvest in Burgundy, the same vines from which, so many thousands of miles away, he had once, not so long ago, drunk the wine. He saw Dijon with its cathedral of chequered roofs, the canals with pollarded trees forming geometric patterns, and free men fishing for trout in the streams by Moulins des Ruarts. The women he passed with their roughened hands and their gingham sunbonnets, the crouched men with their strange wooden shoes and wine-traced cheeks were, like him, French; but no friend greeted him as the coach lumbered on, the dust from its wheels coating the hedges. He had believed once that he was a part of these people, a part of France; and here, just as in his own country, the lowest peasants had rebelled, had freed themselves from oppression and he saw that there they were still free. So why should his people, because they were black, return to slavery? Laveaux, his mentor, had convinced him that liberty and equality were for all men, that 'Liberté, Egalité' was more than just a phrase, a slogan created by scheming politicians or an idealist's dream. As he sat, a prisoner, in the stale heat of the coach, the contrast between Napoleon's intentions for the white people of France and his intentions for the people of St Dominigue must have seemed painfully clear to Toussaint. Only once during the long journey did he receive any human recognition; the coach passed through a small garrison town whose regiment had once been stationed in St Dominigue, and a party of officers who had been alerted of his passage through the area surrounded the coach and, opening the door, clasped Toussaint by the hand and embraced him, wishing to pay their respects to an old and brave soldier.

At last came the final stage of the journey, then the coach drew into Besançon, there was no further to go; Switzerland, the Jura mountains rose behind the town. Toussaint, who had studied so painstakingly the history of Caesar's battles may have been wearily aware that it was here that the great general, whom he so much admired, drove off the Leonari fifty-eight years before the birth of Christ. The coach and its party drove over the ancient bridge that spans the River Doubs, through the cobbled medieval town with its arches of stone, and up the steep climb to the citadel of Vaubun.

He was allowed to rest for a while and then was taken once more to the coach and driven up the winding road that hangs perilously over great gorges, leading through, to him, strange pine forests, and almost ends in the walled town of Pontarlier; almost, but not quite, for there is a further stop – the last – and if you ever took that road you would know it.

14   1802-3: Imprisonment and Death

'He should be enclosed in a fortress in the centre of France, so that he will never have the opportunity to escape and return to St. Domingo where his influence is that of a religious leader. If this man were to return he could still undo all that has been accomplished. You cannot keep him far enough from the sea or in too secure a prison, this man has so inflamed the country that only his presence would be sufficient to rekindle it again.' LeClerc's letter to Napoleon was duly and competently acted upon. The First Consul showed his customary efficiency and instructions were issued to the Ministries of War and Marine and the selection of a suitable fortress was made.

Three thousand feet up in the Jura mountains stands the Fort de Joux. Built at the time of the Crusades, it pinnacles a sheer rocky summit 500 feet high, looking down upon the mountains and the clouds drifting like smoke below it. Eight months of the year the snow softens its harsh outlines, seeping as ice water through the cracks and fissures of its massive stone walls. The walls are twelve feet thick, and even in the four months of summer the cold never leaves the fort's narrow passages. In its grim, dark interior centuries of accumulated misery remain, chilled, fresh, preserved for ever. The fort was a cleverly cruel choice in which to imprison a man of the sun, a man who had never before known cold, had only heard of snow as an unconvincing traveller's tale, had never in his life seen his own breath caught and suspended before him, floating on icy air.

At two o'clock in the morning on 25 August 1802 the berlin carriage with its mounted escort of troopers of the Second Chasseurs clattered onto the pavé of the outer courtyard.

The utmost secrecy and precautions were taken in case of a last-minute bid by Toussaint's supporters to snatch him to liberty, which accounts for his wait in the jail in Besançon, during the daylight hours. It was planned that he should arrive in the early hours of the morning. Toussaint and Mars Plaisir stepped from the carriage, a gendarme and an officer to each side, and Toussaint saw as he glanced above him the monolithic outline of his prison against the cold night sky. Under the lanthorns he confronted his jailers. Toussaint was familiar with the military ceremonial, the ranks, the marching and the shouted command, but now he was a prisoner under guard. His uniform, a French general's, was still the one that he had worn when captured at his home so many thousands of miles away, had worn in the small, cramped cabin of the *Héros* as he crossed the Atlantic, and in it he had travelled the dusty roads of France. It must have been crumpled and stained, and his linen soiled. The brave blue coat with its lavish gold lace and heavy epaulettes, and the flamboyance of the colonial cut, must have seemed garish and out of place to the men he now confronted, under the flickering lights. To them he was not one of the great generals of the French Republic, but a mameluke in creased and fancy clothes, an elderly, tired black man with grey wool hair thinly plaited under his large round hat. The Antilles, his Governmental Palace, his bodyguard of men, were far away.

Wrest any man from his home environment and he will appear at a loss, even ridiculous. If you are black, the clothes that you wear, the cock of the hat, the heel of the shoe proclaim you the man. Deprive him of these attributes and you go a long way towards undoing him as a man. Toussaint's dignity was humbled, at the moment when he needed it most, because he himself was in a dishevelled state.

Baillé, the commandant of the fort, appears to have been a very ordinary man, an old soldier, who as Toussaint's jailer was simply doing his duty and following the orders from the First Consul and the Minister of the Marine. The importance of keeping his prisoner under constant vigilance had been impressed upon him as two of his former prisoners had managed to escape. A repetition would have meant the end of his career. Basically a kind man, he was a reluctant jailer and showed, from the outset, a brusque consideration for his charge.

Baillé and an officer marched Toussaint up the sloping stoop through the heavy medieval doors. How strange, how old and worn everything around him must have seemed in the shadowed light to a man from a land where everything in the sunshine is new, where the past could still be measured in years, not countless centuries.

Toussaint appeared 'calm, quiet and resigned' according to Baillé as he was taken through the narrow passages that led to his cell, passages where hundreds of years of seeping water had arrowed the walls with chevrons of green slime, where his boots splashed through stagnant puddles and his spurs left echoes in the dark.

When the officer unlocked the door of his cell and stood aside for him to enter, Toussaint seemed aware for the first time that he was trapped; he turned, teeth bared, and then was calm again.

The cell was nine metres long by four metres wide with a low, slightly domed roof, a replica of the interior of a West Indian mausoleum. Tombs, that to this day crowd the burial grounds throughout the islands and stand on the sea shores right to the water's edge. A large window had been bricked up, leaving only a narrow slotted square high up on the wall. The cell contained by order of the Ministry of Marine 'a bed, two wooden chairs, a small table and a commode'. There was an open fireplace but the walls were shiny with damp.

Inside the cell Toussaint was immediately ordered to take off his clothes. The orders were exact and explicit. All signs of former rank were to be removed. Napoleon's revenge upon 'this gilded African' was meticulous. His promise that 'he would not leave an epaulette on a single black in the colony' was first carried out upon the greatest of all the blacks of St Dominigue. It was a small cruelty but a skilled one in the process of humiliating one's fellow man. 'Give him warm clothing, grey or black, large and commodious and a round hat that will be his covering. Let him remember his crimes when he was a general, his hideous and tyrannical conduct towards Europeans. He merits only deepest contempt for his ridiculous arrogance.' In fact these precise orders were not carried out by Baillé. Toussaint was handed a private soldier's worn uniform and half-worn shoes. 'I have received,' he wrote later to Napoleon, 'the old worn clothes of an enlisted man and shoes in the same condition, was it necessary to add this humiliation to my misfortunes?'

He was not to be addressed by any rank or prefix, simply as Toussaint. His food, prepared under contract by a blanchisseuse in Pontarlier, was to be soup, salt meat and a biscuit with a glass of wine. It was to be handed into his cell once a day at nine o'clock in the morning. He was never to be allowed to leave his cell, even for exercise. Baillé permitted him, against orders, to keep his watch, some personal letters, a few coins and, as one soldier's gesture to another, his spurs.

Mars Plaisir was put in a separate cell next to Toussaint; the walls were thick but Toussaint must have felt a thin thread of comfort as the door was shut and barred, at least there was one familiar dark face left to him. But the comfort was short-lived for, by Napoleon's personal orders, Mars Plaisir, Toussaint's faithful mulatto servant and friend, was dismissed after four months. A servant for the General was considered an unnecessary luxury.

Mars Plaisir wrote to Isaac, Toussaint's son, on 3 October 1803 from Paris:

Monsieur,
    When we left the vessel at Brest they took us by carriage to Moray escorted by two companies of cavalry with an adjutant, where we

stayed one day. The constituted authorities came and paid us the homage due to your father and I was treated as his aide-de-camp for the moment, but that did not last long. They thus made us traverse a large part of France and they rendered us the same honours as far as the Jura fort. I stayed there with him for about four months and to enter into another room one had to pass three bolts. On going in there I thought I was entering a cave. We saw no one and the doors were only opened at meal-times. I played games to drive away your father's worries, but sometimes when he saw that after doing everything to bolster up my courage I was about to lose it, he revived me in turn. I, seeing the greatness of his spirit, threw myself on his neck and kissed him. Then, often, his tenderness for me made him say these flattering things: 'My wife, Isaac, Placide, Saint Jean and Plaisir, these are my four children', and in our captivity we did not cease to talk to each other nor to shed tears deprived of seeing you.

At the end of about four months in spite of the sufferings caused me by my captivity with your father, the day that they came to tell me that they were separating me from him, saying to him: 'General, I am ordered by the government to withdraw your servant', they hardly gave me the time to embrace him and for him to say to me: 'Do the same to Isaac and all your brothers'. In short, our cruel and hasty separation was for us a bolt from the blue. Then they put me in chains to lead me on foot and so on to Nantes and without a penny in my pocket, it being then prison and in secret while awaiting an opportunity to have me taken to San Domingo. They maintained to me that your father had a treasure to hide there, that he could only have me there who knew it and that I must point out the place where it was, and as I knew that it was not so, only that it was not me even out of fear of pain.

Note – Toussaint must see no one and can under no pretext leave the room where he is shut up.

Autumn came, the weather grew colder, the wood for his small fire was strictly rationed. Toussaint was always cold, day and night. Used to the glaring sun of St Dominigue whose heat makes the great plains shimmer with a dancing haze and where even on the high mountains it is always stickily warm, he suffered in this new, strange climate almost unbearably. He was, it was reported by his jailers, constantly trembling with cold. On 5 October 1802, Baillé reported to the Sous-Prefet at Pontarlier that 'for the last twelve days the prisoner has continually asked to be given a hat against the cold, he has continual headaches caused by the effect of a wound received from a musket-ball in the head. He wants to put a hat over the large kerchief that he wraps it in. He also asked for six of these kerchiefs in Madras or Bayonne.'

This was not a frivolous request; to the West Indian a head covering is a necessary protection against cold and damp, and Napoleon should have been humane enough to realize this, to remember Josephine in her bed and his teasing delight in her bandana. Toussaint found them necessary not only for comfort but for survival. He had not yet realized that no one intended him to survive. When he was provided, at last, with only four, not six as he had requested, he became childishly pettish. It was understandable, he lived in a prescribed area of frustrating, stultifying detail, the small square of light high on the wall that showed the sky, a passing cloud, his only freedom. The incessant, unrelenting cold, the soul-destroying ennui, the complete lack of exercise for a physical man, for the 'Centaur of the Savannahs', eroded both his body and his spirit.

His moods alternated between brief periods of strength of mind and hope, and despair; hope as when he asked Baillé to provide him with writing paper – Baillé was also indulgent enough to lend him his own secretary so that he might write to the First Consul to make an appeal for clemency, make a statement of self-justification, and demand justice in the name of the Republic in which, in spite of all, he continued to believe.

On his good days he felt it possible to pierce through the walls of his jail and to reach the implacable ear of Napoleon. He wrote a memorandum of his actions, his 'memoirs', dictating it to the secretary Jainnin, for Toussaint did not wish to write to Napoleon in Creole. His first letter stated his cause emotionally.

Citizen First Consul,

I will not deceive you of my faults. I have had some. What man is exempt? What man is blameless? Yes, I am quite ready to confess them. Following the word of honour of the Captain General representing the French government, after a proclamation in which he promised to throw a veil of forgetfulness on the events which took place in San Domingo, when you created the 18th 'brumaire' (month), I retired to the bosom of my family. Barely a month passed before some malicious people decided to call me to the mind of the Commander-in-Chief. I received from him a letter which ordered me to unite with General Brunet. I obeyed. He had me arrested. The next day, my house was looted. My wife and my children were arrested. They have nothing, not even clothing. Citizen First Consul, a mother of a family aged 53 years should merit the indulgence and goodwill of a generous and liberal nation. She has no countermand. I, alone, should be responsible for my conduct to my government. I have too high an ideal of the greatness and justice of the first magistrate of the French people to doubt for one moment his impartiality. I like to think that the balance in his hand will not move more to one side than to the other the appeal to his generosity.

Farewell and Respects,
Toussaint L'Ouverture.

Then he started on his memorandum, a statement of what he had achieved for the island of St Dominigue. It is also a plea for justice. 'It is my duty to put before the government of France an extra account of my conduct. I will relate the facts with true simplicity, the frankness of a former soldier. Adding to them my own comments as I progress. In fact, I shall tell the truth even if it is to my own disadvantage.'

What is the truth? Toussaint told it as he saw it. Napoleon under similar circumstances, the same humiliating duress, also believed he told it in his memoirs, but both their truths were different in history.

He pleaded for his family. 'My wife and my children were seized without respect for their station, their sex, without humanity or charity. They have done nothing, they are blameless, they must be returned.'

He could not comprehend that he would not find justice from Napoleon from the Republic. 'I had hoped that I would be brought before a tribunal to give an account of my conduct and by my peers to be judged, instead of which I have been brought to a fort on the very frontier of the Republic and locked up in a frightful dungeon. It would appear that from within this dungeon, is my only recourse to justice from the magnanimity of the First Consul, who is too generous and too great a leader to let an old soldier who is covered in wounds from the service to his fatherland die in a prison, without even giving him the opportunity to be vindicated and to pronounce upon his own destiny.

'I demand again to stand trial before a tribunal or court martial at which should be included General LeClerc and to be judged after all the facts are known.

'Reason, equity and the law of this country assuredly cannot refuse me this right.'

Finally, from a depth of bitter knowledge, he wrote what in his heart he knew to be true: 'Without doubt, I have received this treatment because of my colour. But my colour did not prevent me from serving my country faithfully and zealously. What has the colour of my skin to do with my honour or my valour?'

Then there were the days of increasing despair, of more than despair – acedia – when he wrote nothing, did nothing, when the unremembered but atavistic fatalism of his forefathers possessed him: Africa, where a man with no hope can turn his face to the wall and will himself into disease and death. Long days with no occupation but adding a careful log of wood to the fire, eating his meagre meal, winding his watch, studying his calloused horseman's hands as they pleated his coarse borrowed breetches. Sometimes, his jailers observed, he would sit immobile for hours, simply gazing up at the little space of sky high on the wall.

Once a day he saw Baillé, whom he would detain for as long as possible with fractious complaints: 'Every day the prisoner makes new demands.' Baillé became increasingly alarmed at the deterioration in his prisoner's health, by his headaches, upset stomach, painful rheumatism, and constant cough. He tried to encourage him and humour him, by giving Toussaint little gifts of extra sugar. Toussaint seems to have possessed the universal sweet tooth of the black man.

There was no word from Napoleon. Toussaint resorted to cunning, informing the First Consul that he had something of importance to reveal to him and Napoleon rose to the bait. This is not surprising; there were several things he hoped Toussaint might be persuaded to reveal, among them, certainly, details of the convention between Maitland and Toussaint. For his ambitions in the new world to be successful, Napoleon needed to be forearmed against any British schemes. It could also be an opportunity to disclose an act of treachery on Toussaint's part.

Napoleon was obsessed by the rumours of Toussaint's vast store of hidden treasure, a baseless story popular in St Dominigue at the time but one which Napoleon evidently believed. He was also interested to know how much money Toussaint had sent abroad to supposed accounts in Jamaica and America.

The invasion of St Dominigue was proving not only a military disaster but politically embarrassing, and so it was politically expedient to prove Toussaint's disloyalty, not only to France but to the Colony, to stress that he intended to make St Dominigue independent. If Napoleon could do this it would discredit Toussaint with the planters – powerful lobbyists in France – of whom Josephine was a vociferous member. They were becoming increasingly discontented by the losses they were incurring through LeClerc's invasion and were looking back regretfully to the time under Toussaint when prosperity had flourished. Napoleon was working his way towards total power from First Consul to Emperor. This was a time to consolidate his position – not a time to be criticized for his colonial policy.

On 27 September 1802, the door of Toussaint's cell jarred open and a tall, elegant stranger of obvious rank stepped inside. He presented himself as General Caferelli, aide to Napoleon Bonaparte. Caferelli was only thirty-six years old but was a trusted aide of Napoleon, so trusted that two years later Napoleon used his services in trying to persuade the Pope to crown him Emperor.

Tactfully ignoring the cell and its condition, the passages under water that he had just walked through and the fact that the man in front of him was his General's prisoner, he told Toussaint that it was a pleasure to meet a man of such renown, one who had achieved so much. The First Consul had received his letter and he, as his aide, had journeyed to the Fort de Joux to ask him some questions.

Later he wrote in his report that he had found the prisoner 'trembling with cold and illness, suffering greatly and having difficulty in speaking'. But, in spite of this, he appeared 'firm, dignified and master of himself'. Caferelli could not help but admire 'the spirit which he showed in the circumstances'.

The General delicately offered Toussaint a promise and a threat. If Toussaint's answers to his questions were satisfactory his lot would most likely to be improved; if not . . .

Toussaint's answers were not satisfactory . . . He replied to Caferelli's questions but admitted to nothing that Caferelli did not already know. Any account he might have had in Philadelphia was to buy arms to defend the colony from its enemies. But the enemy, of course, was France. He denied the existence of any treasure; his only personal money was in land, in his cattle and estates.

He grew angry when Caferelli repeated the rumour that the guards he had ordered to hide his hoard were later shot. He finished the questioning by saying with sad dignity 'what I have lost is of more consequences than money.' No treasure of Toussaint's has ever been found.

Caferelli wrote in his report that 'the man is wilfully deceitful, self-possessed, cunningly adroit. He appears sincere but admits nothing but what he chooses.'

On the second day of Caferelli's visit Toussaint handed him his 'memoirs', asking him to deliver them to the First Consul. Caferelli commented, 'It is not difficult to realize that my conversations with the fellow are simply an abridged version of this writing in which he has framed all his defence.'

Toussaint, before he handed over his 'memoirs', wrote a postscript in his own hand and in his own French to Napoleon.

Premier Consul, Père de toutes le militre, Defanseur des innosant . . .

First Consul, father of all soldiers, Defender of the innocent. Judge of integrity, consider now a man more sinned against than sinning, tend my wounds for they are very deep, you alone can heal them. Greetings, and never forget, you are the doctor, my plight and my record merit

your concern. I am relying entirely upon your justice and integrity.
Greetings and respects

Toussaint L'Ouverture

Toussaint knew that Caferelli was leaving him once more alone.
In his final postscript, he no longer made demands, only a plea for help
and humanity.

He also asked Caferelli to convey a letter to his wife.

Au Fort de Joux, 17 September 1802
My dear wife,

I am profiting by the occasion given to me by the good general to
give you my news. I was ill when I arrived here, but the commandant
is a humane man and has given me all the help possible, thank God,
I am better now. You know of my affection for my family and my
attachment for my wife whom I love so dearly. Why have I no
news of you?

Say hello to all from me. I beg them to behave well, virtuously and
wisely. I have already told you that from here on you are responsible
for the welfare of the family before God and your husband.

Let me know about Placide and about yourself.

With all tenderness I embrace you, I am everlastingly your faithful
husband.

Toussaint L'Ouverture

Toussaint was not feeling better, he was feeling worse. Did he really
wonder why he had not heard from her, that it could be her remissness?
It was a husband's letter, concerned with not worrying his wife, protecting
her, guiding her, remaining in her eyes the man she remembered. She can
never have received it. It is in the National Archives together with
Toussaint's last letter to Napoleon, which he handed to Caferelli on the
same day.

17 September 1802
General and First Consul,

The respect and obedience that I have always rendered to you is
second nature and carved upon my heart. If I have failed in my duty,
I have done so unwittingly, if I have been unsuccessful in the promotion
of the constitution, it is because of an overwhelming desire to achieve
perfection, if I have served with too much zeal and too much pride, it
was with a blind unthinking belief that by so doing I would please my
government. If these duties which were my responsibility have been

neglected the oversight was inadvertent . . . but, when it comes to fidelity and probity my conscience is clear. I would wish to say to all men in this state, I was one of your soldiers and the first servant of St Dominigue. Today I am miserable, cast aside, dishonoured, a victim of my own dedication. Please out of justice consider my desperate plight. You are too just and too compassionate to turn your back on my destiny. I have commanded General Caferelli, your aide-de-camp, to convey to you this document, I trust you will consider it carefully. Your well-known fairness and frankness has left me no alternative but to pen my heart to you.

Greetings and respects
Toussaint L'Ouverture

It was Toussaint's last appeal. Did he truthfully still believe in Napoleon's fairness and compassion? The tragedy was that he did. He believed in the Republic of France, so how could he not also believe in the man who ruled it? His imprisonment, his humiliation still appeared to him as a nightmarish mistake, one that Napoleon must and would rectify. It still seemed an impossibility to him that he could continue to be ignored, abandoned. Toussaint still suffered the pain of hope.

The winter crept on slowly. There was no word from Napoleon. Toussaint wrote to Caferelli.

General,
    I pray you to refresh the memory of the First Consul. You know my position, my suffering is great, my health is deteriorating. I still hope for justice. You will be helping a man who is more unfortunate than blameworthy . . . Please send me a word in reply.

There was no reply.

In October, Toussaint received another visitor, a man named Dormoy, professing to be a doctor. How and why he was allowed to see Toussaint is a mystery. He was not, when inquiries were made, a doctor at all, but an ex-priest turned schoolmaster. After the visit he was arrested. It was thought that he might have been helping Toussaint to escape or, at the least, that he was a supporter bringing him comfort. Perhaps he was merely curious. Whatever the reason, this visit had a grave effect upon Toussaint's treatment by the authorities. Napoleon's displeasure was patently clear. 'You are answerable with your life for the safe-keeping of the prisoner.' Under this alarming threat, Baillé was quick to act upon any instructions received. He was told to search Toussaint's room and to remove any personal belongings that he still possessed.

Stung to fury, Toussaint wrote to the Ministry of Marine – the last
letter he was to write.

Nothing can equal the humiliation that has been meted out to me
today. You have despoiled my cell, torn my palliasse to shreds in your
vain attempt to find money which I do not have. Mercifully there was
nothing to find. All I have are the quadruples that you had sent me
which you have confirmed are my property.

You have confiscated my watch and stolen the gold pieces which
were in my pocket. You have even taken my spurs.

I am forewarning you that a detailed account must be kept by you
of all my belongings that you have seized, because this will be checked
by me on the day that my anguish and imprisonment are over. You
must send everything to my wife and children. When a man is already
desperately miserable, it is too inhuman to harass and humiliate him
further. You must have the charity and consideration towards me as a
servant of the Republic and not treat me as if I am an outrageous
criminal. I have already told you, and I repeat it again, that I am an
honourable man and if I had not faithfully served my country in an
exemplary manner, I would not now be imprisoned here on the orders
of my government. I salute you from the dungeon of Fort de Joux.

The instructions for the confiscation of Toussaint's watch were
deliberate, detailed and clear. 'Take away Toussaint's watch if he appears
to enjoy its use. Procure and put in his room the cheapest possible clock
of wood which will be enough to indicate the passage of time.'

Toussaint's watch now lies in a glass case beside his sword in the museum
in Port au Prince, Haiti. It is a pretty thing of amethysts, enamel and
golden cherubs, more suited to a man of fashion than a soldier; he must
have associated the only thing of value left to him with the period of
luxury and plenty that he knew only too briefly. His spurs held more
memories – memories of his favourite stallion, Bel Argent, his ceremonial
parades through throngs of smiling, cheering faces, his triumphs as a
warrior. The last insignia of General L'Ouverture was also gone.

He was to be allowed no more pens, ink or writing paper, as his constant appeals were becoming annoying to the government. He was to
be allowed no further voice from his tomb. Baillé in his apprehension
allowed no jailers near him but himself. He brought him his food, emptied
his slop pail. All further doctor's visits were stopped. 'The constitution
of Negroes bears no resemblance to that of Europeans. I have dispensed
with the services of a doctor and surgeon as they are of no possible use to
him.'

In spite of all this, Toussaint's spirit still occasionally showed and he protested to Baillé about the injustice of his treatment at the hands of the 'wicked and unjust' French.

He never mentioned St Dominigue – it was too near to his heart. Baillé was becoming restless, his duties onerous. It was increasingly cold in the passages of the Fort de Joux that led to Toussaint's cell. Baillé asked for permission to lay planks on the floor to make his walk through the flooded corridors easier. He also asked for an assistant, as he had no time to himself any more because of the vigilance required of him in guarding the prisoner. He complained that not only did he have his duties as Commandant of the fort but also those of jailer and innkeeper.

Baillé was not sent an assistant. Instead he was relieved of his post and a younger man put in his place: Amiot, an officer whose 'devotion to duty was unlimited'. Amiot was also without pity. He harassed Toussaint continuously. He woke him constantly, night after night and, on the pretext of searching his cell, made him get out of bed and stand shivering in the bitter cold. Jailers watched him, humiliatingly, as he used the slop pail in the corner to perform his natural functions. They watched as he ate his food and shone a lantern on his face as he slept.

In March 1803, Amiot reported: 'the condition is about the same, he complains continuously of stomach pains and has a continuous cough. He has an arm in a sling and his voice is curiously changed. He does not ask for a Doctor.'

Much of the time Toussaint lay in his bed. The snow settled against his window, muffling the sounds of the world outside. St Dominigue was only a memory. He must have realized now, at last, that he would never see it again, never ride his horse between the high rows of waving sugar or gallop up the green valleys, never see the bare mysterious mountains turn suddenly to gold in the setting sun, never again look into the comfort of a black face or see his wife's soft round features, her eyes so full of pride for him, or see Isaac and Placide grow into men.

He had no news of his country, did not know how his people whom he loved so much were faring in the war that was splitting his land apart and had no knowledge of whether his generals, his soldiers, his army, were hopelessly defeated, whether there was still hope for his nation or whether it would once again return to slavery. He was never to know.

On 3 April 1803, Amiot left the Fort to go to Neuchatel leaving Toussaint to be guarded by a Captain Colounier. He was ordered not to enter Toussaint's cell. Toussaint was given no food while Amiot was away; no one emptied his slop pail or gave him fresh supplies of wood.

During those four days he must have made some effort to follow the usual pattern of his life; he had attempted to put the last of the wood allowed him on the fire, but when Amiot returned at eleven o'clock on 7 April, he found Toussaint sitting in his wooden chair with his head leaning against the side of the stone fireplace. Toussaint L'Ouverture was dead.

Epilogue

The Times, 2 May 1803

'Toussaint L'Ouverture is dead. He died, according to letters from Besançon, in prison a few days ago. The fate of this man has been singularly unfortunate. He died we believe without a friend to close his eyes. We have never heard that his wife and children, though they were brought from St. Dominigue with him, have ever been permitted to see him during his imprisonment.'

Toussaint died on 7 April 1803. It was stated in the autopsy that he died of 'sudden apoplexy and pneumonia'. Apoplexy is, of course, the old-fashioned word for what we now call a stroke or cerebral haemorrhage. The medical advice of today believes that it is more likely that he died of pneumonia following a stroke.

He was buried in the vault of the small chapel of St Pierre attached to the fort. The grave was unmarked, but not long after his death the old concierge of the fort, when showing a visitor around, pointed to the floor of the chapel and said, 'There lies buried here below the King of the Blacks.'

In about 1880 Marshal Joffre, who was commander of the fort before becoming Marshal of France, ordered the chapel to be demolished in order to form new fortifications, and the skeletons of former prisoners were used among the rubble as building material. Toussaint's bones lie somewhere in the walls or the floors of what is now called the Chateau du Joux. *Requiescat in pace*.

Madame L'Ouverture remained for a while in Bayonne. She was penniless and lacked even a change of clothing. Fortunately the officer in charge of the surveillance of the family, General Dudos, took pity on them and appealed on their behalf to the Ministry of Marine: 'This family is really in a pitiful condition, without money, without clothes and, in a word, without a change of shirt. I must out of humanity take an interest in their position. Were I wealthy I would come to their aid. I am sure that were you, like me, in a position to judge their fate you could not do less than concern yourself'; after which they were at least adequately cared for. Poor, tragic Suzanne L'Ouverture lost Jean-Paul, her youngest who had never been strong, for he died when the cold of winter struck on 7 January 1803, before the death of Toussaint. The family were moved to Agen where Placide joined them. Isaac married Louise ·Chancy, his cousin, and Placide also married, so there must have been moments of happiness for this sad little group, but neither Isaac or Placide left heirs and both died young.

Throughout the years Madame L'Ouverture kept her family of exiles as united as she could, for example when Isaac and Placide quarrelled over their attempts to claim the remnants of Toussaint's estate in St Dominigue. Madame L'Ouverture lived till she was seventy-four and died on 19 May 1816. It is not hard to believe, as she sat in her chair by the fire and dreamed of the past and of Toussaint, that she regretted the rebellion, even regretted his rise to power and the driving force that had inspired him to greatness, and that she looked back to those days when as slaves she and Toussaint had walked to work on their land 'hand in hand', when 'on Sundays after a pleasant meal, we passed the rest of our day with the family, finishing the day with our prayers.'

In St Dominigue after Toussaint's death there was growing insurrection amongst the cultivators, since they were not, as LeClerc had expected, glad to see him go; in fact his capture spurred them on, until their fervour became fanatical. Their chiefs, Dessalines and Christophe, had abandoned them, but the memory of Toussaint was with them and they fought as they had never fought before, as if possessed. LeClerc wrote to Napoleon: 'They laugh at death, the men die with a fanaticism which is unbelievable. It is the same with the women.' Their battle cry was 'death, rather than surrender.'

LeClerc resorted to more savage measures. He made the decision to put 'all men, women and children who have fled to the mountains to the sword, only children under twelve shall be spared, as for the Negro of the plains, half of those must be killed' and, repeating Napoleon's orders, 'not a Negro who has ever worn an epaulette should be left in the colony.'

His black soldiers were deserting him for the guerillas, including Dessalines and Christophe. His forces were becoming too weak numerically to control the rise of power of the rebel army. The creeping menace of yellow fever was also gaining its own victory over the French. No one, whatever his rank, escaped it; 20,000 soldiers died, 15,000 officers, 9000 sailors, 700 doctors and five generals.

On 22 October 1802 LeClerc was suddenly taken ill, and his doctor broke the news to Pauline. LeClerc became delirious and then comatose, but shortly before he died he regained consciousness and asked his doctor to beg Pauline and Dermide to return to France; he died quietly, speaking her name but, ironically, before the man who he had so hated, ill-wished and ill-treated.

LeClerc was replaced by General Rochambeau, who was a human monster, a man of such sadistic cruelty as to make Jeannot appear an innocent. He had blacks torn to pieces by dogs in an old monastery which he used as a ballroom. The dogs were ordered from Cuba specially for this sport. His plans to exterminate the Negro race did not last long. The reinforcements of 20,000 men he had demanded from Napoleon, like LeClerc's army, vanished away.

In November 1803 Rochambeau surrendered, with the proviso that he be allowed to leave the colony in safety. Napoleon's ill-advised, ill-fated venture to seize the island and return it to slavery was over. The largest expeditionary force Napoleon had ever sent abroad had been routed, defeated by an army of 'brigands' and by the climate of the island itself which came to their aid.

His bid to extend his Empire to include Jamaica and the United States was also finished. The history of the United States might be very different today if it had not been for one man, Toussaint L'Ouverture, and the people of St Dominigue.

On 29 November 1803 Dessalines, Christophe and Clairveaux issued the proclamation of the Independence of St Dominigue; later, when Dessalines became the island's first ruler under Independence, he was to change the name to Haiti. These three men may have declared the Independence but it was Toussaint L'Ouverture and Toussaint L'Ouverture alone who envisaged it and created it.

When he made his farewell to the island, when he spoke his famous words 'in overthrowing me, you have cut down in St Dominigue only the trunk of the tree of liberty. It will spring up again from the roots, for they are numerous and deep' he was proved to be right; his own island became the first free Black Republic, but that spirit spread till it encompassed the world. It was Toussaint who brought the torch of liberty to his race – they should always remember him and be grateful.

Sources

Ardouin, B. *Etudes sur l'Histoire d'Haiti* (6 vols), Haiti, Paris, 1853

Brutus, E. *Révolution dans Saint-Dominigue* (2 vols)

Burns, Sir A. *History of the British West Indies*, 1954

Deschamps, L. *Les Colonies pendant la Révolution*, Paris ,1898

Descourtilz, M-E. *Voyages d'un Naturaliste*, Paris, 1809

Desfosses, G. *La Révolution de St Dominigue*, 1893

Edwards, Sir B. *West Indies* (2 vols), 1794

Garran-Coulon, J-P. *Débats entre les accusés et les accusateurs dans l'Affaire des Colonies*, 1798

Harvey, W. W. *Sketches of Haiti*

James, C. L. R. *The Black Jacobins*, 1963

LaCoste, G. *Toussaint L'Ouverture*, Bordeaux, Paris, 1877

LaCroix, Baron F-J-P. *Mémoires pour servir à l'Histoire de la Révolution de Saint Dominigue*, Paris, 1819

Laurent, M. *Le Document*
Toussaint Louverture et l'Independance de Saint-Dominigue

Leyburn, J. G. *The Haitian People*

Madiou, T. *Histoire d'Haiti* (2 vols), Haiti, 1817

Métral, A-M-T. *Histoire de l'Expédition militaire des Français à Saint Dominigue, sous le Consulat de Napoléon Bonaparte*, 1825

Metraux, *Voodoo in Haiti*

Nemours, Gen. A. *Histoire militaire de la Guerre Independance de Saint-Dominigue*, 1925
Histoire de la Captivité et de la mort de Toussaint L'Ouverture, Paris, 1929
Histoire de la Famille de Toussaint Louverture, 1941
Toussaint Louverture, Fondé à Saint Dominigue la Liberté et l'Egalité, 1945
Histoire des Relations Internationales de Toussaint Louverture, 1945

Nugent, Lady. *Jamaica Journal*, London, 1907

Poyen, Col. A. de. *Histoire militaire de la Révolution de Saint-Dominigue*, Paris, 1891

St John, Sir S. *Hayti or the Black Republic*, 1884

St Remy, *Pétion et Haiti*, 1950
Mémoires du General Toussaint L'Ouverture, 1951

Saint-Anthoine, J-H. D. *Vie de Toussaint L'Ouverture*

Saintoyant, J. *La Colonisation Française pendant la Révolution (1789-1799)*, Paris, 1930

Sannon, P. *Histoire de Toussaint L'Ouverture* (3 vols), Haiti, 1920-33

Schoelcher, V. *Vie de Toussaint L'Ouverture*, Paris, 1899

Vaissière, *Saint Dominigue. La Societé et la Vie Creole sous l'Ancien Régime*, Paris, 1909

Williams, Dr E. *From Columbus to Castro*

Wimpffen, Baron A. S. de *Voyage à Saint Dominigue pendant les années 1788, 1789 et 1790*, 1790

Les Archives du Ministère des Affaires Etrangères
Les Archives du Ministère de la Guerre
The correspondence of General LeClerc
Papers and archives in *Bibliothèque des Frères d'Instruction Chrétienne*, Port au Prince, Haiti; *Bibliothèque de l'Armée*, Paris; and the library of the British Museum, London